COLUMBIA UNIVERSITY
STUDIES IN THE
SOCIAL SCIENCES

252

The Series was formerly known as
Studies in History, Economics and Public Law.

The Humane Movement in the United States, 1910-1922

AMS PRESS
NEW YORK

Bulletin of Social Legislation

on the Henry Bergh Foundation for the
Promotion of Humane Education

No. 6

EDITED BY

SAMUEL MCCUNE LINDSAY, PH.D., LL.D.

Professor of Social Legislation in Columbia University

The Humane Movement in the United States, 1910-1922

BY

WILLIAM J. SHULTZ

AMS PRESS
NEW YORK

Library of Congress cataloged this title as follows:

Schultz, William John, 1902-1970.
The humane movement in the United States,
1910-1922. [1st AMS ed.] New York, AMS
Press [1968].
    319 p. 23 cm. (Bulletin of social
legislation on the Henry Bergh Foundation for
the promotion of humane education, no. 6)
(Columbia University studies in the social
sciences, 252).
    Reprint of the 1924 ed. Bibliography: p.
307-310.
    1. Animals, treatment of. 2. Child welfare—
United States. 3. Children—Law—United
States. I. Title. (Series) II. Series:
Columbia studies in the social sciences, 252.
HV4705.S5   1968   68-57581
                    636.08/3
ISBN 0-404-51252-6

Reprinted from the edition of 1924, New York.
First AMS edition published in 1968.

MANUFACTURED
IN THE UNITED STATES OF AMERICA

EDITOR'S PREFACE

DURING the academic years 1908-09 and 1909-10, beginning just one year after the acceptance by Columbia University of the Henry Bergh Fund donated by General Horace W. Carpentier for "the promotion and dissemination of humanitarian principles and the repression of cruelty (not limited to the protection of animals), by lectures, prizes and publications and in other ways," Professor Roswell C. McCrea, then Associate Director of the New York School of Philanthropy, devoted about eighteen months to research in preparation of a descriptive survey of the humane movement in the United States. This survey was published for the Henry Bergh Fund by the Columbia University Press in 1910. It furnished in the main an analytical and descriptive account, and only incidentally an historical interpretation, of the legislation pertaining to cruelty to animals and children and of the activities of public officials and private societies having to do with the administration of such legislation and with anti-cruelty work and animal and child protection. It gave a comprehensive picture of the existing situation in the United States in humane work and covered recent legislation up to and including the year 1909.

The legislation of some of the intervening years and many special problems of administration have been studied under the direction of the Henry Bergh Fund. Some of these studies have appeared in this series of the Bulletin of Social Legislation; cⁱ ers are in manuscript, notably, an interesting report on Legislation for the Protection of Animals and Children, 1916-17, prepared by Frederick C. Hicks, A.M., LL.B., and other memoranda prepared like Professor Hicks' work under the supervision of the Legislative Drafting Research Fund of Columbia University.

All of these materials were used as the basis of the study and research of Dr. William J. Shultz which was begun in the academic year 1922-23 and continued through the greater part of the current year 1923-24. Dr. Shultz has attempted a survey and appraisal of the humane movement in the United States beginning where Professor McCrea left off at the beginning of the year 1910 and covering the legislation and activities of the thirteen years ending with 1922.

The self-imposed limitations in the subject matter considered are for the most part the same as those adopted by Professor McCrea, and the unavoidable limitations in the available materials, reports and records of anti-cruelty work are not very different from those found in the earlier survey.

In the very clear picture that Dr. Shultz presents of the present status and problems of anti-cruelty efforts — legislative and otherwise—substantial progress during the last decade is indicated, but much remains to be done that was just as clearly apprehended a decade ago as now and we must await for its achievement the slow processes of education, especially of children and of public opinion which they in time will be the chief factors in making, and an aroused and better enlightened public conscience. It would seem that the dissemination of just such information as Dr. Shultz has here collected and the placing of it in the hands of teachers and of the large number of agents, directors and workers in the manifold animal and child protective activities ought to hasten the coming of the better day when these social responsibilities will receive more adequate attention from the average citizen. In any event, I am sure that the aim and effort of Dr. Shultz's survey is exactly such as the donor of the Henry Bergh Fund would have approved and that it will be helpful in spreading a knowledge of what has been done to protect animals and children from cruelty and what may still be done.

The information contained in this volume. and especially the classified analysis and summary of legislation for animal protection (Appendix 1) and child protection (Appendix 2), has another and perhaps even more important use in the guidance of legislators and those who administer the law. To illustrate what I mean I cannot do better than to quote from a memorandum by my colleague, Professor Thomas I. Parkinson, late Acting Dean of the Columbia University Law School, who has by his studies and practical work for the Legislative Drafting Research Fund done so much for the improvement of legislation, both state and national, and for its better enforcement.

In commenting on the administrative features of the humane legislation of the years 1916 and 1917, Professor Parkinson said:

"Improvement of social conditions through legislation is largely a problem of formulating legislative standards which are on the one hand consistent with constitutional guarantees and on the other capable of reasonably efficient enforcement. The difficulty will be quickly realized by one who attempts to formulate a standard of humanity which is to be imposed and enforced by law.

" A recent legislative effort in the field of humane legislation presents an interesting illustration. A Maine statute authorized the destruction of any animal ' abandoned *and* not properly cared for '. Under such a statute the right to destroy an animal is dependent on proof that it was not properly cared for and was abandoned. If either a private citizen or a public officer destroyed an animal which he in good faith and after reasonable investigation believed to be not properly cared for, he would be liable in damages if in subsequent proceedings in court the owner could prove that the animal was properly cared for or at least had not been abandoned. The difficulty in such a situation of proving to the court's satisfaction that a particular animal was one of those the destruction of which was authorized by the statute tends to discourage or dissuade action. The Maine legislature, therefore, amended this statute in such manner as to decrease the difficulty of justifying destruction of an animal. It simply substituted ' or ' for ' and ' so that the statute authorized the destruction of any animal ' abandoned *or* not properly cared for '. Under this amended statute the citizen or officer who in the interest of humanity destroyed an animal would be able to justify his destruction if he could prove that the animal was not properly cared for without proving that it was actually abandoned. The amendment improved the statute from the point of view of its enforcement. It decreased the chances of the owner's recovering damages; but it also raised the question of the constitutionality of summary destruction of an animal which had not been wholly abandoned by its owner.

" In the case of Randall *v.* Patch. (118 Me. 303-1919) the court held that the statute, as amended, was unconstitutional; that if the statute had only authorized the killing of an animal abandoned and not properly cared for it might have been justified on the theory that an abandoned animal was not property of value; but that when ' or ' was substituted for ' and ' the statute authorized the destruction of an animal which might have value, which was not abandoned, but which the agent alleged was not properly cared for. From the point of view of its enforcement and the probability of humane destruction of animals the statute had been improved, but this very improvement had carried it over the borderline which separates constitutional regulation of private property in the public interest from unreasonable and, therefore, unconstitutional interference with private rights.

" In humane legislation, as in other social legislation, the difficulty of formulating definite standards has resulted of necessity in legislative standards expressed in general language. This involves either interpretation and application by the courts or the delegation by the legislature to administrative officers of power to apply the general legislative rule to the specific instance, or, as it is generally called, power to fill in the details. Despite the constitutional limitation which prevents the legislature from delegating its law-making power to administrative officers, the courts have sustained the delegation to such officers of broad power to make rules carrying out a general legislative standard or to determine with finality the application of such general standard to particular facts. To illustrate, the courts sustain legislation requiring places of employment to be sanitary, with power delegated to administrative officers to determine what is sanitary and to require that which the administrative officer determines to be necessary to obtain sanitation. Little use has been made in the field of humane legislation of this device for overcoming the difficulty of framing definite standards by the legislature itself or of leaving to the courts in enforcement proceedings the interpretation of indefinite legislative standards. There is wide opportunity within constitutional limitations for the application of this administrative method of developing, definitizing, and enforcing standards of humanity imposed and enforced by law.

"The enforcement of our humane statutes is seldom entrusted to an administrative body especially devoted to administration of prescribed standards of humanity. Much of the legislation in this field depends entirely on the criminal penalty for its enforcement and upon existing agencies to detect and prosecute crimes. Police officers and prosecuting attorneys are usually so absorbed in detecting and punishing crimes of violence that they have little enthusiasm for the enforcement of criminal punishments provided by law for violation of such regulatory legislation as that contained in humane statutes. It is fortunate, therefore, that the courts have finally sustained the propriety of vesting in humane societies the enforcement of such statutes.

"In the case of Nicchia v. New York (254 U. S. 228) a statute requiring dogs to be licensed authorized the American Society for the Prevention of Cruelty to Animals 'to carry out the provisions of this act'. The Society was authorized to collect fees and apply them to 'defraying the cost of carrying out the provisions of this act and maintaining a shelter for lost, strayed or homeless animals'. The validity of the act was attacked on the ground that it violated the 14th amendment of the United States Constitution by 'depriving a citizen of his property without due process of law, to wit, the liberty of owning and harboring a dog without procuring a license from and paying a fee therefor to the Society, a private corporation'. In its opinion upholding the statute the Supreme Court of the United States said: 'When the state in the reasonable conduct of its own affairs chooses to entrust the work incident to such licenses and collection of fees to a corporation created by it for the express purpose of aiding in law enforcement and in good faith appropriates the fund so collected for payment of the expenses fairly incurred and just compensation for the valuable services rendered, there is no infringement of any right guaranteed to the individual by the Federal Constitution.'

"In view of the extent to which the humane societies have been vested with power to enforce humane legislation it would seem that such societies out of their daily experiences in the administration of such laws should gradually derive material for defining and formulating more specific and, therefore, more readily enforceable standards of humanity. While it is too much to expect that the courts would ever sustain as constitutional legislation giving the force of law to standards formulated by such semi-public agencies, it should not be difficult to secure their adoption by the legislature."

SAMUEL MCCUNE LINDSAY

COLUMBIA UNIVERSITY
JUNE, 1924

TABLE OF CONTENTS

FOREWORD

This study attempts to continue for the brief period from 1910 to 1922 Professor Roswell C. McCrea's descriptive survey of the Humane Movement in the United States, which covered the distinctive features of legislation and organized efforts for animal and child protection. Professor McCrea gave an outline presentation of the historical background and development for at least a generation prior to 1909-1910. While making free use of Professor McCrea's materials and in some cases restating his conclusions, I have made no attempt to cover the same ground, but have begun this study with the year 1909-1910 where he left off.

I wish that it were possible to acknowledge in this place my deep obligations to the many persons whose assistance has contributed so materially to the completion of this study. The annual reports of the several hundred humane and child and animal protective societies, and many score of pamphlets on which this study is so largely based, were furnished to me through the courtesy of the officials of these societies, most of whom were known to me only by name. I wish here to express my gratitude to certain of these officials who gave me special assistance and helped me with valuable advice—Col. Coulter, General Manager of the New York S. P. C. C.; Mr. Lathrop, General Agent of the Massachusetts S. P. C. C., and Mr. Carl C. Carstens, who formerly held that office; Mr. Horton, the General Manager of the American S. P. C. A.; and the officials of the Massachusetts S. P. C. A. Above all, I appreciate the sympathy with this work and the suggestions accorded me by the late Dr. William O. Stillman, president of the American Humane Association.

Professor Samuel McCune Lindsay of Columbia University, the director of the Henry Bergh Foundation under whose auspices this study was written, assisted and advised me at every step of my work, and these printed words are but inadequate acknowledgment of my indebtedness to him. I owe much to the assistance of the librarians of the Economics Division of the New York Public Library. The chapter on Anti-Vivisection could not have been written in its present form without invaluable suggestions and help from Dr. Frederick S. Lee of the College of Physicians and Surgeons of Columbia University. The Legislative Drafting Bureau of Columbia University was of material assistance in compiling the legislative digests in Appendices I and II. Mr. Agostino Viggiani and my wife helped me in the reading of manuscript and the correction of proof.

CHAPTER I

INTRODUCTION

THE movement for the prevention of cruelty to animals usually dates its beginning in the United States from the year 1866. On April 10th of that year, thru the efforts of Henry Bergh, the American Society for the Prevention of Cruelty to Animals was incorporated by the legislature of the State of New York.[1] Similarly, the movement for the prevention of cruelty to children dates from 1874, when, their sympathies aroused by the brutality of the Mary Ellen case, Mr. Bergh, Mr. Elbridge T. Gerry and Mr. John D. Wright launched the New York Society for the Prevention of Cruelty to Children.[2]

It should be borne in mind, however, that these dates represent only the commencement of *organized* humane activities. The history of American protest in word and in act against cruelty to animals and to juveniles began in colonial days. Wanton cruelty had always been punishable under the common law. The Massachusetts Body of Liberties in 1640 made reference to cruelty to animals, and other statutory regulations and prohibitions may be traced to colonial legislation. An early published protest came from the pen of Thomas Paine. There appeared, for example, in the Pennsylvania Magazine for May 1775, a poem from his pen bearing the title, *Cruelty to Animals Exposed*. The poem describes the author's vigorous deliverance of a little kitten from the fate of being destroyed by dogs to whom a

[1] Roswell C. McCrea, *The Humane Movement* (New York, 1910), p. 11.
[2] *Ibid.*, p. 135.

"wretch" had thrown her.[1] In his *Age of Reason* he wrote,
" Everything of persecution and revenge between man and
man, and everything of cruelty to animals is a violation of
moral duty. . . . The only idea we can have of serving
God is that of contributing to the happiness of the living
creation God has made." [2]

There was little early specific anti-cruelty legislation, but
it was possible to prosecute " cruelists " [3] under the common
law as committing " nuisances ". A Baltimore paper of
1816 noted the following item:

A cartman in Philadelphia has been indicted and found guilty
of cruelly beating his horse, and sentenced to pay a fine of
thirty dollars with costs of prosecution, and give bond for his
good behavior for one year.[4]

One of the earliest anti-cruelty laws was passed by the
New York legislature in 1829 as follows:

Section 26. MAIMING AND CRUELTY TO ANIMALS.
—Every person who shall maliciously kill, maim or wound any
horse, ox or other cattle, or any sheep, belonging to another,
or shall maliciously and cruelly beat or torture any such
animal, whether belonging to himself or another, shall, upon
conviction, be adjudged guilty of a misdemeanor.[5]

In Massachusetts a statute similar to the above was pro-

---

[1] Rowley, *op. cit.*, p. 37.

[2] Thomas Paine, *The Age of Reason* (Eckler edition, New York, 1915),
pt. i, pp. 67-68; *cf.* Francis H. Rowley, *The Humane Idea* (Boston,
1912), p. 36.

[3] The term " cruelist " is used here and in later chapters to denote the
perpetrator of a cruel act. The term is widely used in humane circles
and will be found in the annual reports of most anti-cruelty societies.
Its adoption into current use is only a matter of time.

[4] *Federal Republican* (Baltimore), Dec. 30, 1816.

[5] *N. Y. Rev. Stat.*, vol. ii, title 6, pt. iv, ch. 1.

posed in 1834 by a commission appointed by the governor to revise the general statutes of the commonwealth, and was enacted in 1836.[1]

In recommending this provision to the legislature, the commissioners said in their report on the general statutes of the commonwealth (1834) :

It probably is not generally known in the community that extreme cruelty to animals even when inflicted by the owner, is an offense punished by the common law. Almost every one must have witnessed very revoltable instances of such cruelty, particularly with regard to horses. There seems to be less excuse for the commission of this offense than most others; and the commissioners submit for the consideration of the legislature the expediency of adopting some reasonable provision on the subject.[2]

Until the last quarter of the nineteenth century, there was no distinct current of protest against cruelties practiced upon children. The eighteenth-century philosophy of natural rights, from which was drawn the expression of the Rights of Man in the *Declaration of Independence*, by implication made protest against such cruelty,[3] but including it, denied it individual expression.

The first half of the nineteenth century witnessed the crusade against slavery, a controversy so all-inclusive that little reforming energy could be spared for a cause which did not obtrude itself upon the public attention. Here and there an individual did take opportunity to point out the sufferings imposed upon a large share of the child popula-

---

[1] *Mass. Rev. Stat.*, sec. 22, ch. 130; cited in Rowley, *op. cit.*, p. 40.

[2] *Ibid.*, p. 40.

[3] " The avoidance of pain for other beings capable of feeling it, as well as for oneself, comes to be thought as a duty "—an interpretation of this phase of the natural rights philosophy in David G. Ritchie, *Natural Rights* (London, 1895), p. 111.

tion. One such was Samuel J. Pratt, who also protested against the infliction of wanton pain upon animals.[1]

The term " humane " as technically used includes both animal and child protection. So it is used in this study. Tradition sanctions this. As has been indicated above, the organized movements in both fields were begun by the same individual, moved by the same humanitarian feelings. During his lifetime, Henry Bergh bestowed fostering care upon the two societies organized by him, although the greater part of his attention was claimed until his death by the American S. P. C. A.

Moreover, at the present time, most humane organizations devote themselves to both fields and entitle themselves " humane societies ", rather than societies for the prevention of cruelty to either animals or children. In 1922, of the five hundred and thirty-nine active humane organizations that were members of the American Humane Association, one hundred and seventy-five confined themselves exclusively to animal work, and fifty-seven exclusively to child work. The majority, three hundred and seven, included both activities.[2]

Nevertheless, there is fundamentally a wide divergence between the two types of activity.[3] It has become more and more pronounced with the passage of time, and will continue so in the future. To shield animals from undue pain and suffering is an end and aim in itself. Economic motives and factors of public health are accessories in accomplishing desired reforms, not true agents in motiv-

[1] Samuel J. Pratt, *Humanity, or Rights of Nature* (1838), cited in Rowley, *op. cit.*, p. 37.

[2] *American Humane Association, Forty-Sixth Annual Report* (1922), p. 62.

[3] *Cf.* George B. Mangold, *Problems of Child Welfare* (New York, 1914), p. 462.

ating them. The true animal lover regards as incidental the
loss of millions of dollars when herds of range stock die
every winter for lack of shelter and fodder; he feels their
death pangs: he is more concerned over the sufferings of
the cows in an ill-kept dairy than at the possibility that their
milk may be tainted. In seeking to pass legislation to
remedy such abuses, he is ready to make use of the economic
and public health arguments, but the problem for the solution of which he is striving, is emotional.[1]

The early child-protective movement was similarly motivated; today many of its most active workers represent additional ideals. The humanitarian consideration is
overlaid by the economic and social.[2] Appeal is made not
only to our humanity, but to our sense of citizenship.[3]
We are asked to consider the injured child not only as an
individual who suffers, but as an integral part of our social
system; his loss is our loss, for we shall have to pay out of
our own pockets to right the injury done to him. It is
forced upon our attention that the neglected or delinquent
child of today is the citizen of tomorrow, that the present
perversion of his character is a distinct moral loss to the
state a generation hence, the state in which he will be
our co-partner.

This difference of approach to the problems involves a
growing difference of methods. In the infancy of the
animal and the child protective movements, the most impor-

[1] *Cf.* Henry S. Salt, *Animals' Rights Considered in Relation to Social
Progress* (2nd edition, London, 1915), ch. i.

[2] *Cf. infra,* ch. xi.

[3] Taking random examples, Dr. William Henry Slingerland begins his
study *Child Welfare Work in Pennsylvania* (New York, 1915) with the
figures for the costs of child institutions in Pennsylvania and New
York, $75,879,100 in the former state and $56,745,000 in the latter. A
similar attitude is to be found in Nora Milne, *Child Welfare Work from
a Social Point of View* (London, 1920).

tant activities of each were identical and concerned with the most pressing problem—the prosecution of offenders.[1] This initial duty performed, the ways separate. The animal societies find fields of constructive work in providing watering places, rest-farms, shelters and hospitals for animals, and recently, in forwarding the cause of humane education. Their duty lies clear before them; they need have no fear of overlapping the activities of other organizations.

Those child societies that feel themselves required to do more than prosecute offenders,[2] have before them no such simple program. Once they admit a social responsibility in their work, they find themselves obliged to measure up to very broad standards. They are not relieved of responsibility when an offender is haled into court; the question as to the disposition of the child remains. Perhaps there are other social agencies which will accept responsibility for his destiny; the child-protective societies must have means of easy and rapid communication with them. Perhaps such other agencies do not exist; the child protective societies must develop agencies to meet the problem.

Good-will alone will not produce results; specialization and specialized knowledge are necessary; " case work " becomes a requisite. The instruments of prosecution do not apply here. The agent with police power must be supplemented by the social worker, the list of convictions by case data.

This differentiation between animal and child work is not academic. It is an acute problem before every one of the three hundred and seven humane societies today combining both types of activities. The personnel and material

[1] Cf. McCrea, op. cit., p. 33, et seq.
[2] Cf. infra, ch. xi.

equipments required in each field preclude the possibility of satisfactory combination. In a small society where means are limited, one or the other field will be slighted. If the society be large and have sufficient means at its disposal to allow of specialization in each field, it becomes essentially two separate organizations, each jealous of the possible supremacy of the other, and always threatening division.[1]

Divergent though they be, the two activities must often be united. More than one humane society has begun its history as either a child or an animal protective organization; at some period, it has had abuses in the other field brought sharply to its attention and has generously expanded itself to remedy these abuses. As a single example, the Arkansas Humane Society, now inactive, was originally organized for the protection of animals. In 1909 after a startling case of brutality to a child, it was given jurisdiction over children as well, and was reincorporated as a state-wide organization. From then until the entry of America into the World War, it struggled to maintain both fields with varying success until its demise.[2]

In most small towns and rural districts, it would be practically impossible to support two independent organizations, one to protect children and one to protect animals. Not only would difficulty be found in appealing to residents to provide sufficient income for both, but the necessary interested personnel would be lacking. Therefore, it is the policy of wisdom to combine both activities. Which will be subordinated to the other, will depend upon the personal inclinations of the leaders of the society. Usually animal protection predominates. The problems are simpler, and more capable of direct and immediate solution. The human appeal is uncomplicated by other considerations.

---

[1] Cf. McCrea, op. cit., p. 137.

[2] Manuscript letter of April 4, 1923 from the former secretary of the society.

It is usually found that small humane societies with resources of $2000 a year or less, devote themselves almost exclusively to animal protection. Cases of obvious cruelty are prosecuted, visits are made to stables and farms where animals are improperly kept. An animal fountain may be erected, and some educational and propaganda work done through the schools and children's organizations. The maximum that such a society accomplishes for the children of the district is to initiate prosecution where cruelty is known to exist, and to bring cases of neglect that necessitate attention to the notice of the proper public authorities.

There is thus a distinct cleavage between efforts to protect animals and efforts to protect children. This study must of necessity reflect this cleavage. Insofar as possible, all humane societies will be classified as either animal or child organizations according to the field wherein their efforts preponderate. Mention will, of course, be made of their other activities where essential.

This study, insofar as it deals with the Humane Movement in general, divides itself into two distinct parts. The first is an exhaustive examination of almost the entire field of animal welfare; the second deals with one rather sharply defined and limited group of activities relating to child welfare.

In the first division of this study, it is necessary to draw a line between protection of animals from cruelty, and certain phases of the conservation movement as applied to animals. Every state has on its statute books many game laws. In every volume of session laws, amendments to and modifications of these game laws fill many pages. Within them are sometimes to be found sections which regulate kinds of traps to be used for animals, and time periods for their visitation, and types of rifles to be used for bird hunting so as to insure a speedy death. The humane import of these sections is very clear and in Appendix I summarizing humane animal legislation, note has been taken of them.[1] But the purpose of the game laws as a whole is not to prevent cruelty but to preserve our rapidly vanishing wild life from immediate extinction. Game laws are more closely allied with regulations for reforestation and the shutting off of tne minerals of Alaska from exploitation, than to anti-cruelty legislation.[2]

There are societies and organizations that are doing valuable work in this field of preservation of wild birds and animals. The Audubon Society is the best known; the Campfire Club of America and the League of American Sportsmen should be mentioned. Professor McCrea included in his *Humane Movement* a detailed account of the activities of these organizations, considering their work so closely allied to protective activities as to deserve mention with organizations for the prevention of cruelty.[3] For the reasons mentioned above, the study of this movement is omitted entirely from this volume.[4]

[1] *Vide infra*, app. i.

[2] For information in this field, see the summary of game laws issued by the Biological Survey of the United States.

[3] McCrea, *op. cit.*, pp. 127-134.

[4] The Migratory Bird Act of 1918 and a more recent Supreme Court decision upon it, raise issues of no small interest to humane workers, and in particular to those laboring for more humane conditions in animal transport, insofar as they relate to the possibility of a congressional statute based on a treaty overriding existing state legislation in this field —legislation that notoriously lags behind even the moderate provisions of the Federal Act of 1906 (*vide infra*, p. 109).

By the Act of March 4, 1913, certain migratory birds were taken under the custody and protection of the United States government and the game laws of the various states were set aside by a federal statute. On August 17, 1916, by treaty between the United States and Great Britain on behalf

A similar distinction has been drawn between humane work proper, and organized animal activities and legislation motivated by economic considerations and factors of public health. Animals are property and laws relating to property apply to them. They are a specialized form of property, being animate, and hence there are fields of legislation devoted to them in this relationship. Such legislation, which considers animals as property possessing value, is not primarily humane. In protecting animal property from injury, it certainly protects the animals concerned from suffering, but this is only incidental. In this study, only legislation whose motivation is directly humane is considered. For example, in Arkansas, the owner of a dog which

of Canada, the protection for certain of these birds was made international. The statute being subsequently held unconstitutional in *United States v. Shauver* (214 Fed. 154, see 39 Sup. Ct. Rept. 134), Congress on July 3, 1918, passed a new act regulating the shooting of migratory birds and declared that it was for the purpose of carrying out the treaty. The President promptly promulgated regulations under the statute. Congress, therefore, clearly assumed that under the treaty power it could take control of a subject otherwise not within its power in order to carry out a treaty and the Executive endorsed the opinion of the Legislature. The statute was reviewed by the Supreme Court (*Missouri v. Holland*, 252 U. S., 416, 433), and the Court unequivocally negatived the argument that a treaty cannot go further than an act of Congress in derogation of the reserved powers of the states. Mr. Justice Holmes replied to this contention, " No doubt the great body of private relations usually fall within the control of the State, but a treaty may override its power. . . . Here a national interest of nearly the first magnitude is involved. It can be protected only by national action in concert with that of another power. The subject-matter is only transitorily within the State, and has no permanent habitat therein. But for the treaty and the statute there soon might be no birds for any powers to deal with. We see nothing in the Constitution that compels the government to sit by while a food supply is cut off and the protectors of our forests and our crops are destroyed. It is not sufficient to rely upon the States. The reliance is vain, and were it otherwise, the question is whether the United States is forbidden to act. We are of opinion that the treaty and statute must be upheld " (*ibid.*, pp. 434, 435).

worries or chases another man's sheep is liable to damages.[1] Examination of the statute shows that the sheep are considered not as animals subject to suffering but as property liable to damage.

An important portion of human sustenance is supplied by animals. Diseased or imperfect animal foods carry the possibility of disease and ill health to those who eat them. Inasmuch as the health of its citizens is a care of the modern state, legislative attention has been bestowed upon the living conditions of our food and dairy animals. In ensuring a supply of healthy animals at the slaughter houses and pure milk from the dairies, the well-being of great numbers of animals has been improved. But again, such legislation has no more right to be considered primarilarly humane than the Pure Food and Drugs acts similarly motivated. In this study, therefore, it is considered only in passing, and analysis of it has been omitted from the legislative summary in Appendix I.[2]

The problem of humane education presents a not dissimilar difficulty; in this case, however, a summary of the laws on humane education has been included. Statutes providing for the teaching of humaneness in the public schools of a state are not fundamentally dictated by the desire to add an extra subject to the school curriculum; their primary intention is to prevent possible suffering to animals—by means only slightly less direct than laws punishing cruelists.[3]

The protection of children from cruelty is but a specialized portion of the broader field of child welfare, and any attempt to limit it must be arbitrary. There are some who would accept a definition confining child protection to

---

[1] *Ark., S. & H.*, secs. 7296, 7300.

[2] Compare with the similar summary in McCrea, *op. cit.*, pp. 321-387.

[3] *Cf. infra*, ch. viii.

" protection from neglect, and physical and moral injury ".[1]
Undoubtedly, such a definition would hold true for the child
protective movement in its early phases. But this movement, as must all such, has undergone a form of evolution,
and the above definition would appear to many as alto-
gether too narrow.

To avoid fruitless academic arguments as to what con-
stitutes child protection and what does not, we must approach the problem from another direction. If there are
child-protective societies which confine themselves to the
narrower definition, there are others that have spread themselves far afield. We shall study the activities of all,
accepting them as child protective societies upon their own
identification, for such identification reveals their intent.
Where we find other agencies occupying themselves either
entirely or as a part of a greater plan of work with the
protection of children from neglect and physical and moral
injury, we shall consider them also as doing child-protective
work and study them.

In the summary of legislation for the protection of
children included in Appendix II, these principles have been
followed as closely as was practicable. Legislation in the
fields of public health, institutional provision for dependent
and delinquent children, procedure in juvenile courts, illegitimacy and bastardy, is omitted from this summary
except where its import is distinctly protective. Nevertheless, more than passing mention is given to this legislation
in the body of this study,[2] as several very important protective societies are active in these fields.

The four chapters following this introduction deal with
organized agencies for animal protection. The subject
matter of Chapter II is the development of societies for
animal protection from 1910 through 1922. The problems

---

[1] *Vide infra*, p. 201.   [2] *Vide infra*, ch. x.

which the entry of the United States into the World War in 1917 brought to these societies, are considered in Chapter III, in which is also included an account of the organization of the Red Star. Chapter IV deals with those societies which seek to further animal welfare in other ways than specific protection from cruelty. Chapter V deals with official state agencies for animal welfare.

Chapter VI generalizes the organizational and financial policies of the animal welfare movement. Chapter VII indicates some recent developments of this movement and deals with animal protective legislation.

Since 1910 an ever-increasing share of the energy of animal societies has been devoted to the field of humane education. Consideration is given to this topic in Chapter VIII. A study is made first of all of the activities and accomplishments of humane education societies and those protective societies that make humane education a part of their program. Secondly, attention is paid to humane education as included in public school curricula.

Chapter IX is devoted to the anti-vivisection movement. As no satisfactory study has hitherto appeared in this field, an account is given of the development of the antivivisection movement before 1910, which is continued to date. Differing in this respect from the subject matter of the rest of this study, antivivisection is the center of a heated and bitter controversy. Every effort has been made to avoid partisanship or the writing of an exposition in favor of either group of contestants. Insofar as is possible, explanations of the controversies are included as an integral part of the history of the movement.

Chapters X, XI, XII are concerned with child protection. The growth of the child protective societies is dealt with in Chapter X. An analysis of their aims and accomplishments is made in Chapter XI. Chapter XII treats of official state activities in this field.

CHAPTER II

SOCIETIES FOR THE PREVENTION OF CRUELTY TO ANIMALS

IN the year 1910, the American Humane Association reported that six hundred and fifty-nine societies had been formed in the United States for the prevention of cruelty. Of these, one hundred and two were dead and ninety-five were noted as inactive, no reports having been received from them. This left a total of four hundred and thirty-four anti-cruelty societies active in their respective fields. Of this number, two hundred and forty-seven were humane societies for both children and animals; one hundred and thirty-one were for the protection of animals only.[1]

Compare the statistics of 1910 with those included in the report for 1922. There is a total of nine hundred and thirty-eight anti-cruelty societies noted in the later report; two hundred and ninety-eight are dead, one hundred and one are inactive, leaving five hundred and thirty-nine reported as active. As has already been stated, three hundred and seven combine animal and child protection; one hundred and seventy-five confine themselves to the protection of animals.[2]

This represents a decided increase in the intervening twelve years, an increase the more marked when we turn our attention to figures other than those for the total of societies. The following table will indicate this:[3]

[1] *American Humane Association, Thirty-fourth Annual Report* (1910), p. 178.

[2] *A. H. A., 46th Ann. Rpt.* (1922), p. 62.

[3] The figures are taken from the *Annual Reports* of the American Humane Association for the period covered. These figures are neces-

[24

STATISTICS OF HUMANE ORGANIZATION, 1910-1922

	Number of active societies	Member-ship	Annual dues and contributions	Public funds received	Total income from all sources	Number of children handled	Number of animals handled
1910	434	117,442	$361,308	$262,726	$1,348,297	171,799	1,347,185
1911	471	76,262	386,381	426,609	1,198,809	136,493	1,463,123
1912	515	124,743	616,082	456,997	1,869,167	245,857	1,367,367
1913	528	141,334	618,651	448,506	1,999,425	178,016	2,553,162
1914	558	143,396	592,650	572,182	2,211,458	243,937	2,844,721
1915	562	161,562	690,334	623,971	2,130,022	212,215	2,394,721
1916	577	157,118	632,188	608,544	2,275,418	215,046	2,892,535
1917	583	91,550	792,460	602,170	2,251,871	219,909	2,218,385
1918	599	92,520	577,207	577,332	2,125,440	231,425	2,452,230
1919	575	23,228	707,796	721,170	2,378,142	217,954	2,635,496
1920	535	89,665	779,538	799,020	2,817,477	222,469	1,238,746
1921¹	...	......	....	....	....	....	....
1922	539	202,524	841,072	845,080	3,329,820	234,577	2,621,804

¹No statistics in American Humane Association, 45th Annual Report.

These figures taken together show a fairly steady growth through 1915 and into 1916. Then the period of war intervened, and there was a check to this progress. War charities competed with anti-cruelty societies for financial support. Humanitarian energies were diverted to other fields than animal protection. During the next four years, the different series vary with little apparent relation to each other; the number of active societies grew until 1918 and then decreased; membership fell as did the total of dues and contributions. The statistics are too inaccurate to permit the drawing of any conclusions. We shall make a more thorough analysis of this period based on the experiences of individual societies in Chapter III. After 1920, however, we find that all series agree in indicating a resumption of the progress of the first half of the previous decade.

Satisfactory as these figures may appear compared with the extent of the humane movement a generation ago, they by no means should be taken to indicate that a limit to its growth has been reached. There are regions in this country equal in size to continental states unserved by humane organizations. Idaho, Mississippi and New Mexico are without either animal or child societies.[1] South Dakota

sarily inaccurate. Few societies are at all careful in the keeping of accounts and of statistics of work—despite repeated prayers for greater accuracy on the part of those officials of the American Humane Association who year after year vainly try to compile some sort of statistical tables of the progress of the humane movement. This added to the incompleteness of returns, makes the figures only the roughest possible estimates, but nevertheless valuable in gaining a very general idea of our problem.

[1] In the humane directory of the United States included in the A. H. A. reports, Idaho is credited with a state humane society with five branches. A circular letter and a personal letter brought no replies from them, nor have the offices of the Amer. S. P. C. A. or the Mass. S. P. C. A. records of correspondence with them during the past three years. A similar situation exists in the case of the Mississippi Humane Society. A letter from the former secretary of the Roswell Humane Society of New Mexico stated that it no longer existed.

has a humane society for both child and animal work in Sioux Falls that finds its resources inadequate to cover more than the immediate neighborhood.[1] Repeated letters sent since September 1922 to the two humane societies credited to Arizona brought no reply.

Even in states that can boast an imposing list of anti-cruelty societies, there are many, many counties left untouched. At a conference of the Federated Humane Societies of Pennsylvania held in 1919, only the counties of Allegheny, Erie, Philadelphia, Dauphin, Bedford, Montgomery, Lycoming and Northhampton were represented. No humane work at all was carried on in the fifty-seven other counties of the state.[2] In these counties, Pennsylvania's anti-cruelty laws are a dead letter, because neither societies nor officers are there to enforce them. Several years earlier, the Western Pennsylvania Humane Society in Pittsburg, Allegheny County, extended its activities to some of the adjoining counties by appointing active agencies therein. These were largely mining districts and single agents were inadequate to serve them.[3] More successful was found to be the system employed in Allegheny and Philadelphia counties of reporting infractions of cruelty laws to central agencies and managing prosecutions from such centers.[4]

The same conditions are true for the state of Illinois. Here, of the one hundred and one counties in the state, only twenty-seven counties in 1915 contained organized societies for the prevention of cruelty to animals. In that year there were thirty-three humane societies outside the

[1] Manuscript letter of Nov. 17, 1922.

[2] *Western Pennsylvania Humane Society, 45th Annual Report* (1919), p. 7.

[3] *Ibid.*, *42nd Ann. Rpt.* (1916), p. 15.

[4] *Ibid.*, *45th Ann. Rpt.*, p. 5.

city of Chicago and four in Chicago itself.[1] The 1920 report of the American Humane Association listed only twenty-three societies for the whole state. Of these only seven answered inquiries for information, two of them to report that they were defunct. It is clearly evident then that Illinois is no better served than Pennsylvania.

The states of Pennsylvania and Illinois were chosen as examples because they are two of the most thickly populated and socially progressive states in the Union. When this is borne in mind, the relative extent to which the humane societies listed in the American Humane Association reports serve the territory of the United States, can be appreciated. The truth becomes apparent that while some half dozen of the largest cities of the country are well and thoroughly covered by perhaps twice that number of large anti-cruelty organizations, in the territory beyond the suburban limits of these cities the anti-cruelty movement is still in its infancy.

Figures of children and animals rescued from cruelty and torture, and totals of contributions and of membership can give no adequate conception of what has constituted the development of the movement for the prevention of cruelty to animals during the last decade. Such development can only be measured by the actual detailed accomplishments of the individual societies. Such an account is clearly impossible for each of the five hundred and forty-nine societies active in 1922. Instead, representative societies have been chosen for different sections of the United States, and their histories summarized. Wherever possible, large city organizations have been selected, for only these can boast individuality. The experience of any of the smaller rural societies is that of all.

[1] F. Morse Hubbard, *Prevention of Cruelty to Animals in the States of Illinois, Colorado and California* (New York, 1916), p. 1, *et seq.*

The American S. P. C. A. was incorporated in 1866 with jurisdiction to operate anywhere within the boundaries of New York State. Its period of maturity was reached long before 1910. It had salaried agents patrolling the streets of New York City to interfere in cases of cruelty and to make arrests when deemed necessary. In 1910 these agents made 1904 arrests [1]—a very considerable total when it is borne in mind that the policy of the Society is not to make arrests if any other method of procedure is warranted.

In addition to patrolling the streets the special agents investigated complaints and inspected stables to ascertain the conditions under which horses were kept; they watched the horse markets to prevent abuses at public sales; they paid regular visits to poultry markets and bird and animal stores; they kept theatrical and circus acts of trained animals under surveillance, and made daily inspections of stock yards, ferries and other places where animals are kept or worked in large numbers. In the course of this work they examined annually several hundred thousand horses alone; in 1910 the number of such examinations was 417,055.

Since 1894, the licensing of dogs in New York City had been another duty of the American S. P. C. A. The fees were retained by the society to meet the expenses of issuing licenses and of maintaining animal shelters; any surplus was applied to enforcing the anti-cruelty laws.[2] The Society had salaried inspectors who made investigations to discover unlicensed dogs and who also looked out for the general welfare of dogs, just as the special agents sought to protect horses.

In 1910 the prosecution of cruelists in New York City

[1] This account of the activities of the Am. S. P. C. A. in 1910 is drawn in large part from F. Morse Hubbard, *Prevention of Cruelty to Animals in New York State* (New York, 1915), p. 2, *et seq.*

[2] *Vide infra*, p. 95.

took a strange development. A group of East Side black-mailers operating for the most part among the petty pedlers of that district adopted the procedure of poisoning the horses of their victims to enforce their demands. The American S. P. C. A. took upon itself a large share of the responsibility of hunting down this band and breaking up its activities.[1]

In the same year the relief work of the Society was greatly expanded. Two motor ambulances were presented by one of its patronesses, and the Society purchased two new horse ambulances. Shelter work was increased to such an extent as to burden resources, 318,000 dogs and cats being attended to during the year. A " travelling state agent " with general duties was appointed to serve the rural territory around New York City and to aid weaker organizations in that territory. This extension of activities threatened to cause the expenses of the Society to exceed its income for the year, and the Board of Managers empowered the officers of the Society to make expenditures in excess of the annual income to the extent of $25,000.[2]

In 1911 it was decided to build a new animal dispensary for Manhattan which was opened in August, 1912. It embodied the most advanced ideas in dispensary construction, and was thoroughly equipped with modern facilities for treating the diseases of all animals and birds.[3]

In 1914 a new dispensary was opened in Brooklyn. In the same year, fear of the further spread of an epidemic of glanders caused the closing of all the watering troughs in New York City. As the City neglected to make any provision for the watering of horses by other means, this

[1] *American S. P. C. A., 45th Ann. Rpt.* (1910), pp. 5-8.

[2] *Ibid., passim.*

[3] 1911 and 1912 *Reports; vide* also Hubbard, *Prevention of Cruelty to Animals in New York State,* p. 5.

duty fell upon the animal society. It installed a drinking pail service at all the old fountains and at many hydrants in various parts of the city.[1] (This glanders scare was nation-wide and similar action was taken in many of the larger cities. In Boston the Angell Memorial Fountain erected under the auspices of the Massachusetts S. P. C. A. and considered absolutely hygienic and epidemic-proof, was closed by the City, much to the chagrin of the society.)

During the summer of 1916 the New York society suffered from another epidemic scare. New York City found itself in the grip of infantile paralysis and the report was circulated that cats carried the germ of the disease. A panic spread among cat owners. The Society tried to check it, but parents were terror-stricken and tens of thousands of cats were hastily ejected from their homes. The Society found it necessary to make prompt response to all calls if the animals were not to be turned adrift to shift for themselves. To prevent this abuse, the Society increased its force, added to its equipment, and for several months maintained an all-day, all-night, Sunday and holiday service.[2]

During the same year, by a gift of five autos, the Society's vehicle equipment was increased to twenty-seven. Work was extended to rural districts about the city where conditions were even worse than within city limits. Agents were sent to county fairs, and to road construction and logging camps.

The outbreak of the war presented new problems to the Society. Lecture work was carried on in the army cantonments around New York City, and aid extended to the veterinary service. A building strike in the fall of 1917 forced the suspension of construction, and great numbers of horses had to be kept idle in their stables. The S. P. C. A.

[1] *Amer. S. P. C. A., 49th Ann. Rpt.* (1914).
[2] *Amer. S. P. C. A., 51st Ann. Rpt.* (1916).

provided for a constant inspection of these stables for the duration of the strike.

In 1918 addition was made to the horse-relief service. Two watering carts ordinarily used to sprinkle the streets were purchased and fitted with faucets permitting the water to be drawn into pails. They were put into service along the water-front to supply water to the dock horses. A bubbling cup was also provided on each wagon for the drivers.

1919 and 1920 saw a development and expansion in all lines of the Society's activities. During these years, more attention was given to humane education. In 1918 a lecture service was established; in 1921 a Department of Humane Education was developed.[1]

The 1921 *Annual Report* of the society carried an account of the activities of the Society's Veterinary Department. Valuable medical research and study of animal diseases were pursued at the dispensary during that year, particularly in the field of radium treatment for cancer in animals. The kinds of animals operated upon was also noted; the list included monkeys, bulls, deer, rabbits, goats, guinea pigs, ferrets, canaries, geese, turkeys, ducks and opossums.

In 1922, so much had the demand for hospital service increased, that the capacity of the dispensary and hospitala was doubled by a second-story addition. Much valuable laboratory equipment was added. The finances of the society for this year were as follows:

Expenses		*Income*	
For prevention of cruelty to animals	$73,558.82	For prevention of cruelty to animals	$66,646.73
Shelters and humane disposition of animals ...	167,760.64	Shelters and humane disposition of animals ...	165,722.00
	$241,319.46		$232,368.73

[1] *Vide infra*, pp. 126-128.

The figures below indicate some of the society's activities during the year:

Retired police and fire horses placed in homes 108
Horses examined at auction sales 22,515
Horses condemned at auction sales 1,367
Sick and injured animals treated at Society's hospital 10,046
Dogs restored to their owners and placed in homes 1,831
Permanent drinking fountains in operation summer and winter .. 70
Temporary watering stations maintained during summer 25
Temporary receiving stations for animals 5
Animals received at these stations 24,719

Offenders arrested and prosecuted by the society 792
Offenders arrested by police and prosecuted by the society 40
                                                            _____
        Total arrests and prosecutions 832

Animals suspended from labor 4,340
Horses, mules and other large animals, disabled beyond recovery,
    humanely destroyed 819
Disabled horses removed from the streets in ambulances 692
Complaints received 5,930
Cases investigated 10,228
Calls made for unwanted, sick and injured animals .... 84,484 [1]

In addition to the American S. P. C. A., New York City supports the Humane Society of New York. This second organization was incorporated in 1904 as the Henry Bergh Humane Society, whose purpose was mainly humane education. In 1906, changing its name to the New York Humane Society, it was reorganized as a prosecuting organization. In 1908 its name was again changed to the Humane Society of New York, and it was authorized to receive fines in the cases it prosecuted, and its officers and agents were to have the power of police officers.[2] Its course has not been smooth. It has been subjected to criticism for its methods of prosecution since it was founded, and has had to bear with the

[1] *Amer. S. P. C. A., 57th Ann. Rpt.* (1922).
[2] Hubbard, *op. cit.*, p. 8.

disapproval of the American S. P. C. A. To the latter it
has retorted with counter charges of inefficiency. For example, in its report for 1911-12 [1] the number of arrests made
by the American S. P. C. A. are tabulated beside those of
the Humane Society with the annual income of each appended, so as to make it appear that in proportion to its
income the latter was the more active. Of course, this
does not take into account the non-prosecuting activities of
the larger society.

In 1914 action was brought to have the charter of the
Humane Society of New York annulled, which was unsuc-
cessful. An attempt to have the City withhold fines likewise failed.[2] The Humane Society has continued active in
prosecution. In 1921 its ten agents brought 2,694 cases
into the magistrates' courts. It has supplemented this work
with stable inspection, and lately has engaged in horse watering. In 1921 it watered 70,867 animals. Its income for
the year was $17,767.17, of which the larger part was
expended in the salaries of its outside and office forces. For
distribution of humane equipment for horses, it disbursed
$432.03.[3]

The 1922 report of the American Humane Association
lists fifty S.P.C.A.s and humane societies engaged in animal
protection in New York State exclusive of New York City.
This number includes independent and branch organizations.
In importance, they range from infant societies struggling
along on an annual income of a few hundred dollars to the
Mohawk and Hudson River Society with its ten branches,
serving the central district of the state.[4] These have pro-

---

[1] *Humane Society of New York, 8th Ann. Rpt.* (1912), p. 3.

[2] Hubbard, *op. cit.*, pp. 10-13.

[3] *The Hum. Soc. of N. Y., 18th Ann. Rpt.* (1922), p. 8.

[4] These are studied in Hubbard, *Prevention of Cruelty to Animals in
New York State*, p. 18, *et seq.* Readers interested in them are referred
to that study.

gressed since 1910 without notable developments, except for the Rochester Humane Society. In 1918 the duties of dog registration and the income from the resultant fines were taken away from this society. At this period it entered the Rochester Community Chest and found its income still further reduced. As a result the society has had to give up its activities in humane education which it had previously considered the most important part of its work.[1]

The history of the Massachusette S. P. C. A. is very similar to that of the American S. P. C. A., allowance being made for local differences. It is the second oldest humane society in the country, having been incorporated in Massachusetts in March 1868 through the efforts of Mr. George T. Angell of Boston.[2] As in the case of its sister organization, by 1910 the prosecution of cruelists was only one branch, and not necessarily the most important, of its activities.

Because of its preeminent position in Massachusetts, it was more nearly a state-wide organization than the New York society, having salaried agents in various counties under whom were numerous volunteer local agents.[3] During 1910 the society was very active in investigating the stock yards about the city of Boston and particular efforts were made to prevent the shipping of "bob veal"—unweaned calves a few weeks old—between the states of Massachusetts and New York.[4]

[1] *Humane Society of Rochester, Ann. Rpt. for 1918, passim.*

[2] McCrea, *op. cit.*, p. 11.

[3] By 1917 these local agents numbered about 350, representing nearly every city and town in Massachusetts. *Mass. S. P. C. A., Ann. Rpt. for year ending March 1917.*

[4] *Mass. S. P. C. A., Ann. Rpt. for year ending March 1911,* appearing in *Our Dumb Animals,* vol. xliii, p. 191. The earlier reports of the Mass. S. P. C. A. will be found in this periodical; after 1915 they are published in pamphlet form.

In 1911 it was decided to construct the Angell Memorial Hospital for Animals, in which edifice would be housed the offices of the Massachusetts S. P. C. A. and the American Humane Education Society. Ground was bought in one of the suburbs of Boston, close to the Harvard Medical School, for $35,000, and plans were drawn up. During the year the Society found itself forced to combat a vigorous attempt by interested parties to repeal an act of 1910 allowing the Society to inspect slaughter houses.[1] A similar attempt to legalize "bob veal" traffic was thwarted. In connection with this last, the Society began a campaign against the transportation and use of aged and worn-out cows for "canners" and "bolognas".[2]

Construction of the Angell Memorial Hospital was delayed for a couple of years in the hope of being able to raise the required fund before commencing building operations. This hope proved vain, and in the fall of 1913 it was decided to begin construction without full funds in sight, but with the hope that they would be forthcoming. This decision was justified, and a year and a half later the hospital was opened.

To this hospital have come animals not only from all parts of Massachusetts but from the entire country. The problem of how to ship these animals—mostly dogs, and often extremely valuable—has been met by the construction of a special non-patented shipping crate, designed especially for the Society. The facilities of the hospital have been more than once overtaxed, so that it has been necessary to establish a waiting list and to refuse cases for which no room could be found.[3] During the year 1922, 4,592 small animals and 416 large animals were treated at the hospital,

[1] *Mass. Sess. Laws*, 1910, ch. 590.
[2] *Mass. S. P. C. A., Ann. Rpt. for year ending March 1912.*
Mass. S. P. C. A., Ann. Rpt. for year ending March 1922, p. 7.

making a total of 26,350 cases since the opening of the hospital on March 1, 1915.

The activities of the Society have expanded year by year. In 1917 one great need was met by the gift of a rest farm for horses at Metheuen. In 1920 a Women's Auxiliary was formed to assist in the financing of the Society and to help it meet the strain upon its resources occasioned by its new growth. By means of fairs and social events they made possible in 1921-1922 the refitting with modern equipment of several of the small animal wards in the hospital.

Some of the activities of the Society during 1921 within the limits of the city of Boston are indicated by the following table:

Complaints investigated	8,197
Animals (all kinds) examined during such investigation	54,343
Horses taken from work	1,281
Horses humanely destroyed	967
Other animals humanely destroyed	5,723
Animals inspected (stockyards and abattoirs)	725,734
Animals sick or injured, humanely destroyed	1,764
Horses watered on Boston streets during summer	77,488
Prosecutions	233
Convictions	216

During the year, the income of the society totaled $191,-332.88, of which nearly $67,000 was from bequests and $31,092.42 was from members and donors. The expenses totaled $164,457.79. Of this total, $17,224 went towards expenses of *Our Dumb Animals.* Salaries and agents' expenses absorbed $63,328, and the hospital department $39,-682. The Rest Farm including implements, live stock, etc., cost $13,042.[1]

The Connecticut Humane Society divides its activities between animals and children. Its agents are active in both

[1] *Mass. S. P. C. A., Ann. Rpt. for year ending March 1922,* p. 12.

fields, investigating child cases and animal cases according to the order in which they present themselves. Lack of means has prevented the Society hitherto from dividing the work between two separate departments, though this intention has several times been expressed. In 1912 the president announced, " Humane work is naturally segregated into two departments—that of animals and that of persons. Each should be generalized in a separate department as means are provided." [1] In 1917 he again said, " We are now seeing more and more, not only the necessity of creating two departments, but also the advantages of special agents in each, and an adequate equipment of the nature that each department needs. Progress must lead to special agents in each department, although both will be applying the same humane principles and have much in common, whereby there is a great saving in expense." [2]

The Society has followed a conservative policy, extending its activities little by little in its various fields as means were provided. In its animal work, it has sought " something higher than the prosecution of offenders ".[3] It believes rather in the probationary treatment of cruelists and in actively furthering the welfare of the animals themselves. In 1909 it founded the Frances Bereford Home for Animals for the boarding of horses and smaller animals. It has paid no little attention to the matter of humane education, forming and maintaining Bands of Mercy in the public schools of the state; in 1916 there were 691 of these Bands in 119 public schools with a membership of 27,000. The following figures give its finances for three representative years:

[1] *Connecticut Humane Society, 32nd Ann. Rpt.* (1912).

[2] *Conn. Hum. Soc., 37th Ann. Rpt.* (1917).

[3] *Conn. Hum. Soc., 30th Ann. Rpt.* (1910).

SUMMARY OF INCOME AND EXPENSES

	1910	1915	1921
State appropriation	$2,000	$2,000	$3,500
Membership dues and contributions	6,000	5,852	11,996
Income from invested funds............	5,100	5,833	16,560
Total income including bequests and miscellaneous receipts	$14,551	$22,810	$38,277
Total expenditures	14,126	15,468	36,778

The Society has always financed itself conservatively. All bequests are invested, and expenditures are never allowed to exceed the net income. It looks forward to becoming a state-wide society, but is careful not to over-expand itself upon an insufficient foundation.

The experience of other large societies in the eastern and central parts of the United States is practically the same as that of those described. In almost every case, the larger societies have experienced a growth during the last dozen years and have more or less expanded their activities. In several cases they have formed societies which, growing strong, have become independent organizations. Some anti-cruelty societies of which the Pennsylvania S. P. C. A.[1] is an example, have formed Ladies' Auxiliaries to which were entrusted administration of such activities as animal dispensaries, horse-watering stations, work-horse parades and other special fields, or which, like the Ladies' Auxiliary to the Massachusetts S. P. C. A., have aided in their financing.

Every society has its own local problems and its own way of meeting them. In Chicago, before the adoption of the 18th Amendment, many saloon keepers had constructed

[1] *Vide Pennsylvania S. P. C. A., 50th Ann. Rpt.*

horse-watering troughs before their doors as an added
attraction to teamsters. After the advent of prohibition,
these were neglected with the closing of the saloons. In
1920 the Chicago Anti-Cruelty Society decided to take over
and maintain these troughs.[1] The Nebraska Humane
Society, a recently formed but very active and progressive
organization in Omaha, which devotes most of its attention
to animals, has organized a Pet Owners Association to
arouse humane interest among children as a part of its
humane education work.[2]

In the South the most important humane organization
is the Louisiana S. P. C. A. It has classified its activities
under six heads: (1) prevention of cruelty on the streets
and the investigation of complaints sent in by members
and others; (2) the ambulance service; (3) humane destruction of diseased or homeless small animals; (4) the
operating of the pound and the dog wagon; (5) the maintenance of drinking fountains in the streets of New Orleans;
(6) the humane educational department.[3]

Previous to 1912 the society confined its activities to
the city of New Orleans. In 1912 the president stated:
" As the Louisiana *State* S. P. C. A., it is clearly our duty
to extend our operations over the entire state. There should
be a branch of our society in every good sized town in the
state." [4] During the year an attempt was made to carry out
this program, with the result that again, as during several
previous years, the expenses of the society exceeded its in-

Anti-Cruelty Society, 21st Ann. Rpt. (1920), p. 11. For a full account
to 1915 of the anti-cruelty societies in the city of Chicago and throughout
the state of Illinois, *vide* F. Morse Hubbard, *Prevention of Cruelty to
Animals in the States of Illinois, Colorado and California* (New York,
1916), pp. 1-36.

[2] Manuscript letter of April 24, 1923.

[3] *Louisiana S. P. C. A., 25th Ann. Rpt.* (1912).

[4] *Ibid.*, p. 21.

come, and the floating debt rose to nearly $8000. The following year resolutions were adopted that the president and executive committee of the society must personally meet any annual deficit they allowed to arise. The executive committee of the year accepted the responsibility and in 1913 the state-wide program was abandoned and the income exceeded the expenses by $854.26.[1]

In 1915 the society again planned state-wide expansion. This time their assistant secretary was sent to visit the larger towns of the state, remaining in each community as many days as he found it necessary to organize a society there. It was also suggested that he visit the already established societies within the state, and render assistance where they were not upon a firm foundation. During 1915 two new societies were organized within the state, one at Lake Charles and one at New Iberia;[2] the latter is still active.

In the western states, with the exception of California with its large San Francisco and Los Angeles societies, there are few important anti-cruelty organizations.[3] This is not surprising when the sparsely settled condition of this region is taken into consideration.

While many of the smaller societies noted in the reports of the American Humane Association are active and vigorous, accomplishing an unexpected amount of work with very limited resources, some exist only on letter-heads and in the American Humane Association lists. One letter received from the secretary of such a society reads: " I regret to say I cannot send you a copy of our Humane Society's report,

[1] *La. S. P. C. A., 26th Ann. Rpt.* (1913), p. 4.

[2] *La. S. P. C. A., 28th Ann. Rpt.* (1915), p. 10.

[3] For the discussion of the Colorado, Washington and Wyoming state humane bureaus, *vide infra*, ch. v. For an account of the California animal societies to 1915, *vide* F. Morse Hubbard, *Prevention of Cruelty to Animals in the States of Illinois, Colorado and California*, p. 69, *et seq*

because we have made none. There are only two members
in the Society, the President, and myself, the Secretary."
From Alaska comes a letter from the secretary of the
humane society accredited to that territory: " Our Humane
Society, as an organization, is something of the past. There
are a few of us left, but the principal number of old-timers
has left." [1]

Besides the regularly organized anti-cruelty societies,
there are here and there other organizations and groups
which interest themselves in this work. In several cities
and towns Women's Clubs have organized anti-cruelty committees. For the most part, the work accomplished by these
committees is negligible, as there is lacking the interested
personnel of an S. P. C. A. membership and the financial
backing that such a membership ensures. What income
such committees do receive, is only a meagre grant from the
Women's Clubs. The Women's Club of North Carolina
provides an example. It has a special committee for the
Prevention of Cruelty to Animals, which during 1922 distributed some cards and posters. In addition one or two
cruelty cases were investigated and reported. Usually the
work fell on one or two interested individuals.[2] In Corpus
Christi, Texas, the City Federation has a humane committee,
receiving its income from the city, which cooperates with
the city and county officials in prosecuting cases of cruelty
to animals and children.[3]

The Humane Animal Commission of Los Angeles, California, functions like the Corpus Christi Committee. In
1908 the city of Los Angeles made a contract with the
Humane Animal League of that city for the conduct of

[1] Manuscript letter of Nov. 11, 1922.
[2] Manuscript letter of April 23, 1923.
[3] Manuscript letter of May 1923.

the city pound. The validity of the contract was at once attacked on the ground that it violated the provision of the city charter, which required contracts involving the expenditure of money by the city to be let only after competitive bid. The courts upheld this contention, and declared the contract void. In the following year, after the arrangement with the Humane Animal League had been declared illegal, the city council established a Humane Animal Commission consisting of three persons appointed by the mayor and council. The conduct of the pound under the Commission as then established did not prove entirely satisfactory, and in 1912 the city council authorized the Humane Animal Commission to appoint a secretary who should have immediate supervision of the pound and of the work connected therewith.[1]

In 1913 the city council of Los Angeles decided to vest authority to perform this work in a new commission. Accordingly, an ordinance was passed creating the present Humane Animal Commission and providing that, in addition to the maintenance of the public pound, it should be the duty of said commission to enforce all ordinances of the city of Los Angeles and all humane laws of the state concerning the care or treatment of dumb animals or for the prevention of cruelty to such. Since that time, practically all the animal welfare work in the city of Los Angeles has been carried on by the Humane Animal Commission.[2]

The Commission is a city department, with five commissioners appointed by the mayor and confirmed by the city council. They each serve for a term of four years. The Commission has no membership and receives no donations.

[1] Hubbard, *Prevention of Cruelty to Animals in the States of Ill., Col., and Cal.*, p. 94.

[2] The Los Angeles S. P. C. A. serves the rural territory outside the city limits.

Its income is voted as a budgetary allowance from the city. In addition it collects and credits to its account the city dog-license fees. It has always kept a careful check on its expenditures, with the result that it has never had to draw its full appropriation. Its income and expenditure for three representative years were as follows:

	July 1910–11	*July 1915–16*	*July 1921–22*
Receipts	$30,190.25	$36,716.80	$56,621.50
Expenditures	13,140.77	15,864.37	22,778.82

During the calendar year of 1922 fifteen hundred and sixty-five cases involving large animals were investigated, five thousand three hundred and eleven animals were examined, and one hundred and seventy-four were destroyed; there were thirty-eight arrests and twenty-eight convictions.[1]

In several cities instruction in the essentials of the prevention of animal cruelties is given in the police training schools. In Philadelphia, New York, Chicago and St. Louis, police officers and patrolmen receive instruction as to their duties when cruelty cases are brought to their attention. In addition they are supplied with catechisms relating to the most frequent abuses witnessed on the city streets.[2] In Chicago the members of the police force are provided with a set of instructions of which four sections deal with their duty where animals are involved.[3]

In nearly every state there is some one humane society incorporated as a State Society with statewide jurisdiction. With very few exceptions, these state societies have not at present found it possible to expand much outside the limits of their home cities. At the most, they send out field

---

[1] Manuscript letter of April 11, 1923.

[2] *A. H. A., 41st Ann. Rpt.* (1917), p. 12.

[3] F. Morse Hubbard, *op. cit.*, p. 7.

agents to cover large stretches of rural territory as best they may, and to organize branch societies or independent groups where they find sufficient local interest. Only in Illinois and Wisconsin and to a limited extent in New York have state societies been successful in building up extensive branch organizations, and in this manner somewhat unifying activities for animal protection in different parts of their states.

Other states have sought to gain a unity in their work by means of State Humane Conventions or Federations. In 1910 there were five of these federations—in New York, Pennsylvania, Michigan, California and Indiana.[1] By 1922 the number was eight; in addition to the five already mentioned, associations had been formed in Florida, Minnesota and Ohio.[2]

Of these federations, the three most active are in California, New York and Pennsylvania. The California association was organized in September 1908 and incorporated the following year with a membership of twenty-eight anti-cruelty societies.[3] The aims of the association were " to advance the humane cause through the promotion of fellowship and effective cooperation between societies and humanitarians, to centralize the humane strength of the state in one working body, and to inspire each society with an appreciation of its possibilities and to aid in realizing all of its opportunities through conventions, correspondence and moral support ".[4]

The membership of the association consists of individuals and anti-cruelty societies. Voting power is based upon a

[1] McCrea, *op. cit.*, p. 29. The Michigan association, then as now, was only a " paper " association and no meetings have been held since 1910 (manuscript letter from secretary, May 1923).

[2] *A. H. A., 46th Ann. Rpt.* (1922), p. 63.

[3] *A. H. A., 34th Ann. Rpt.*, p. 128.

[4] Hubbard, *op. cit.*, p. 104.

system of proportional representation; societies are grouped
in classes according to their respective membership and are
entitled to representative members in the state association
in proportion to such membership. These individual representatives are required to pay dues so that in effect, the
contributions made by each society are in proportion to its
membership. In addition to the representative members of
the societies, individuals interested in humane work may
join the state humane association. In 1915 this individual
membership numbered eighty-five.

One of the first problems before the California state
association was to separate the goats from the sheep among
the California anti-cruelty societies. A number of these
organizations during the early years of the association were
" nothing more than frauds ".[1] At the time, humane officers
had the right to carry arms. The larger cities in California
were visited by a wave of strikes, and strike breakers and
strikers met in numerous clashes. Both sides enrolled themselves in certain of the humane societies in large numbers in
order to obtain permits to carry arms, and were sworn in as
humane officers by judges of the superior court in lots of
fifty and seventy-five at a single sitting, no effort being made
to investigate the character of the prospective officers. One
San Francisco paper commented that nearly every platform
man running a street car in San Francisco during a strike in
the winter of 1907 wore an anti-cruelty society badge.[2]
These wild-cat organizations were refused membership in
the state association and through its efforts a bill was passed
in the legislature taking away the right of humane officers to
carry arms. The spurious societies immediately questioned
the constitutionality of the act, but the superior court upheld
the law and the decision was confirmed by the Appellate

---

[1] *A. H. A., 34th Ann. Rpt.*, p. 128.

[2] Hubbard, *op. cit.*, p. 85.

Court. With the desire to further weed out spurious societies the state association in 1913 sponsored legislation annulling the granting of fines to prosecuting anti-cruelty organizations.

The association has also sought to secure the organization of new societies in California, and to assist and strengthen weak ones. For a few months in 1914 a special officer was employed to visit various parts of the state which needed attention, to take action for the prevention of cruelty, and to make arrests wherever necessary, and also wherever possible to arouse local sentiment and bring about the organization of local societies. Lack of funds, however, made it necessary for this project also to be abandoned.

The New York State Association has likewise been very active, though never forced to meet such acute situations as have faced the California organization. Its chief function has been to bring all the New York societies into cooperation, with the result that of the large states, New York is the most thoroughly covered by humane organizations. In the winter of 1917 a state humane agent was appointed by the association with duties similar to those of the California agent.[1]

In Pennsylvania there exists the Federated Humane Societies of Pennsylvania which has a nominal membership of thirty-six societies (actually only fifteen are represented in meetings) and meets once a year for conference and consultation. It does no other work.[2] For a time, an unofficial federation existed in New Jersey. The S.P.C.A.s of this state maintained a state legislative committee to observe and report on humane legislation. It made reports from 1913 to 1916, becoming inactive in that year upon the death of its secretary.

---

[1] *National Humane Review*, vol. vi, p. 53. The idea comes from New England where the first state agent was employed to attend to rural work in Maine (*Nat. Hum. Rev.*, vol. vii, p. 90).

[2] Manuscript letter from secretary of May 23, 1923.

At various times a movement has been set on foot to have a broad federation of the humane societies in the western part of the United States.   In 1916 the field representative for the Northwest of the American Humane Education Society sent the following letter to several of the larger western societies and state bureaus:

I am writing the societies of the North-West organized for the broader humanity, relative to the federation of such societies for the purpose of getting together at least once a year for the discussion of plans and untangling some of the problems that are peculiar to our situation. Would your society be glad to be identified with such a movement? [1]

The reply of the secretary of the Wyoming State Board was very favorable.   He added, moreover, that in 1915 he had discussed the matter with the secretary of the Colorado Humane Bureau and had partly arranged a plan of cooperation.   Apparently nothing came of this suggestion.

In 1920 the proposal was raised again, this time by the president of the Los Angeles S. P. C. A.   In the annual report of the Society for that year, she suggested cooperation between the animal societies of southern California in particular and if possible a broad coordination of all the western societies.   Such a federation would be a clearing house for humane problems and would be able to meet the big crises occasioned by droughts, pests, etc., to which the western animal movement is subject.   The Los Angeles S. P. C. A. offered to inaugurate such a movement. [2]

To some extent unity is given to humane work for both animals and children throughout the United States by the American Humane Association.   This organization was

[1] *Wyoming Humane Society and State Board of Child and Animal Protection, Biennial Report for 1916.*

Los Angeles S. P. C. A., 43rd Ann. Rpt. (1920), p. 5.

founded in 1874 and was incorporated in the District of Columbia under Federal laws in 1903. Its purposes as stated in its certificate of incorporation are:

(a) The prevention and suppression of cruelty, especially of cruelty to children and animals, and the enforcement of all national laws therefor; and the enforcement of national and state humane laws in any state or territory of the United States in which exists no society having for its object or one of its objects the enforcement of such laws in such state or territory, respectively, and in any state or territory of the United States, in which such a society exists, with the written consent of such society thereto.

(b) The association and coöperation of individuals and societies and corporations (organized in the United States and Territories for the purpose of preventing and suppressing cruelty, especially cruelty to children and animals), by making such individuals, societies and corporations members of this corporation.

(c) The promotion of the enactment and enforcement of humane laws.

(d) The organization, assistance and encouragement of humane societies and societies for the prevention of cruelty, especially of cruelty to children and animals.

(e) The owning, manufacturing, making, publishing, buying, selling, distributing and giving away of humane books, papers, periodicals, tracts, pictures, lanterns, slides, medals and other things conducive to humane education.

(f) The receiving, acquiring, holding, owning, investing, and reinvesting, collecting, selling and conveying and using in the promotion and carrying out of any of its objects, and in accordance with its by-laws and the directions of grantors, testators and benefactors, all kinds of property, real, personal or mixed.[1]

---

[1] For complete copy of the certificate of incorporation, *vide* McCrea, *op.. cit.*, pp. 221-222.

Since 1877 the American Humane Association has held annual meetings, which serve to bring together workers in both fields of humane activity. These meetings are not only business meetings, but serve also for the exchange of ideas and the stimulation of interest. Their programs include papers and addresses on subjects relating to child and animal protection, the discussion and adoption of suitable resolutions on these subjects, and reports from special committees which have been appointed to investigate such matters as slaughter-house reform, animal transportation, model forms of state dog-license laws, and other humane legislation.

The American Humane Association as an organization, is controlled by a board of directors elected by qualified members. It is managed by officers selected by this board. Its activities are divided among several departments. There is first that of the executive and general management. Next in importance is the department which publishes the *National Humane Review* with its growing monthly circulation of 50,000 to 60,000 at present, and which conducts general propaganda. During the period of American participation in the World War, one of the most important departments was that of the Red Star.[1] Foreign work has a department of its own. Finally, there is a special fund which provides for a humane revivalist who encourages and assists weak societies and endeavors to prevent them from becoming inactive.[2]

In connection with this last department, it had long been the desire of the president of the Association that a field agent should be appointed. In addressing the 1911 meeting, he stated as third among the needs of the Association, " a

[1] *Vide infra,* ch. iii, pp. 60-63.

[2] *National Humane Review,* vol. xi, p. 83. This article is reprinted by the Association as a pamphlet entitled *Outline of Work* (1923).

field agent who can go around among our societies and help the weak ones; who can study their needs; who can go to the universities and present our cause to the young men and women who are about to go forth in life; who can act as a recruiting agent for our work; and who can lay the foundations for a school and a magazine." [1] During recent years, the Association has found it possible to maintain such a field agent, most of whose time has been spent in the West.

For a time there were hopes of a still broader international federation of humane societies. One plan that was presented at the 1910 International Conference provided for: (1) a central bureau, headquarters of the federation, probably in London or New York, with branches; (2) a federation secretary, a man of keen insight and wide knowledge; (3) a library to contain reports and copies of the laws of different countries on all subjects relating to child and animal life; (4) interchange of ideas; (5) active propaganda; (6) arranging visits between members of federated societies; and (7) international congresses. [2] The 1910 Conference passed a resolution that an international bureau be formed as a first step toward such federation. [3]

In July 1914 representatives of societies in various countries met at London at the invitation of the Royal S. P. C. A. The American Humane Association was represented by its president. After discussion, an international organization to promote animal welfare was formed and officers elected. Dr. William O. Stillman, the president of the American Humane Association, was elected its first president. Membership was limited to societies created for the legal prevention of cruelty to animals. Any such might

[1] *A. H. A., 35th Ann. Rpt.* (1911), p. 12.
[2] *A. H. A., 34th Ann. Rpt.*, p. 46.
[3] *Ibid.*

belong on the payment of $5.00 annual dues. Biennial congresses were decided upon and a permanent " Bureau of Information " was established where advice in regard to anti-cruelty laws in different countries and copies of literature and reports might be secured. The first congress was to be held in July 1916, conditions permitting.[1] The outbreak of the World War and subsequent events precluded the development of this international organization.

The first step since the War towards internationalizing humane activity was taken in an international humane conference held in New York City in October 1923 in connection with the 47th annual meeting of the American Humane Association. At this conference, which devoted three days to the discussion of animal protection and three days to child protection, there was a large attendance and representatives were present from the leading countries. A resolution was adopted calling on the humane societies in all countries to cooperate in the reorganization and effective functioning of the International Association formed in London in 1914.

During the dozen years from 1910 to 1922, there were no outstanding changes of policy in the protection of animals from cruelty. Instead, this work was expanded on lines already laid down. The S. P. C. A.s in the large cities grew in size and resources, increased their forces of agents, and made their machinery for animal protection more effective; they also added substantially to their material equipment. In every case, their financial policies were conservative, and they preferred to regulate their expenditures by their ordinary annual income, putting bequests aside for investment.

Less can be said for the host of smaller S. P. C. A.s and humane societies serving towns and rural districts. Their number increased as did their membership, but very many

[1] *Nat. Hum. Rev.*, vol. ii, p. 221.

of them rested on fragile foundations. As a group, they showed no such development and growth as did the larger city organizations, although several of their number, under brilliant individual leadership, became important anti-cruelty agencies.

There can be no question of the benefits of confederation and inter-organization to the anti-cruelty societies. In 1910 the California, New York and Pennsylvania state associations, while active, had not realized their full capabilities. During the following decade they contributed materially towards the development of humane work in their states. The state associations organized after 1910 learned from their experience and profited thereby.

The American Humane Association, under the presidency of the late Dr. William O. Stillman also made its work more effective through the establishment of the *National Humane Review* and the employment of field workers.

CHAPTER III

THE EUROPEAN WAR AND ANIMAL PROTECTION

As may be seen from the table on page 25, the first two years of the World War affected the activities of the American societies for animal protection little if at all. In the annual reports of many of the societies for 1914, slight reference was made to it. During 1915 and 1916 the *National Humane Review* and some of the other humane publications carried notices of the sufferings that animals were necessarily undergoing in the battle zone. The American Humane Association in its annual conferences of these years did not discuss this subject at great length and made only passing reference to the English organizations that were endeavoring to relieve this suffering.

Some few societies succeeded in raising a rather impracticable issue during this period. All animals sent to European battlefields were certain to suffer; these societies sought to confine such animal agonies to European horses and mules insofar as this could be accomplished by preventing the shipment of American transport animals. Several letters to this effect were published in the *National Humane Review* and in *Our Dumb Animals*. Letters from one or two of the smaller societies stated that their secretaries also corresponded with various government officials to this effect. Societies located in the larger ports and terminal centers met this problem by making certain that the condition of the animals congregated in stations awaiting transportation was not unendurable.[2]

[1] *Vide Annual Reports* of Amer. S. P. C. A. and La. S. P. C. A. for 1916.

As early as 1914 the Connecticut Humane Society foresaw a problem that would arise if the war should be of such duration as to cause a steady shipment of draft animals from this country.   In the *Annual Report* of that year, the president of the Society said: " By sending horses abroad for war, our own supply will be seriously diminished.   The price of horses will be high.   Fewer new horses will be put into service.   More old and poor ones will continue in use and carry the burden.   Thus demands upon S. P. C. A.s for their relief will be largely increased." [1]

The *National Humane Review* during 1915 and 1916 noted the mounting price of horses and mules and commented on the poor condition of many animals in use during the latter part of that period, particularly the type of horses appearing at the auction block.[2]   The Louisiana S. P. C. A. in its 1915 report specifically referred to this phenomenon:

We find more old animals on the streets now than heretofore, caused by the scarcity or the terribly high cost of animals at the present time, resulting from the European War drawing on the American market.   The price of horses has advanced 35% during the year.   The best grades are no longer obtainable at any price and the poor owner has to purchase decrepit animals at the auction block.   Firms who heretofore sold their stock at the end of each year have ceased to do so, holding on to the old ones, they being better than the present supply that is offered.[3]

This degeneration in the quality of animals used continued right through the war period, increasing the labor of all anti-cruelty societies.   After the spring of 1917, many societies found another drain upon their resources in the aid

---

[1] *Conn. Hum. Soc., 34th Ann. Rpt.*, p. 11.

[2] *Vide Mass. S. P. C. A., Ann. Rpt. for 1916.*

[3] *La. S. P. C. A., 28th Ann. Rpt.*, p. 16.

they extended to the veterinary service of the government
and to the Red Star. In the matter of assisting the War
Department, several societies allowed local pride to out-
weigh common sense. At least two bought animal ambulances which they desired to present to the Government,
but which proved impossible of transportation to France.

After America's entry into the War, some societies
found themselves weakened in another direction. The
American S. P. C. A. noted in 1918 that " many old employees entered the military service and it was impossible to
replace at short notice men who by reason of long years of
training had become proficient in their particular line of
work. Others were forced by the high cost of living to
seek the larger salaries paid by the commercial world. All
organizations supported wholly or in part by public gener-
osity also suffered financially from the stress of war." [1]
The Massachusetts S. P. C. A. and the Pennsylvania S. P.
C. A. felt the same loss.

This blow fell heaviest on the larger organizations with
more or less extensive salaried staffs. In small local societies the age of the members for the most part precluded
war service. Far more serious to all societies, large and
small, were the falling-off of contributions and the increase
of costs due to the rise of prices. As was only to be expected, animal societies suffered heavily from the competition of war-time charities. This was felt even before the
entry of the United States into the War. The 1915 report
of the Louisiana S. P. C. A. remarked, " In point of membership, I think we are still feeling the effects of the European War to some extent, as calls upon the charitable public
of New Orleans have been frequent and urgent during the
past year." [2]

[1] *Amer. S. P. C. A., 53rd Ann. Rpt.* (1918), p. 5.
[2] *La. S. P. C. A., 28th Ann. Rpt.* (1915), p. 5.

A little later the *National Humane Review* commented upon the effect of the War: " Recently, several societies have written to the American Humane Association stating that their work has practically ceased; that they have no money left with which to do humane work and that they will have to close their doors." [1]

The following table showing the income of the Hudson District S. P. C. A. of New York State makes clear how seriously the War affected the finances of a moderately large society:

RECEIPTS OF THE HUDSON DISTRICT S. P. C. A. FROM ALL SOURCES

1913	$22,500.57
1914	18,431.81
1915	15,576.66
1916	10,574.84
1917	10,348.48
1918	7,003.97
1919	13,366.54
1920	10,488.86
1921	16,234.76

In the Far West, the Los Angeles Society reported difficulties in raising its income traceable to the War: " During the War, the purchase of Liberty Bonds and contributions to agencies which were helping in the Great Cause made it impracticable for the Society to call upon the public at large for funds."[2]

The rise in prices beginning in the spring of 1915 after the temporary depression in this country at the outbreak of the War, likewise worked hardship upon anti-cruelty societies. During 1915 the pressure of European war orders and the high prices paid for them caused an increase of production in several fields of industry. This gained momentum throughout 1915 and 1916, carrying with it a

[1] *National Humane Review*, vol. iii, p. 205.
[2] *Los Angeles S. P. C. A., Ann. Rpt. for 1920.*

gradual increase in the prices of all commodities. The war finance policy of the United States government augmented the inflation which continued, except for a short interruption in the winter of 1918-1919, until the summer of 1920. The early stages of the price increase aroused no comment; by 1918, however, its effects were felt by anti-cruelty societies as by all other organizations and individuals. Those societies maintaining shelters and doing animal relief work were the hardest hit. Again the large societies were the worst sufferers. The Louisiana S. P. C. A. complained that "the high cost of dog-catching has reached such altitudes that it cost the Society more to operate the dog-pound last year than the total receipts from dog licenses have amounted to." [1]

One branch of the activities of the Rhode Island Humane Education Society since its founding has been to issue an humane art calendar. In 1919, although the company that supplied these calendars to the Society did so at cost, the directors of the Society were uncertain whether they could afford to continue the distribution of them. In the end they compromised by sending out 1919 pads to be attached to 1918 backs. In 1920 their calendar bill was four times the pre-War figure, and the precedent of the previous year was followed; the 1920 backs were made so that 1921 pads might be attached to them if necessary. [2]

A financial problem that faced more than one city society was whether it should enter the local Community Chest. This organization was an outgrowth of war charity needs. In effect, it was a financial federation of the charities of the neighborhood. A simultaneous drive was made for all these charities, and the resulting fund was then apportioned among them according to their needs. In return,

[1] *La. S. P. C. A., 32nd Ann. Rpt.* (1919), p. 5.
[2] *Rhode Island Humane Education Society, 16th Ann. Rpt.* (1920), p. 6.

each society had to pledge itself not to make a separate appeal for funds upon its own account. Several animal protective societies entered their respective community chests. A few among them, the Arizona Humane Society being one, found the plan advantageous and advocated it.[1] A larger number duplicated the unfortunate experience of the Rochester Humane Society which found its income greatly decreased by dependence on the Rochester (N. Y.) Community Chest.[2] In most community chests animal protective societies found themselves out of favor; "people before animals" was a natural slogan. Moreover, under the rules of the community chests, these societies had to sacrifice their membership lists, losing thus the support that comes from an enthusiastic personnel.[3]

The American Humane Association set its face against community chests from their very initiation. During 1917 and 1918 every number of the *National Humane Review* carried an editorial by President Stillman criticizing the idea. In one such he quoted with approval the following: " I believe that the Community Chest is unwise, un-American, and undesirable. It puts the brake on individual initiative, and shackles progressive and immediate improvement. It has been particularly injurious to societies for the prevention of cruelty to animals." [4]

In brief, the World War distinctly increased the labors of the animal protective societies by enlarging the opportunities for cruelty through the use of poorer draught animals and the additional labor forced upon them by the exigencies of the War. Many societies also felt that one of the psycho-

[1] *Humane Monthly*, vol. i, p. 11.

[2] *Vide supra*, p. 35.

[3] *National Humane Review*, vol. viii, p. 175.

[4] *Ibid.*, vol. x, p. 171.

logical reactions of the War was to release many of the more brutal instincts of mankind, and that animals suffered thereby. On the other hand, the financial burdens of the War—Liberty Bond drives and war charities—cut off no little financial support from anti-cruelty societies. American societies were not prostrated as were those of some of the belligerant countries, but they suffered severely. Some of the weaker ones collapsed entirely, the stronger in many cases found it necessary to limit their work.

Out of the sufferings of animals in the World War grew a new organization, the Red Star. As early as October 1914, there was a humane movement for the protection of the animals in the war zones. In that month President Stillman of the American Humane Association wrote in the *National Humane Review:*

What is now needed for the horses is an adequate international convention which will undertake to do more to protect those unfortunate brutes which have become the victims of battle. Great Britain and Germany already have had orders issued that men shall be designated to destroy war horses which have been wounded or severely injured. A new world-wide international agreement should be instituted whereby each country will undertake to have equine Purple Cross veterinarians present on the field of conflict to care skillfully for battle horses and to relieve their sufferings as humanely and promptly as possible. An international movement is already under way seeking to accomplish this end.[1]

The Purple Cross referred to by President Stillman was started in England at the outbreak of the War by the anti-vivisection societies. It never functioned actively and was soon superseded by the international organization known as the Red Star. At the commencement of hostili-

---

[1] *Ibid.*, vol. ii, p. 229.

ties, Swiss federal and cantonal authorities organized the Red Star Society to look after the care of war animals. A meeting of the friends of animals was held and the humane organizations of all countries asked to cooperate.[1] No action was taken by American societies during the first two years of the War, although each of the combatants organized its own Red Star service.

On May 22, 1916, Secretary of War Baker wrote to President Stillman as follows: " It is believed that plans similar in tenor to those of the Red Cross could be very advantageously adopted by your Society for rendering organized aid to injured animals in time of war, and if your Society will undertake this work, the War Department will be very glad to cooperate with you." [2]

On July 26, 1916, the American Red Star Animal Relief was organized as a department of the American Humane Association to cooperate with the United States Veterinary Corps. The first Red Star branch was formed in Newport, R. I.[3] The branch organizations were expected to assist in furnishing supplies and equipment for the veterinary service of the army and to endeavor to secure a suitable personnel for war-time volunteer field service. In addition, all branches were asked to contribute to the Red Star Fund of the American Humane Association.

During the winter of 1916 a few branches were formed. The spread of the Red Star was much more active after the entry of the United States into the War. In 1917 its organization was extended to include auxiliaries and junior leagues. In 1918 in Los Angeles alone, there were 28,179

[1] *Ibid.*, vol. iii, pp. 156-157.

[2] *American Humane Association, 41st Ann. Rpt.*, p. 14.

[3] *National Humane Review*, vol. iv, p. 193.

members of the Junior Red Star League, and they contributed $8,182.53 to the Red Star Fund.[1]

With the cessation of hostilities the main program of the American Red Star came to an end. Nevertheless, it was a powerful organization with the impetus of success behind it. It had a strong financial foundation and it was easy to divert its resources into peace-time channels. At the 1919 conference of the American Humane Association the president said:

The special function of the American Red Star Animal Relief is to meet conditions of suffering that exist on too large a scale to be handled successfully by local anti-cruelty societies. Examples are the Halifax explosion, the fire near Duluth, epidemic disease as in Colorado in 1919, and Texas coast storms. It is for situations such as these that the Red Star was founded and will be maintained.[2]

Since the War most of the attention of the Red Star has been devoted to bettering the condition of the western range stock.[3] In 1919 a representative visited the range country and carefully investigated conditions. The matter was then taken up with the U. S. Department of Agriculture. Leaflets were published on range stock shelter.[4]

Apart from this, the broad peace program originally mapped out for the Red Star has not been followed out. With the cessation of its war activities, much of the enthusiasm that helped to launch it has died. It exists today as a skeleton organization rather than as an active one. Its finances for 1922 were as follows:

[1] *A. H. A., 42nd Ann. Rpt.*, p. 23; *vide* also *National Humane Review,* vol. v, p. 144.

[2] *A. H. A., 43rd Ann. Rpt.*, p. 4.

[3] *Vide infra*, pp. 118-119.

[4] *A. H. A., 43rd Ann. Rpt.*, p. 15.

Balance, Sept. 1, 1921 .... $2,438.79

RECEIPTS

Donations and contributions $1,931.18
Memberships 7,076.16
Branches and auxiliaries 1,052.32
Leaflets and supplies 174.46
Memorial Tablet fund 828.75
Refund on convention expense 109.63
Interest on Liberty Bonds 12.75
    Total receipts .... ———— $11,185.25

    Total $13,624.04

DISBURSEMENTS

Salary of Director General $1,500.00
Salaries of office employees 5,257.69
National Humane Review and printing 3,699.16
Rent, heat, light and janitor 600.00
Postage, expressage, telephone and telegraph 817.65
Miscellaneous 226.93
Office supplies 397.48
Convention expense 150.00
Auditing 104.00
    Total disbursements .... ———— $12,752.91

    Balance $871.13

Additional expenditures of $1,752.96 for range stock relief literature, a memorial tablet, and repairs and storage for an animal ambulance were made out of a special fund.[1]

[1] *A. H. A., 46th Ann. Rpt.,* p. 51.

CHAPTER IV

ANIMAL WELFARE ASSOCIATIONS

THERE is a large and growing number of humane organizations which take no part in prosecuting cruelists, but which devote their entire attention to other specific forms of animal welfare. Included among these are the animal rescue leagues, the animal shelters, and the workhorse parade associations. Of these three types of organizations, the first two accomplish the broader work.

The animal shelters, in which classification the animal rescue leagues may be included, and the S. P. C. A.s occupy separate fields. They can, nevertheless, be operated together or separately, as experience has shown, without doing injury to each other. In fact, once an S. P. C. A. has passed a certain stage of its growth, some sort of shelter for animals that come under its protection or into its charge becomes absolutely essential.

As has been pointed out, the larger organizations such as the American S. P. C. A. and the Massachusetts S. P. C. A. maintain completely equipped animal hospitals in which shelters are necessarily included. Those S. P. C. A.s such as the Louisiana organization and a number of others, which manage the dog pounds of the municipalities in which they are located, must make provision for the care of many small animals. Young organizations whose resources are limited often believe it a wise policy to provide rest quarters for at least a few small animals.

There is a broad field, however, for societies devoting

themselves exclusively to animal shelter work, chiefly for the benefit of small animals. Several also include as annexes dispensaries and rest farms for worn-out horses.

The plan most widely adopted for these associations is that of the Elizabeth Morris Refuge—first, the maintenance of homes where animals may be temporarily sheltered or boarded by owners; second, the equipping of an animal hospital; third, the maintenance of temporary homes for suffering and homeless animals, and where unwanted animals may be humanely destroyed.[1]

Until the Elizabeth Morris Refuge for small animals was incorporated in Philadelphia in 1888, there had existed no organization making the care of small animals its special work, and thereafter practically no efforts were made on their behalf outside of the city of Philadelphia until the Animal Rescue League of Boston was organized. This, the first of animal rescue leagues, was started in March 1899 through the efforts of Mrs. Huntington Smith, who has since organized more than a dozen similar institutions.[2]

The Boston League began with a small house, shed and yard, and an aged married couple were hired to do the work. By 1910 it had grown until there were five houses and a stable in the city, and a country annex for horses. The policy of the League was stated in this year as follows:

We keep all dogs we receive, unless very sick or vicious, five days; then those unclaimed are humanely put to death except a limited number of desirable ones for which we can find good homes. We keep from twenty to thirty of the best of the cats and kittens to place in homes and the rest are put to death. We let no cat nor dog go without the payment of one dollar, and with the dog we supply a collar and a leash. For an extra good dog, we tell the purchaser that we expect a

[1] *National Humane Review*, vol. i, p. 223.
[2] *A. H. A., 38th Ann. Rpt.*, p. 29.

donation of from two to five dollars. This is to prevent men from obtaining good dogs for the purpose of selling them. Accurate records are kept of the placing out of all animals, and strict accounts of all money received and spent. We have a regular system of records for every part of our work and record every dog, cat, puppy or kitten received. We do not keep a large number of animals alive, nor to give away. Our object is to prevent and to release animals from suffering.[1]

The activities of the Boston League increased greatly during the next decade. In the city of Boston at present, several receiving stations are maintained. The aim of the League is that every settlement house in Boston should have a receiving station connected with it so that the children may be interested in the work.[2] In the late fall, winter and spring months, a travelling agent is employed to visit the rural territory about the city of Boston. Unlike the travelling agents of the S.P.C.A.s, his task is not to seek out cases of cruelty and bring the offenders to justice, but to relieve the residents of the territory of their surplus pets. As his coming is looked forward to, there is less cause to turn such animals adrift to shift for themselves, for most of the people are willing to put up with the temporary inconvenience that such animals may cause them until the arrival of the agent when they know that they will be humanely disposed of.

Since 1902 the League has maintained a patrol of the beaches within twenty-five miles of Boston from October 3rd to November 5th of each year. It has found that many families take dogs and cats with them to their summer homes at the beaches or else adopt stray animals during their stay there. When the time for departure arrives, no thought is given to these creatures. They are left to struggle to

---

[1] *A. H. A., 34th Ann. Rpt.*, p. 133.
[2] *Animal Rescue League of Boston, 23rd Ann. Rpt.* (1922), p. 5.

maintain life for a miserable month or two until they perish during the winter months. The extent of this practice may be judged when it is noted that during 1921 the League collected four hundred and one such deserted animals from the Boston beaches.[1]

Within the city of Boston the League carries on a horse rescue work similar to that of the Massachusetts S. P. C. A. These two organizations have always worked in harmony; more than once during severe winters they have willingly pooled their resources so as to be able to handle as many cases as possible. As a branch of its horse work, the League maintains a stable-inspection service compelling owners of horses unfit for labor either to give them proper treatment or to surrender them for humane destruction where cure is impossible. Every Christmas Eve several thousand dinners are provided for the horses of Boston.

During the year of 1921 the Animal Rescue League cared for the following animals:

Dogs 5,162
Cats 45,383
Other small animals 80
Birds 419
Horses taken from sales stables or from owners who were persuaded to give them up 652
Horses cared for at Pine Ridge 76

Total 51,772

The League has nine branches in and about the city of Boston. At Dedham is maintained the Pine Ridge Home for horses. At this home are to be found horses of two classes; the first consists of worn-out animals to whom the League grants a brief holiday in the fields before humanely putting them to death. The second class consists of

[1] *Ibid.*, p. 6.
[2] *Ibid.*, p. 3.

"boarders". These are usually the horses of pedlers and small dealers which have been overworked for a long period, but whose owners cannot afford to pay for their recuperation. The League has proved that a week or two at the Pine Ridge Home gives new life to such animals, conferring a benefit both upon horses and owners.

In addition to the above work the League distributes numerous pamphlets and publishes a magazine *Our Four-Footed Friends*. The income of the League for 1921 was $44,376.63. $3,896.05 came from membership dues, $15,-608.87 from donations, and $15,440.68 from interest on investments.

Within Massachusetts there are nine other rescue leagues, modeled upon the Boston organization. Of these, the League of New Bedford is the most important with an expenditure during 1921 of $8,229.54.[1]

The state with the second largest number of rescue leagues is Pennsylvania, where the Morris Refuge was the initial organization. There are now two within the city of Philadelphia and three in the western part of the state.[2]

In September 1921, after a long period of inactivity, the Kentucky Annual Rescue League was reorganized. The Kentucky Humane Society had long been requested to take over the Louisville pound and add rescue work to its program, but it felt that it had enough to do with the investigation and prosecution of cruelty cases. Upon its refusal to act, some of its members resurrected the Animal Rescue League and took over the pound. From the beginning, it has had financial difficulties. Louisville has a Community Chest which the Animal Rescue League refused to enter because the Chest had never raised its full quotas.

---

[1] *Animal Rescue League of New Bedford, Ann. Rpt. for 1921.*
[2] *A. H. A., 44th Ann. Rpt.,* p. 81.

The League has had to meet criticism from some quarters because of this decision.[1]

Although differently titled, the New York Women's League for Animals performs a work very similar to that of the rescue leagues. It had its inception in 1906. At that time the need was felt for an organization which would materially assist in humane work for animals while not interfering with the work of the American S. P. C. A. It was then known as the Women's Auxiliary of the American S. P. C. A. and occupied itself with certain special fields of the Society's work. Its first interest was in the holding of a workhorse parade, which was done in 1906 as also in the following years. In 1908 an entirely new branch of work was undertaken in the establishing of temporary shelters for small animals during the summer months. Two shelters were opened, one in the Bronx and one on the lower East side. From June to November of that year there were received six hundred and ninety-eight dogs, four thousand one hundred and eighty-six cats, and two parrots. During the winter the Auxiliary worked in co-operation with the American S. P. C. A., arranging with drug stores to supply free telephone and post-card service for notifying the Society to call for unwanted animals.

Realizing the importance of training children in habits of kindness towards animals, the Auxiliary from its start devoted its efforts in that direction. Boys' clubs were organized, Young Defenders' leagues maintained, and illustrated lectures given. During 1909 courses of lectures on humane education were established at five different settlements, and about one thousand boys and girls were enrolled in clubs for the protection of animals against ill-usage.

The Auxiliary established the first clinic and dispensary

[1] Manuscript letter of May 24, 1923.

for the treatment of all animals in New York City, which was opened in January 1910. During the winter non-slipping chain shoes for horses were given to truck drivers. Watering and sprinkling places were also established.[1]

In 1910 the Auxiliary incorporated itself under the general law as the New York Women's League for Animals in order that it might become the beneficiary of a legacy which it had been informed a friend was desirous of making.[2] It now had a membership of one hundred and twenty-five with special committees on workhorse parades, juvenile animal leagues, summer shelters and protection of small animals, protection of horses, the free dispensary for animals, and an inspection committee. Soon after the Mountain Rest Farm for horses was established by the League. It had no special police power nor right to receive fines, but it did, however, interest itself in the prosecution of what it deemed flagrant cases of cruelty.

During its early years, the growth of the League was extraordinarily rapid. By 1911 its membership had increased to over six hundred. It expanded its dispensary work and continued its program of workhorse parades and lectures on humaneness.[3] In 1914 it completed its $135,000 animal hospital which expanded on the work of the former dispensary, continuing its ideal of free treatment wherever the finances of the animals' owners did not warrant a donation.

During the war period the League, like so many other animal welfare societies, found its finances severely restricted by the competition of war demands on charity. At times one or another feature of the League's work had to be

---

[1] *A. H. A., 34th Ann. Rpt.*, p. 112.

[2] *Amer. S. P. C. A., 45th Ann. Rpt.* (1910), p. 7; *cf.* also *New York Women's League for Animals, 1st Ann. Rpt.* (1910), *passim.*

[3] *New York Women's League for Animals, 2nd Ann. Rpt.* (1911).

curtailed, but in most cases, additional efforts on the part
of friends of the League and the organization of pet brigades
tided over the stringency.[1]   After 1918 the League, in cooperation with the American S. P. C. A., devoted an increasing share of its attention to humane education, arranging
contests and offering prizes.   This work has continued with
success up to the present.[2]

By 1922, the twelfth year of its existence, the New York
Women's League for animals had developed into one of
the most active and successful animal welfare organizations
in this country.   Throughout this period it has enjoyed
high praise, with very little adverse criticism.   It has succeeded in winning men and women of prominence for its
friends, and they have been of incalculable aid in the
League's development.   Much of its work does not appear
in printed figures; in its hospital, however, during 1921 it
treated 1,352 animals and in the dispensary 9,279.   Its
total hospital expenses during the year were $19,899.85.
The expenses of the horse-watering stations it maintained
during the summer, its humane education campaign, and
administration outlays, brought the total to $30,835.33.
Its income is almost entirely from dues and the donations
of friends as it has not had time to build up a strong
endowment.[3]

The Women's Auxiliary for the Pennsylvania S. P. C. A.
is similar in organization and activities to the New York
Women's League.   It was organized in 1917 to relieve the
Pennsylvania S. P. C. A. of the care of the horse-watering
stations in Philadelphia and the annual workhorse parades.
It started with an income of $6,475.38.   Year by year this

---

[1] *New York Women's League for Animals, 9th Ann. Rpt.* (1918).

[2] *Cf. infra*, p. 128.

[3] *New York Women's League for Animals, 11th Ann. Rpt.* (1921),
p. 15.

has increased. In 1919 it was $8,374.31, the next year
$9,700.63, and in 1921 $9,830.98. During its first two
years it confined itself to organizing workhorse parades
and to caring for the watering troughs, fifty-two in 1917
and sixty in 1918. In 1919 a watering wagon was purchased and equipped with gravel sprinklers to be used on
the slippery streets of the city during the winter months.
During 1919 a large number of new troughs were established. By 1920 there were two hundred and forty-four in
operation, and in 1921 two hundred and seventy-one.[1]

In a few cities, the police and the mail carriers have been
organized into S. P. C. A. auxiliaries. The South Bend
(Indiana) Humane Society interested the Board of Public Safety of South Bend in this plan and they agreed to
secure the signatures of the Chief of Police and of all the
policemen to the pledge: "We the undersigned, hereby
promise to try to be kind and to protect the children, the
horses, and all helpless creatures from brutal treatment."
This agreement was signed by forty policemen. The Society agreed to pay $2.00 into the pension fund of the
police system for each item of information which should
lead to a conviction for violation of humane laws. A similar agreement was also made with the mail carriers of the
city. Each group was then formed into an auxiliary of the
society.[2]

One type of the auxiliary work under consideration, the
workhorse parade, has been developed by a large number
of special organizations. The first workhorse parade held
in the United States was in Boston in 1903. The idea was
drawn from the English cart horse parades. In this first
parade it was discovered that all the prizes for good appear-

[1] *Auxiliary to the Pa. S. P. C. A., Annual Reports,* 1917-1921.
[2] *A. H. A., 42nd Ann. Rpt.,* p. 17.

ance of the horses went to the entries of large corporations, and that the result was a severe discouragement to the owners of individual entries. This was remedied in the parade held in the following year by the introduction of an Old Horse Class, whose ranks were recruited almost entirely from the entries of drivers who owned their own horses.[1]

The Boston Work Horse Parade Association which organized the 1903 parade was the first of its kind. It held that the existence of such an organization was justified if the public could be interested in the condition of the work horses which appeared on the city streets. The president of the Boston Association said in 1910:

Nothing has done more to uplift the condition of the work horses of Boston than the fact that the public looks upon the horses as an advertisement of the business of the owners. The hope of the work horse parade is generally to influence the drivers. To reward and encourage the driver rather than the owner should be the great object. We give a medal to the driver who has shown the same horse in two successive parades. . . . The great difficulty in the management of the parades is to secure judges who are competent and thoroughly honest in making the award.

A few years later he Association decided to expand its activities and renamed itself the Boston Work Horse Relief Association. Besides holding its annual parade, it now maintains a free hospital for horses and a receiving station for dogs and cats. It employs agents, provides for stable inspection, and publishes literature, approaching more closely the type of animal relief associations already discussed.[3]

[1] *National Humane Review*, vol. i, p. 52.
[2] *A. H. A., 34th Ann. Rpt.*, p. 111.
[3] *A. H. A., 44th Ann. Rpt.* p. 59.

In 1920 there were in addition to the Boston Association, workhorse parade associations located in Chicago, Cleveland and San Francisco. As has been pointed out, both the New York Women's League for Animals and the Auxiliary to the Pennsylvania S. P. C. A. began as work horse parade associations.[1]   In addition, many of the other anti-cruelty societies have interested themselves in these parades, and the 1922 report of the American Humane Association noted fifty-four such parades held in as many cities in the United States.[2]

There can be no question of the significance of the animal *welfare* movement, in distinction to that for the *protection* of animals from *cruelty*. That efforts should be made to further the *welfare* of animals, shows that a great advance has been made since the days when Henry Bergh had to labor so valiantly to convince people that animals had a moral right to be protected from even the grosser forms of cruelty. It is one with the movements for prison reform, for better institutional care of children, for the restriction of child labor, and for various types of social insurance.

The animal *welfare* movement is an indication of an important development in our view of what we consider our duties towards the animal world. It is also an acknowledgment of the fact that much of the fight to protect animals from cruelty has been won, and that it is now possible to divert efforts and resources from this more elemental task to what is, after all, a much broader work. The data of Chapter II are proof that there is still much to be done in this field, that there are still many people as yet unreached by humane propaganda, and broad regions where laws for the protection of animals are not enforced; nevertheless,

[1] *Cf. supra*, pp. 69 and 91.
   A. H. A., 46th Ann. Rpt., p. 65.

welfare work can from now on develop concomitantly with *protective* activities, and possibly in time supersede them.

It is worth noting that most of the societies for animal *welfare* have developed since 1910. The first animal rescue leagues were founded many years earlier, it is true, but their greatest growth has occurred during the last generation. During these later years, they have expanded the field of their activities—they have opened animal hospitals and dispensaries, they have organized work-horse parades, they have established drinking fountains, etc. It is significant, too, that the New York Women's League for Animals, incorporated in 1910, has enjoyed such an astoundingly rapid development, and that protective organizations such as the American and the Massachusetts S. P. C. A.s have entered so largely into welfare activities during this period.

CHAPTER V

STATE ACTIVITIES FOR ANIMAL WELFARE

SEVEN states—Colorado, Minnesota, Montana, Washington, West Virginia, Wisconsin and Wyoming—have state agencies for the enforcement of anti-cruelty laws and the protection of animals and children. Of these, the Colorado State Bureau of Child and Animal Protection formed in 1901,[1] has achieved the best organization.

Before 1901 there had been a state humane society with powers to establish branch organizations throughout the state. Lack of necessary means, however, confined its activities entirely to the city of Denver. It was felt by the officers and directors of this society that it was not a charitable or benevolent organization but an arm of the law, and as such, should be supported by general taxation. Accordingly, bills were introduced in the legislatures of 1897 and 1899, designed to make the Society an official state agency supported by legislative appropriation. Because of apathy rather than active opposition, both bills failed to pass. Finally, in 1901, after considerable agitation, sufficient interest was aroused to secure the passage of a law constituting the Colorado Humane Society a State Bureau of Child and Animal Protection.[2]

The act did not change the society's organization, nor

[1] *Cf.* McCrea, *op. cit.*, pp. 216-217.

[2] Except where otherwise indicated this account of the Colorado Bureau is drawn from F. Morse Hubbard, *Prevention of Cruelty to Animals in the States of Ill., Col. and Cal.*, p. 37, *et seq.*

did it in any way interfere with its internal affairs. Those were still controlled by its by-laws. It did, however, provide that the governor, the superintendent of public instruction and the attorney general, should be ex-officio members of the Bureau's board of directors. It also provided that the Bureau should hold annual meetings at the state capital for the transaction of its business and the election of its officers, and for the consideration of questions relating to child and animal protection; and that the Bureau should make annual reports to the secretary of state in regard to its work, which the secretary of state should publish in pamphlet form and distribute to certain of the state and county officers, newspapers, and state and educational institutions. The law was accepted by the Society and straightway went into effect.

Under the present organization of the Bureau, the board of directors consists of eighteen members, three of whom are the state officers mentioned in the act creating the Bureau. The policy has been to divide the other fifteen members as equally as possible between the two leading political parties. The officers and employees are selected with a view to fitness and experience and not because of political affiliations. They are subject to recall and to civil service rules as are other officers and employees of the state. The salaried officers are a secretary, a clerk and three state officers. Two of the state officers are occupied for the most part with work in the city of Denver, and the other devotes his entire time to traveling about the state. As occasion demands, he is assisted in this state-wide work by one or both of the other officers.

Naturally this small force is not adequate to meet the needs of the state. Consequently, great dependence is placed upon the system of volunteer officers which was inaugurated by the Colorado Humane Society. Any person of good standing and judgment may be appointed a volunteer officer after making a sworn application to the Bureau and obtaining the endorsement of at least four reputable citizens of his town or county, one of whom must be an official.[1]

According to its act of incorporation,[2] the duties of the Bureau are; (1) to secure the enforcement of the laws for the prevention of wrongs to children and dumb animals; (2) to assist in organizing branch societies and to appoint local and state humane agents; (3) to assist such societies and agents in the enforcement of anti-cruelty laws; (4) to promote the growth of education and sentiment favorable to the protection of children and dumb animals. Before its incorporation as a state bureau, the Colorado Humane Society had organized five branch societies. After 1901 this branch organization collapsed and the sole remaining branch located at Colorado Springs incorporated itself in 1906 as the El Paso County Humane Society. Since 1910 two new societies have been formed at Boulder and Leadville under the auspices of the State Bureau.

From the time of its founding, the Bureau has not always maintained friendly relations with the state administration, and the resulting unpleasantness amounted to open conflict in 1903, in 1906, and again in 1915.[3] This last disagreement, arising out of a controversy between the Bureau and Judge Lindsay of the Denver Juvenile Court dating back to 1911, had most serious consequences for the Bureau. In May 1915, Governor Carlson vetoed the appropriation made by the legislature for the work of the Bureau, suggesting that the Bureau's work for children

[1] Manuscript letter of July 1923.
[2] Col. Sess. Laws, 1901, pp. 191-192, sec. 3.
[3] Hubbard, op. cit., pp. 61-64.

could well be taken over by the State Home for Dependent Children, and its animal work by the game wardens.[1]

The Bureau was faced with two alternatives—either to discontinue its activities until Governor Carlson's term should end and so lose its prestige, or else to appeal to the public for its entire financial support and so run the risk of dissociating itself from the state government. It denied the governor's charge of duplication of activities and made a direct appeal to the citizens of Colorado for private support to carry its work over until 1917, when Governor Carlson's term would end. As part of this program of appeal, pamphlets were issued, explaining in vivid terms the work of the Bureau to the citizens of the state, and it is believed by the officers of the Bureau that this type of publicity brought the work of the Bureau to the attention of many people in Colorado for perhaps the first time.[2]

The Bureau weathered this crisis by radically curtailing several departments of its work, and since 1917 has experienced no further trouble. Moreover, whereas before 1915 it received an annual appropriation of only $7,800, since 1917 it has received $10,500 each year. In addition, it has been able to count on varying contributions from private sources, resulting from the appeal made from 1915 to 1917; during 1921 and 1922 these contributions amounted to $2,662.50.

The Colorado Bureau has always prided itself on being an efficient organization. Its secretary writes, " The system of a State Board of Child and Animal Protection, free from political influence but responsible to the State, is so far superior to any other system of child and animal protection yet tried, that there is in many important ways but little ground for comparison. The per capita cost of

[1] Pamphlet, *To the Fathers and Mothers of Colorado*, issued by the Colorado State Bureau of Child and Animal Protection in 1915.

[2] Manuscript letter of July 1923.

dealing with our cases is the lowest known." Several
authorities corroborate the Bureau's estimate of itself.[1]

In 1907 the Wyoming Humane Society was constituted
a State Board of Child and Animal Protection.[2] In 1910
it was still in the stage of development, and spoke of its
work as " just getting under way ". It operated through a
state agent, a special officer, and a force of eighty-five volunteer officers to cover the state. During the year it
handled cases involving five hundred and sixty-eight children and four thousand three hundred and thirty-three
animals.[3]

During the following year it followed a double program.
On the one hand it began a campaign to force the attention
of the school authorities to the statute providing for humane
education; in this it had the cooperation of the Colorado
Bureau. It also endeavored to prevent as much as possible
the cruelties then practiced in sheep-shearing.[4] The sheepmen's and rangers' associations of the state lent it all assistance.

In 1913 a reorganization of the Board was effected.
It now became known as the Wyoming Humane Society
and State Board of Child and Animal Protection. Its government was now vested in a board of nine directors, a
majority of whom had to be appointed by the governor of
the state; they controlled the election of the president, vice-
president, state humane officer and secretary. Three members of this Board were designated an executive committee
to transact the current business of the Board when the

[1] *Cf.* William Henry Slingerland, " Child Welfare Work in Colorado ",
in the University of Colorado Bulletin, vol. xx, no. 10, p. 75, *et seq.*

[2] *Wyo. Sess. Laws,* 1907, ch. 82.

[3] *Wyoming State Board of Child and Animal Protection, Biennial
Report for 1911 and 1912.*

[4] *Cf. infra,* p. 120.

Board was not in session. It was expected that the state
humane officer and the secretary would organize local auxiliary societies throughout the state.[1]

The governing board of nine directors proved to be an
unwieldy institution, as in practice it was found difficult
to obtain a quorum at regular intervals. On the suggestion
of the governor of Wyoming, it was decided in 1919 to
free the Wyoming Humane Society from state ties, and in
its place to create the office of Commissioner of Child and
Animal Protection. Legislation to this effect was passed.[2]
The term of the Commissioner's office is two years, and his
salary $2500 a year. He is expected to cooperate with the
Wyoming Humane Society. Recently a new Commissioner,
formerly with the Salvation Army, and very much interested
in child welfare, has been appointed, and it is to be expected
that in the future, more emphasis will be placed on child
rather than animal protection.[3]

The Montana Bureau of Child and Animal Protection is
similar in organization to that of Colorado.[4] However,
because of insufficient appropriations during recent years,
it has not been able to accomplish its work effectively. In
Washington the state humane society was likewise constituted a state bureau in 1913.[5] It too has languished through
insufficient appropriations.

In West Virginia a state board was organized in 1899
to be known as the " West Virginia Humane Society ".

[1] *Wyoming Humane Society and State Board of Child and Animal
Protection, Biennial Report for 1917 and 1918*, p. 5.

[2] *Wyo. Sess. Laws*, 1919, ch. 32.

[3] *Wyoming Commissioner of Child and Animal Protection, Biennial
Report for 1921 and 1922.*

[4] By *Sess. Laws of 1903*, ch. 115, the state humane society was constituted a state bureau.

[5] *Wash. Sess. Laws*, 1913, ch. 107.

It had the same duties as the Colorado Bureau, but its annual appropriations were much smaller.[1] In 1919 its child work was taken over by the State Board of Children's Guardians. The Minnesota Society for the Prevention of Cruelty was constituted a state bureau in 1905.[2] It has a board of directors consisting of thirty members, the governor of the state, the attorney-general and the superintendent of public instruction being ex-officio. Current business is transacted by an executive committee of seven. The Society receives a biennial appropriation of $13,000.[3]

In 1919 the Wisconsin legislature passed an act providing for a State Humane Officer with powers of a police officer and constable, who should superintend and assist in the organization of humane societies in the counties of the state and who should administer and enforce the humane laws and promote humane education.[4] Wisconsin differs from the other states thus far noted which participate in humane work by not providing a bureau or state board to cooperate with the officer, although in many ways the arrangement is similar to the provision for a Commissioner in Wyoming.

The object of the legislation was to localize humane work and make it a distinct activity of each county. In this way it was expected that humane work would be made more effective through gaining the interest and support of members of the organized local humane societies; immediate relief in cases of cruelty would thus be provided locally, and the expense would be saved to the state which would have been incurred in attending to details which might be performed by county organizations.

[1] McCrea, *op. cit.*, p. 19; *cf. W. Va. Code of 1906*, sec. 15J, amended by *Sess. Laws*, 1907, ch. 40.

[2] *Minn. Sess. Laws*, 1905, ch. 274.

[3] Manuscript letter of May 26, 1923.

[4] *Wis. Sess. Laws*, 1919, ch. 359.

By means of personal visitation, correspondence, newspaper publicity and other public notices, a public meeting is arranged for within the county to be organized, generally at the county seat. At this meeting, which is usually under the direction of the State Humane Officer, the purpose and plan of a county humane society is explained, a society is organized, officers and a board of directors elected, by-laws adopted, and plans made for the incorporation of the society. These county humane societies are formed either as independent organizations or as branches of the Wisconsin Humane Society.[1] Seven were formed or reorganized during the first year of the Officer's activity.[2]

Where county societies do not at present exist, the State Humane Officer undertakes the enforcement of the anti-cruelty laws through county humane agents, and in his own words, " wherever practicable, a policy of admonishment rather than a policy of arrest of the offender " is adopted.[2] As rapidly as county humane societies are organized and county humane officers are appointed, local humane law enforcement is turned over to them.[3]

In 1921 the biennial appropriation was increased from $6,000 to $10,000.[4]

The taking over by the states of functions usually exercised by private societies has been looked upon with mixed feelings by humanitarians. There are many who have denounced it on the ground that it tied humane activities to party politics, and that the impersonal administration of animal protective and animal welfare activities by the States could never be as keen as when these activities were in the

[1] *Wisconsin Department of Humane Work, Report for 1920*, p. 8.

[2] *Ibid.*, p. 9.

[3] For chart of the activities of the State Humane Officer, *vide* appendix v.

[4] *Wis. Sess. Laws*, 1921, ch. 157.

hands of interested humanitarians. It should also be noted that many of the most progressive humane workers favor it greatly.

The history of the Colorado Bureau, and particularly its controversy with Governor Carlson, lend support to the arguments of those who object to state participation in humane work. Nevertheless the Colorado Bureau can point to a satisfactory record of accomplishment. It is by no means certain that the "bureau" or "state board" is the best organization for state humane administration. Wyoming experimented with it under various forms and eventually rejected it. Wisconsin's "state agent" is considered by many a distinct advance along this line.

The period since 1910 has been one of experimentation, so far as concerns state humane activities.

CHAPTER VI

ORGANIZATION AND FINANCES OF ANTI-CRUELTY SOCIETIES

A careful survey of the annual reports since 1910 of the leading anti-cruelty societies shows that there has been no significant change in the general form of their organization from that described by Professor McCrea in 1910:

In the organization and management of societies for the prevention of cruelty to animals, there is substantial uniformity of outline. The early New York model with its English prototype has been pretty closely followed. With the exception of a few States, in which there is a larger element of public participation in management than in the majority, the organizations are private corporations, exercising delegated police powers. The earlier societies were created by special charter, conferring upon the charter members all of the rights, franchises and powers of a corporation, usually with some specific limitation as to the value of real estate that might be held. The objects and powers of the society were set forth in the charters. Among these powers were usually included the right to appoint and employ agents, to purchase, print, publish, and circulate literature fitted to promote the objects of the society, and to erect and maintain fountains and other conveniences for the comfort of dumb creation. Power to regulate the internal management through the election of officers and the adoption of a proper code of by-laws is likewise conveyed in such charters; and the regular local police are required, as occasion demands, to aid the society, its officers, members and agents, in the enforcement of any laws that may be in force for the protection of dumb animals. Provision is not infrequently added that fines, in whole or in part, collected through the instrumentality of a society for violation of the law (*sic*), shall go to the society involved.

More recently, societies have been quite regularly incorporated under the provisions of general law. The organization and powers in these cases remain the same in general outline as in the earlier instances of creation by special charter.

Under the general grant of powers, thus conveyed by charter or act of incorporation, by-laws, or a constitution and by-laws, are adopted. These prescribe more minutely details of organization and the manner of conducting a society's business. The constitution usually covers such items as the following: the grades of membership, with fees to be received from each grade; provision for officers and directors, with a statement of qualifications for such and of the method of their election; the manner of formation and powers of an executive committee, in whose hands rests the real governing and appointing power within the society; and further provision for periodical meetings (usually annual) of the society.

By-laws deal with more detailed, formal matters connected with the conduct of the society's affairs. These usually prescribe: the times of meeting of the board of directors and of the executive committee; the order of business at such meetings; the appointment of special committees dealing with particular lines of activity; the duties of the various officers, and of the various committees; and the method of amending the by-laws.[1]

There can be no question that the most important item in the development of the anti-cruelty society is the growth of its membership. The main financial reliance of a society for animal protection is the private contributor. In the

[1] McCrea, *op. cit.*, pp. 16-18.

statistics appended to the 1922 *Annual Report* of the American Humane Association, the most important single item of income for the humane societies of the United States was their income from dues and donations, $841,072.34 for the year—this out of a total income of $3,329,820.11.[1] It must be remembered in connection with these figures that it is the large societies in the cities that enjoy income from investments and property. The overwhelming majority of small societies are absolutely dependent upon their income from membership dues and on donations by members and friends.

Moreover, an extended membership signifies that many more people in the community are interested and personally active in the work of the society. Growth of membership is cumulative, as each new member is at once a new advertisement of the society and an added link between it and its community. It is no exaggeration, therefore, to measure the success of a young anti-cruelty organization by the expansion of its membership list.

Of the quality of the types of membership of different societies, Professor McCrea says:

Membership arrangements have been differentiated to meet widely varying possibilities, and the element of flattery involved in the personal mention of a classified membership list, infinitesimal though it may be, is exploited to the utmost. There is an element of truth in the characterization of the annual report of a humane society as " a few pages of statistics, several half-tone cuts and a copy of the Social Register." The backbone of the membership of every society is of course the roll of active members, each of whom pays an annual fee ranging from one to five dollars. Beyond this it would take a considerable list to exhaust prevailing variations of forms of membership. In addition to a not infre-

---

[1] *American Humane Association, 46th Ann. Rpt.*, p. 62.

quent list of honorary members, the other most commonly found grades of membership are the following: life members, with a single initial fee usually of $100; associate members, with a small annual fee; junior members, made up of young people, with a small annual fee for which the receipt is likely to take the form of a badge or button.[1]

In the growth of the society and the obtaining of new members, publicity plays a most important role. As the secretary of one very active society writes, " The failure of so many S. P. C. A.s is caused by not keeping their labors before the public. *We believe that we can sell charity the same as merchandise and we are doing it every day.* The public will support a well-going society every time."

An established institution with all societies is the published annual report, appearing usually in pamphlet form, but sometimes in the local newspaper or, as has been the case with the Massachusetts and Los Angeles S. P. C. A.s, in a humane magazine published by the society. These annual reports vary from brief financial statements to folios containing the entire history of the society and of its surrounding community.

But after all, the annual report has only a limited circulation and most societies have discovered that much greater publicity is to be gained through the local newspapers. There is much news value in some of the semi-routine activities of an anti-cruelty society, and newspapers are only too willing to give space to them. Larger organizations such as the New York, the Boston, and the Chicago societies, have departments or staff members whose duty it is to advertise the activities of the society. The American Humane Education Society established a press bureau at Palo Alto, California in 1910 to give publicity to the activities of the western societies, and in 1917 the decision was made to

---

[1] McCrea, *op. cit.*, pp. 25-26.

start an official humane press bureau with headquarters at Boston.[1]

Some societies consider the paid advertisement placed in the local newspapers a good investment. In 1916 the Western Pennsylvania Humane Society adopted the policy of placing once a week in each of seven English and one German dailies of Pittsburgh, a half-inch advertisement soliciting reports to the Society of all cases of cruelty to animals, to children, and to aged persons. The total cost of this advertising proved to be $265 for the year. The result was a decided enlargement of the Society's work and the addition of a number of new members who confessed that their interest was aroused by these advertisements.[2]

This same society considers the printed circular a valuable form of publicity. In 1918 as the result of mailing two thousand printed appeals for financial help to people believed to be in sympathy with the aims of the organization, $4,150.00 was obtained.[3]

As has been pointed out, the main sources of income for most societies are the membership fee and the personal donation. Nevertheless, these must always be uncertain, even in the most carefully managed and most progressive societies. Therefore, all the successful anti-cruelty organizations have endeavored to build up endowments. The American Humane Association has encouraged this and its president has time and again in the annual conferences and in the *National Humane Review* emphasized the importance of an endowment for every society, in 1917 pointing out that three quarters of the support of the largest and most

[1] *American Humane Education Society, Annual Reports* for 1911 and 1918.

[2] *Western Pennsylvania Humane Society, 42nd Ann. Rpt.* (1916), p. 16.

[3] *Western Pennsylvania Humane Society, 45th Ann. Rpt.* (1919), p. 7.

successful humane societies came from their endowment funds.[1]

Very often a society finds it necessary to spend in excess of its income in the course of a year; the American S. P. C. A. for example, is authorized to permit its expenses to exceed its income up to $25,000 in any one year.[2] The continuation of such a policy for any considerable length of time, except under extraordinary circumstances, would prove disastrous. There are many organizations which, like the Connecticut Humane Society, make it a point to invest in their entirety all bequests received by the Society.[3] The importance of a well-invested endowment may best be realized when it is stated that the income of the American S. P. C. A. in 1922 from interest on investments and income from leased property was $30,576 out of a total net income for the year of $66,646.73,[4] and that during the same year the Massachusetts S. P. C. A. received as interest on invested funds and deposits $31,211.91 out of a total income for the year of $191,332.88 which included bequests amounting to $64,977.70.[5]

Throughout the period under consideration, serious controversy has raged over the question as to whether it is advantageous for anti-cruelty societies to receive the fines for the cases they prosecute. The receiving of fines by a society is closely linked with its exercise of police power. Both questions have been thoroughly discussed by Mr. Hubbard in his study on the societies of New York State under the heading, " Should humane societies perform police duty, and should they receive fines in payment therefor? " His

[1] *National Humane Review*, vol. v, p. 91.

[2] *Vide supra*, p. 30.

[3] *Vide supra*, p. 39.

[4] *Amer. S. P. C. A., 57th Ann. Rpt.* (1922), p. 24.

[5] *Mass. S. P. C. A., Ann. Rpt.* for year ending March, 1922, p. 12.

conclusions as quoted below are as valid today as they were
in 1915.

The proper enforcement of laws for the prevention of cruelty
to animals demands a body of men who give their whole time
to this one thing.   So if it is to be done by the regular police
force, it would have to be through the creation of a special
squad.   This would necessitate an addition to the force, so it
would not be of any economic advantage.   In any case the city
must hire the work done.   It might well be a good investment
for the city to provide such a special squad of policemen: the
more prevention that is provided, the better.   But that is not
to say that the special police power at present vested in the
agents of humane societies should be taken from them. . . . .
Their effectiveness would be quickly diminished.   Certainly if
there is need for special agents to help in stamping out
cruelty to animals, they should enjoy the power of peace
officers.[1]

The need for such assistance has been recognized by the
laws of this state for a good many years, and the need is
not less today.[2]   This is no reflection on the police force.
The agents are the specialists who are needed continually on
the field, even though they be supplemented by a squad
from the city's police force. . . .

It is in fact difficult to see how cruelty to animals can be
effectively prevented in the city or in the country unless the
societies, through their agents, participate immediately in the
arrest and prosecution of offenders.

This brings us to the second question.   If it is necessary
and proper to delegate these public duties to private societies, should the city pay the societies for their services?   If
so, what form should the compensation take?   It hardly
seems necessary to debate the first of these queries.   Tax-
payers do not as a rule object to paying a reasonable price

They do at present in twenty-one states; *cf.* appendix i

[2] Written in 1915, but quite true at present (1923).

for value received; and the proposition that the society which incurs expense to serve the public should be reimbursed therefor is essentially fair.   But how should it be done? This is the crux of the whole situation.

The system of allowing fines to accrue to the society which prosecutes violations has had a pretty general vogue.   That it is liable to abuse is unquestionable, and that it has been abused in many places is unquestioned. . . . The charge has been made by certain horse owners that the agents of the societies in New York City make a practice of arresting without cause and inducing pleas of guilty for the sake of getting fines.   It is also alleged that in one society at least an agent's fines must exceed his salary if he would hold his position. It is admitted that there have been instances of grafting agents: but these sweeping indictments of the societies' policy are strenuously denied.   As a matter of fact, it is difficult to discover evidences of any general or extended abuse of the system in New York City. . . .

While the fine may be an additional incentive to make arrests and while the number of arrests made may bear some relation to the degree of the society's dependence upon fines as a source of revenue, the arrests actually made in this city are not such as to constitute an abuse of privilege, . . . nor are the magistrates in the habit of imposing excessive fines for the sake of enriching the societies.[1]

In California in 1913 the policy of giving fines to the prosecuting society came to an issue.   As has been pointed out, the state of California in the early part of the past decade was infested with numerous wild-cat anti-cruelty societies, whose activities were as much distasteful to genuinely established humane organizations as they were to the public authorities with whom they came into conflict.[2]

[1] Hubbard, *Prevention of Cruelty to Animals in New York State,* pp. 49-55.

[2] *Vide supra,* p. 46.

The actions of these societies brought criticism on the entire anti-cruelty movement. In 1913, on the initiative of the State Humane Association of California, a bill was introduced to remove the incentive for unfair practices by providing that anti-cruelty fines be paid into the public treasury instead of to the societies bringing prosecution; in return, bona-fide societies should receive allowances from the city or county.[1] It became law as an emergency measure on May 30th,[2] and provided that societies might be paid a sum not exceeding $500 per calendar month from the city or county general funds by the board of supervisors or other governing bodies thereof. The emergency declared by the legislature was explained in Section 2 of the amendatory act:

Section 607e of the Civil Code permits societies organized for the prevention of cruelty to animals to make arrests, carry on prosecutions and collect fines, and under the provisions of this section numerous societies have been organized and are being operated in such a manner as to be a menace to the public peace and safety. Arrests are being made and property seized without prosecution of the charges made; citizens are being forced to pay tribute to outlaw societies to escape prosecution, and police officers are urging the immediate withdrawal of the right of these societies to collect fines because of their greatly increased activity in these practices pending a time when this bill may become law.[3]

The California societies are not fully satisfied with the situation created by this law. In 1916 the secretary of the California State Humane Association complained that the city and county boards did not voluntarily appropriate

---

[1] *National Humane Review*, vol. i, p. 66.

[2] *Cal. Sess. Laws*, 1913, p. 638.

[3] *Vide* Hubbard, *Prevention of Cruelty to Animals in the States of Ill., Col. and Cal.*, p. 91.

money for the societies as contemplated by the act of 1913; that when made, the amount of the appropriation was subject to the whims of the politicians; and that not a few of the societies found themselves reduced to the most venal sort of lobbying to be able to continue their existence.[1] The situation has not been altered since then. Very few societies are able to secure any allowance from the county treasurers. Possibly three societies out of twenty-five receive from $100 to $150 a month.[2] The State Humane Association presented a bill in the 1923 legislature providing that the county supervisors must pay a minimum of $50 and not more than $500 a month to humane societies in their county, but the bill, though passing both houses, was vetoed by the governor.

Apart from fines as results of prosecutions, there are two types of aid which is being extended to anti-cruelty work from the public purse. In one case, purely private corporations are being paid for special public work that they perform. Such, for instance, are those societies for the prevention of cruelty to animals that contract with their cities to operate the public dog pounds and enforce dog-license laws, and receive in turn a certain fixed sum or a percentage of receipts. They do the work because they do it better than the city or any other private contractor would do. This certainly seems a legitimate and proper work for an anti-cruelty society to do, and public sentiment seems to approve of the arrangement. An analogous relation is found where societies for the prevention of cruelty to children are paid for caring for children, either in courts or in their shelters, or where humane officers are paid for probation or other special work. In these instances, the

[1] *National Humane Review*, vol. iv, p. 54.

[2] Manuscript letter of Nov. 17, 1923 from the secretary of the State Humane Association of California.

integrity of the humane society as a strictly private corporation is not invaded. It elects its own directors, and manages its own affairs.[1]

The other case where public moneys are expended for humane work is illustrated by such arrangements as the present California law providing for city and county appropriations, the provisions for the distribution of the Ohio " sheep fund ",[2] and the recent Pennsylvania ordinance authorizing the boards of county commissioners to appropriate money, if they see proper, for the support of local humane societies of two years legitimate and active service.[3]

Public support of the first type is well-nigh universal. In nearly every town where there is an active anti-cruelty society or animal-rescue league, the pound work of the town has been placed in the hands of the society. In smaller towns a fixed appropriation is often made to cover the expenses of the pound. In the larger cities the plan is usually followed of allowing the S. P. C. A. to administer the licensing of dogs and to retain the fees to cover the expenses of the pound work and other specified activities. In New York City the American S. P. C. A. performs this duty. The fees collected are to cover the costs of shelters and the humane disposition of animals in New York, Brooklyn and Richmond. Rarely does the total of fees collected cover these expenses; in 1922 the total income from dog-license fees was $165,722.00, whereas the costs of the shelter and disposition of animals were $167,760.64.[4]

The right to receive such fees has been confirmed in the case of the American S. P. C. A. by a United States Supreme

[1] *Cf. A. H. A., 35th Ann. Rpt.* (1911), p. 8.

[2] *Vide infra*, p. 185.

[3] *Pa. Sess. Laws*, 1921, ch. 80. *Vide* the account of this act in *Western Pennsylvania Humane Society, 47th Ann. Rpt.* (1921).

[4] *Amer. S. P. C. A., 57th Ann. Rpt.* (1922), p. 24.

Court decision of December 6, 1920,[1] which reads in part as follows:

When the State chooses to entrust the work incident to such licenses and the collection of fees to a corporation created by it for the express purpose of aiding in law enforcement, and in good faith appropriates the funds so collected for payment of expenses fairly incurred and which is compensation for the valuable services rendered, there is no infringement of any right guaranteed to the individual by the Federal Constitution. Such action does not amount to the taking of one man's property and giving it to another, nor does it deprive dog owners of liberty without due process of law.

The advantages of the second type of support by grants from public funds are open to controversy. The various charges that are brought against it may be summarized in the statement that it forces the society to lobby and engage in political activities to whatever extent it is dependent upon such funds. The fate of the California societies has already been pointed out. No instance, however, has come to light where a society has had an opportunity to receive such public moneys and has declined it. A questionaire on this matter sent to thirty-four representative societies in 1920 elicited the following results:

Number of societies receiving no public funds 12
Number of societies entirely supported by public funds 1
Number of societies partly supported by public funds 20
Number expressing belief that societies should receive public funds 25
Number believing that they should not 7
Number believing that it would destroy initiative 6
Number believing that it would not .... 21 [2]

[1] *Lillian Nicchia v. the People of the State of New York, 254 U. S., 258.*
[2] *A. H. A., 44th Ann. Rpt., p. 10.*

CHAPTER VII

Recent Developments in Animal Protection

Many of the activities of anti-cruelty societies have been indicated in the proceding chapters. Generalization of these activities in this place will be valuable.

In these days the grosser forms of cruelty are exceptional. Where there are active societies, there is a steady though perhaps not always measurable reduction in the extent of the practice of cruelty to animals. A very interesting illustration of this is furnished by the records of the Washington (D. C.) Humane Society. This society serves a sharply defined territory. Its limited field prevents it from constantly expanding its operations. Therefore its reports of prosecutions can be taken as illustrating with rather close accuracy the cruelty conditions in the city of Washington. In 1910 Washington was pointed to by humanitarians as being one of the least advanced cities in the matter of the prevention of cruelty to animals,[1] this despite the fact that the Washington society kept seven agents upon the streets of the national capital and was so active that horse owners formed an Animal Protective Association to combat its efforts. The steady improvement of the conditions from that day to this is indicated by the following table of arrests for all forms of cruelty made by the Society's agents:

[1] *Vide A. H. A., 34th Ann. Rpt.*, p. 112.

Year	Arrests
1910	1,213
1911	2,017
1912	1,824
1913	1,352
1914	909
1915	712
1916	655
1917	490
1918	233
1919	117
1920	102
1921	99
1922	66 [1]

Though not so apparent elsewhere, the same tendency is operative throughout the country. In 1921 the American S. P. C. A. could report: " In former days, an agent would make two or three arrests a day, and suspend a number of horses from duty. Now an agent may walk the streets all day without seeing a case demanding interference. His principal duty is that of investigating complaints." [2] While some of this improvement is doubtless due to the decrease in the use of horses within city limits—within twenty years the number of horses used in New York City has decreased from about 110,000 to 65,000 according to estimates of the officials of the American S. P. C. A.—New York anti-cruelists agree that the growth of a kindly spirit among horse drivers has been the more significant factor. Even in districts where active anti-cruelty societies have not as yet been formed, humane ideas have permeated.

No longer forced to consider every case brought before them one of wilful cruelty, the anti-cruelty societies do not now emphasize immediate prosecution. The manager of the Erie County S. P. C. A. has pointed out in respect to this :

[1] *Washington Humane Society, 1922 Year Book*, p. 12.
[2] *National Humane Review*, vol. ix, p. 187.

Formerly the humanitarian was more concerned about the enforcement of the law and the punishment of the evil-doer than he was in seeking the cause of things. It has taken nearly a half century of waging warfare upon the cruelist to break down his indifference to the rights of the lower creatures by the law enforcement. It is, therefore, only in recent years that organized humane forces have undertaken another line of attack through constructive methods to make certain his defeat. The punishment of the wrong-doer is not so important in this day as the application of a remedy to cure him of his short-comings.[1]

The Pennsylvania S. P. C. A. publishes the following table of the causes of cruelty and their respective remedies:

Ignorance	Education
Poverty	Kindness and understanding
Indifference	Warning
Viciousness	Arrest and prosecution [2]

One of the important functions of many humane societies is to initiate anti-cruelty legislation and to keep a close watch upon the state legislatures to prevent the passage of bills which would either directly or indirectly authorize or permit the increase of cruelty to animals. Usually this latter duty is undertaken by one or two of the larger societies in the state; in New Jersey for a time, all the societies co-operated in maintaining a committee for this purpose.[3]

During the past decade there have been no marked developments in the types of humane legislation that has been passed in the various states. In a few states, the general anti-cruelty statutes have been strengthened by the addition of a word or phrase. In Maine, " dogs " has been included

[1] *A. H. A., 47th Ann. Rpt.*, p. 7.
[2] *Pa. S. P. C. A., 46th Ann. Rpt.*, p. 18.
[3] *Vide supra*, p. 47.

in the statute forbidding overdriving, overloading and unnecessary beating.[1] California has strengthened her general statute which read " cruelly whips, beats, or ill-treats
animal" by the omission of the word "cruelly".[2] Nebraska has added "maltreat" to her general statute.[3] Ohio
has made the overworking of any animal a misdemeanor.[4]
Since 1907, every state in the Union has had a more or
less complete general anti-cruelty act upon its statute books.

All but six states [5] punish the failure to provide necessary
and proper food, drink and shelter for animals. Pennsylvania does not specifically make such neglect a misdemeanor,
but it does provide that any peace officer or humane agent
may relieve the neglected animals and has a lien on them to
recover costs.[6] Not all the states that punish the neglect
of animals have made provision for their relief by others
than the owner. Where such provision has been made, it
usually allows interested outsiders to relieve the suffering
animals after a specified time, usually twelve hours, and
provides that the expenses of relief are chargable to the
owner and constitute a lien on the animals cared for.
Twenty-three states have made such provision.[7] Colorado
makes provision that neglected range stock may be relieved
by the State Board of Stock Inspection Commissioners, and
that the expense shall constitute a lien on the stock which
shall be sold after thirty days.[8]

[1] *Me. Sess. Laws*, 1909, ch. 208.
[2] *Cal. P. C.* (1909), sec. 597.
[3] *Neb. Sess. Laws*, 1911, ch. 174.
[4] *Ohio, Sess. Laws*, 1910, p. 118.
[5] Ga., Ky., Md., Nev., N. H., and Ore.
[6] *Pa. Sess. Laws*, 1911, p. 654.
[7] Ark., Cal., Col., Conn., Id., Ia., Me., Mass., Mich., Minn., Neb., N. J.,
N. Y., N. D., Ohio, Pa., R. I., S. D., Tenn., Tex., Va., Wash. and Wyo.
[8] *Col. Sess. Laws*, 1909, ch. 210; 1913, ch. 152.

All but five states [1] penalize the abandonment of disabled and decrepit animals.   In the majority of cases, it is provided that, within certain limitations, peace officers may kill such animals.   Only a few states have decrepit horse sale laws, although in several others, such bills have been introduced and defeated. [2]   For the enforcement of these sale laws, the vigorous cooperation of the local anti-cruelty societies is necessary.   In Philadelphia, for example, under the act of May 6, 1909, an officer of the Pennsylvania S. P. C. A. examines all horses offered for sale in the horse markets and auction rooms.   Each horse is ticketed with an indication of approval or condemnation.   Where horses are condemned, the owner receives $5 and the auctioneer $1 of the $6 allowed for the carcass. [3]

In connection with the prevention of this form of cruelty, it should be pointed out that several humane societies make it a rule to buy decrepit horses that are offered at the auctions for from $3 to $10.   Even where there are decrepit horse sale laws, these societies consider this alternative method preferable to prosecution.   The Animal Rescue League of Boston buys about 300 horses a year at an average price of $5 each.   It has an arrangement with horse auctioneers whereby horses condemned by it are " knocked down " to it without competitive bidding. [4]

Very few states today lack laws punishing those who maliciously kill or injure another's animals, and a somewhat smaller number provide additional protection in this field by regulating the exposure of poison with the intent of killing pernicious animals.   Only seven states [5] do not

[1] Ariz., La., N. M., N. C. and N. Dak.
[2] In California in 1913, and in Florida in 1915.
[3] *National Humane Review*, vol. iii, p. 5.
[4] *National Humane Review*, vol. ix, p. 126.
[5] Ariz., Kans., La., Md., N. M., Ore. and Vt.

penalize cock-fighting, and in not a few, spectators are also punishable either by direct provision or by implication. Only seventeen states [1] have legislative provision forbidding the docking of horses' tails despite the long and active agitation carried on by all societies against this abuse. The changing mode of fashion, however, and the substitution of the automobile for the carriage as a pleasure vehicle, have been most effective in curing this evil.

Among the miscellaneous offenses forbidden under penalty are the use of the bristle bur on horses,[2] the setting of certain kinds of traps and the failure to visit traps within a specified period (usually 24 hours),[3] the exhibition of bears except in a menagerie,[4] the leaving of horses unblanketed in a public place [5] (in most states this offense is covered only by municipal ordinances), the cutting off of more than half of an ear of a domestic animal,[6] the working of a horse more than 15 hours out of 24 or more than 90 in a week,[7] the preparation of or participation in moving picture films involving cruelty to animals,[8] the sale of feed for livestock in bags with tags attached by metal fasteners which may work loose and get into the feed,[9] the careless exposure of barbed wire near livestock,[10] and the beating or

---

[1] Cal., Col., Conn., Washington, D. C., Idaho, Ill., Ia., Me., Mass., Mich., Minn., Neb., N. H., Ohio, S. D., Utah, Wash. and Wis.

[2] *Cal. Sess. Laws*, 1903, ch. 129.

[3] Mass., Me., Tenn. and Vt.

[4] *Me. R. S.*, ch. 125, sec. 40.

[5] *Minn. R. L.* (1905), sec. 5155; *Neb. Sess. Laws*, 1911, ch. 174.

[6] *Ore. B. & C.* (1901), secs. 2078, 2079.

[7] *Pa. Sess. Laws*, 1913, no. 438.

[8] *Me. Sess. Laws*, 1921, ch. 53.

[9] *N. J. Sess. Laws*, 1920, ch. 121.

[10] *Ore. Sess. Laws*, 1921, ch. 308.

maltreating of a cow's udder to simulate fullness or the leaving it unmilked for 24 hours for the same purpose.[1]

It should be borne in mind that the placing of a law upon the statute book does not automatically secure its enforcement. In the final consideration, the enforcement of the anti-cruelty statutes must depend upon the humane societies. Where they remain inactive, the law becomes a dead letter.

This police duty, then, is a primary activity of all societies, though the enforcement of the laws need not always necessitate prosecution. Many societies engage in secondary activities, some of which deserve mention.

It has been pointed out in Chapter II that a large number of animal societies erect and maintain drinking fountains and watering stations for horses. During the last few years, a number of the larger societies have been adding stable inspection to the list of their activities. In 1911 the American S. P. C. A. reported:

Believing that the condition of the horses in our city would be improved by better stable supervision, and that many of the infirmities with which they are afflicted, as well as their short life in the city service, are due in no small measure to unscientific methods of stabling, feeding, rooming, harnessing, etc., the society has initiated a gratuitous service of " stable inspection " that has appealed strongly to horse owners and has been welcomed by drivers, stablemen, and others having the care of horses. Upon request the Society sends its expert veterinary inspector to make minute examination of stables. A confidential report is made to the owner, pointing out any defects that may be found and suggesting a remedy. Drivers and stable employees are also instructed in regard to these various subjects.[2]

After a thoroughgoing campaign of stable inspection

[1] *Pa. Sess. Laws*, 1911, p. 178; *Wis. S. & B.*, sec. 4445a.
[2] *Amer. S. P. C. A., 46th Ann. Rpt.* (1911), p. 8.

throughout New York City completed by the Society in 1914, the necessity for continuing this program lessened, and since then the Society has sent its agents to stables only upon complaint.

The Massachusetts S. P. C. A. amplifies this stable inspection. The Massachusetts fire law makes it compulsory for all stables where draught animals are kept above the ground floor to provide two means of exit from the ground or street floor at opposite ends of the building unless automatic sprinklers have been installed throughout the stable. The Massachusetts Society includes the enforcement of this law in the routine of its stable inspection.[1]

Several societies have interested themselves in the matter of the paving of city streets.[2] The problem is three-fold: it involves the appearance of the streets, the durability and suitableness of the paving material for the heavy automobile and truck traffic which prevails today, and lastly, what is of significance to humane societies, its fitness for horse traffic. Some types of paving, for example the creosoted wooden block, are admirable in that they deaden noise and provide a cushiony road bed; on the other hand, it is almost impossible for a horse to keep footing on a creosoted block pavement after a heavy rain storm. Individual societies have interested themselves in the problem, and in 1913 it came up for discussion in the annual conference of the American Humane Association.[3] The conclusions arrived at were that granite blocks will stand the heaviest traffic, that macadam is best for the horse's safety, and that vitrified brick is superior in wet and slippery weather. The American S. P. C. A. favors granite blocks for horse traffic and discourages the use of the wooden block and of asphalt.[4]

[1] *Mass. S. P. C. A., 49th Ann. Rpt.* (1917).
[2] *Cf.* McCrea, *op. cit.*, p. 81.
[3] *A. H. A., 37th Ann. Rpt.*
[4] *National Humane Review,* vol. i, p. 7.

Closely allied to the matter of street paving are the efforts of several societies to induce their municipalities to sand the city streets in winter. This has not always been successful and several societies have purchased and operate such sprinklers during the winter months upon their own responsibility. In New Orleans, where the streets are never made slippery by ice or snow coatings, the Louisiana S. P. C. A. nevertheless maintains and operates a sand spreader to use on streets made unsafe for horses by oil and gasoline drippings. The Atlanta Humane Society likewise maintains a sand-blowing apparatus which spreads a thin coat of fine sand on the streets on damp mornings. There has, however, been opposition to this on the part of the local merchants who complain that later in the day the sand blows up and into their stores.[1]

One society has taken upon itself to see that the horses in its city have proper shoeing during the winter months. The Erie County S. P. C. A. in the winter of 1918 began a campaign of education among the large trucking companies of Buffalo which might otherwise have organized to resist legislation to such end introduced without their consent or against their will. When their support was won, an ordinance was introduced in the Buffalo city council and passed without opposition:

No person owning or having the care, custody, or control of, or driving any horse, mule, or other large animal used for the purpose of driving or hauling, shall permit or allow any such animal to be driven upon any of the streets, avenues, or highways of the city of Buffalo between November first of any year and April first of the following year, unless such animal is shod in such manner as will prevent, or tend with reasonable certainty to prevent, it from slipping.[2]

[1] *La. S. P. C. A., 28th Ann. Rpt.* (1915), p. 17.
[2] *Buffalo Ordinances*, 1918, ch. iv, sec. 26.

The American Humane Association has also taken up the matter of road construction outside of the cities in its relation to horse traffic. One of the speakers at the 1918 annual conference predicted the doom of the horse as a means of transport if the present methods of road construction, taking into consideration only automobile traffic, were followed. In New York State the New York State Association of Horsemen, and in Massachusetts the Protective Association for Horses, were organized mainly to meet this issue. Pennsylvania horse associations likewise were agitating at that time various types of road reforms which were embodied in a bill in 1919 providing that the highway commission should take the needs of horses into consideration in its plans for road construction.[1] The Carriage Builders National Association at its convention in Washington in November 1917, adopted a resolution that " special appeal should be made to all associations and organizations interested in good roads to construct them in a way that will admit of the humane use of the horse."[2]

The suggestion made to the 1918 convention of the American Humane Association was the construction of roads that would admit of both horse and auto traffic. The speaker said:

Since the regulation of traffic has been undertaken in our larger cities, it has been an established rule that the slow moving vehicles keep to the curb, giving the faster ones a freer path through the centre. The same system can and should be followed in the country and a roadway of proper surface for horses should be provided at either side of the motor path. The width of this side drive should depend upon the needs, but generally, a six foot drive on each flank of the hard surface

[1] *Vide Western Pennsylvania Humane Society, 46th Ann. Rpt.* (1920), p. 7.

[2] *A. H. A., 42nd Ann. Rpt.*, p. 22.

will care for the traffic, permitting the slow horse-drawn vehicles to keep to the right in each direction. The construction of a stone road of the modern county road pattern adjacent to the hard surface, would form a natural and inexpensive transition from the concrete to the dirt shoulder, and would also give the horse his place.[1]

The transportation of live stock by the railroads has been a matter of great concern to many anti-cruelty organizations located near important railroad centers. One of the first cruelties attacked used to occur within the stock yards at the terminals. There were formerly butchers who specialized in the purchase of crippled stock at a reduced rate, and although it was necessary after slaughtering to discard quantities of bruised meat, they realized big profits on each animal so purchased. When in any shipment there were few such animals, they made smaller profits. It was discovered by agents of the humane societies that they often deliberately crippled healthy animals for their own gain, entering cars at the stock yards and, unobserved, breaking the legs or otherwise injuring whatever animals they could, which they later bought very cheaply. When the humane societies discovered this practice, they brought it to the attention of the stockyard officials and with their cooperation, prosecutions were initiated and the practice checked.[2]

The Massachusetts, Buffalo, Chicago, St. Louis and Los Angeles anti-cruelty societies among others, have long maintained an inspection service at the railroad terminals to examine and dispose of injured stock.[3] The extent of this activity over the decade beginning 1910 may be judged by the agents' records of stock injuries and mortality at the Buffalo yards published in the annual reports of the Erie County S. P. C. A. :

[1] *Ibid.*

[2] *National Humane Review*, vol. ix, p. 228.

[5] *Vide* McCrea, *op. cit.*, p. 73 for table of the activities of the Erie County Society in this field for one year.

STOCK INJURIES AND MORTALITY IN BUFFALO YARDS

	Cattle			Hogs			Sheep		
	Carloads	Crippled	Dead	Carloads	Crippled	Dead	Carloads	Crippled	Dead
1910	2,579	77	2	1,037	1,336	1,119	866	666	795
1911	(600,000)[1]	211	100	(5,800,000)	5,998	4,367	(2,000,000)	2,331	4,416
1912	(300,000)	260	134	(5,400,000)	7,238	6,159	(1,800,000)	3,649	6,145
1913	no report								
1914	8,649	147	63	30,385	6,246	6,280	7,275	1,641	3,215
1915	16,540	160	98	34,843	5,275	5,496	6,442	1,126	2,650
1916	21,073	162	106	32,673	5,149	6,145	6,161	1,383	2,648
1917	13,304	191	170	27,272	4,315	4,414	3,838	994	2,108
1918	21,431	220	200	33,087	3,0?6	5,524	6,846	1,056	2,369
1919	no report								
1920	21,430	201	136	32,631	3,461	2,366	8,964	1,172	1,091

Figures in parentheses give the number of animals arriving at the yards instead of the carloads.

These figures indicate a decided decrease during these years in stock mortality during transportation. Although the total of dead and crippled animals is greater in the later years, this is more than counter-balanced by the increase in shipments, so that the average number of killed and injured animals to each car is actually less. This is to be explained in part by the added care that is given to the animals by the train crews because of the educational propaganda carried on among them by the humane societies, and by the greater cooperation of yard crews. As the result of a propaganda drive begun in 1919 by the Los Angeles S. P. C. A. among the caboose men and caretakers, and by arrangement with the railroad officials so that the office of the Society was constantly in touch with all stock shipments, the Society was able to announce a year later a fifty per cent improvement in stock-transportation conditions in its district.[1]

Little of the improvement noted above can be credited to more progressive transportation legislation, as state legislatures have been notoriously inactive in this field, where they have not passed or attempted to pass actually retrogressive legislation. In Ohio, for example, the legislature in 1913 and 1914 tried to amend the livestock-transportation law, extending the time that stock might be confined on a train from twenty-four to thirty-six hours. It was only by the vigorous action of the Cleveland Animal Protective League that this was defeated.[2]

All state stock transportation legislation has been moulded by the federal twenty-eight hour law of March 3, 1873 as modified by the amendment act of June 29, 1906.[3] The modified act provides that no interstate land or water carrier shall transport cattle, sheep, swine or other animals

[1] *Los Angeles S. P. C. A., 43rd Ann. Rpt.* (1920), p. 18.
[2] *A. H. A., 41st Ann. Rpt.* (1917).
[3] 34 Stat. 607-608.

for a period longer than twenty-eight consecutive hours without unloading the same in a humane manner, into properly
equipped pens for rest, water, and feeding, for a period of at
least five consecutive hours, unless prevented by storm or by
other accidental or unavoidable causes which cannot be anti-
cipated or avoided by the exercise of due diligence and fore-
sight: Provided that upon the written request of the owner or
person in custody of that particular shipment . . . the time of
confinement may be extended to thirty-six hours . . . : Provided that it shall not be required that sheep be unloaded in the
night time, but where the time expires in the night time in the
case of sheep, the same may continue in transit to a suitable
place for unloading subject to the aforesaid limitation of thirty-
six hours.

A proposal to require all stock trains to average a speed of
eighteen miles an hour, though desirable, did not become a
part of the law.

A series of judicial decisions has emphasized the humane
character of the act.[1]   Nevertheless, it should be remembered that the 1906 amendment gave an advantage to the
shippers by providing for the extension to thirty-six hours
on request and several decisions other than those cited in
Note — have provided for the shippers' interest: in *U. S. v.
Pere Marquette Ry. Co.* it was asserted that " the Act has
also in view the protection of the interests of owners of
animals and of the public in preventing their health and
condition being injured in transit ";[2] in *U. S. v. Oregon
Ry. & Nav. Co.* it was stated that the Act was intended "to
subserve the interests of the owner ";[3] in two decisions,

---

[1] *U. S. v. Atlantic Coast-line Ry. Co.*, 173 Fed. 764 (C. C. A. 1909);
U. S. v. Southern Pacific Co. (1900); *U. S. v. the Union Pacific Ry. Co.*,
169 Fed. 65 (C. C. A. 1909); *U. S. v. Oregon Short Line Ry. Co.*,
160 Fed. 526 (1908); *U. S. v. Southern Pacific Co.*, 157 Fed. 459 (1907).

[2] 171 Fed. 586 (1909).

[3] 163 Fed. 649 (1908).

U. S. v. St. Joseph Stock Yards Co., and *U. S. v. Louisville and Nashville Ry. Co.* it was stated that the act was passed not more from considerations of sympathy for the cattle, than to protect the public from imposition and from unwholesome food.[1]

The Act of 1873 had been a dead letter from its passage in spite of sporadic attempts on the part of the Department of Agriculture to enforce it, and many grave abuses had arisen out of the failure of the railroads to live up to the law. After the passage of the 1906 amendment, however, the Bureau of Animal Industry put its agents on the roads to follow the shipments of live stock and to report violations. Hundreds of cases were reported and the law was rigorously enforced. On June 30, 1918 there were 2,831 cases of violations of the act pending in the courts.[2]

The legislation that has been passed on this matter affecting intra-state shipments has been for the most part to bring the state laws into alignment with the federal. In addition, four states have speed minimums: Colorado, ten miles per hour;[3] Kansas, fifteen miles per hour;[4] Nebraska, eighteen miles per hour except on branch lines where twelve miles per hour is permitted;[5] Kansas, fifteen miles per hour;[6] and North Dakota, twenty miles per hour.[7] Iowa requires animals to be carried at the " highest practical speed "; what this is to be is decided by the Board of Railway Commissioners.[8]

[1] 181 Fed. 625 (1909); 18 Fed. 480 (1883). *Vide U. S. Dept. of Agriculture, Bureau of Animal Industory, Order no. 264* (1919) for review of the Act and a review of further decisions bearing on it.

[2] *A. H. A., 43rd Ann. Rpt.*, p. 16.

[3] *Col. Sess. Laws*, 1921, ch. 68.

[4] *Kans. Sess. Laws*, 1907, ch. 276.

[5] *Neb. Sess. Laws*, 1905, ch. 107.

[6] *N. D. Sess. Laws*, 1903, ch. 144.

[3] *Iowa Sess. Laws*, 1907, ch. 115, amended by 1913, ch. 180.

Humanitarians are not satisfied with present conditions of animal transportation and numerous reforms have been projected. These were generalized by Dr. Francis H. Rowley, President of the Massachusetts S. P. C. A., at the 1921 convention of the American Humane Association:

First. We have been told, ever since the days of Bergh and Angell, that the remedy for these evils is the slaughter of food animals near the place of their rearing, and the shipping of their flesh in refrigerator cars. But the hundreds of millions of dollars invested in our present systems of slaughter houses . . . makes their breaking up a dream whose fulfillment lies only in the millenium.

Second. No small part of the suffering of animals in transit is due to the failure of the railroad to maintain a proper rate of speed in their transportation. A freight composed of sentient creatures should have the right of way over shipments of inanimate merchandise. . . . The universal opinion is that a speed should be maintained of not less than from 18 to 25 miles per hour.

Third. Much has been accomplished, chiefly through anticruelty organizations . . . to change the conditions that formerly existed at unloading stations. I have seen yards into which cattle, sheep and swine were forced from cars where they wallowed in mire half-way up to their knees, where hay pitched to them became fouled with mire before it could be a quarter eaten, and where the watering troughs were so full of filth, that, thirsty as they were, the suffering victims could not drink from them. Things have been greatly improved in recent years. Yet here is another point at which humane societies may well concentrate their forces.

Fourth. Years ago there was a hope that improved cattle cars might materially help lessen the suffering of animals in transit—cars so constructed that animals might be provided with food and water in the cars themselves. Who knows anything about the much-talked-of palace cars today, except those for horses? It was soon found that the watering troughs in these cars must be placed at a height which could be reached by the animals.   But this height was just such that the troughs, though filled with water at frequent intervals, were more like sewers than drinking places.   Cattle are cattle.   You can't load them with heads all one way.   You can make it possible for them to lie down and have their food and drink provided for them in cars only at an expense that the trade would denounce as prohibitive.   Here, then, is another point against which humanitarians must concentrate their forces.   They must seek the repeal of the amendment that extended the confinement period to thirty-six hours, and strive for something even more humane than the old twenty-eight hour law.[1]

A special committee of the American Humane Association drew up recommendations for a model Animal Transport Act which were reported in the 1917 Convention of the American Humane Association,[2] but as yet few state legislatures have adopted any of these recommendations.

Closely allied to the problem of stock transportation is that of the humane slaughter of food animals.   It has occupied the attention of humanitarians for the last twenty years,[3] but is little nearer solution today than when first propounded.   The following description of a large American slaughter-house was made to the 1920 American Humane Association conference by Dr. Francis H. Rowley:

In a large room, I saw probably one hundred steers standing with water being sprayed over their backs.   I said to the man who was taking me about, " It isn't hot enough today to spray those animals."   I wondered at the kindness that had suggested that these animals could be cooled by the spray.

[1] *A. H. A., 45th Ann. Rpt.* (1921), p. 10.

[2] *Vide* appendix iii.

[3] *Cf.* the recommendations adopted at the 1908 conference of the American Humane Association, in *A. H. A., 32nd Ann. Rpt.* (1908), also quoted in McCrea, *op. cit.*, p. 258.

He said " We don't spray them to get them cool; but the hair is so thick, until we spray them it is a poor nonconductor (*sic*) for our electric punches."

Then opening from this pen is a door which will bring a certain number of animals in through a passageway perhaps five feet wide. Doors are in it making it into compartments, each one holding four animals. These doors are lifted, and as the animals are started by this electric prod they are rushed in with speed as fast as they can make it, every man standing along the line having one of these electric prods.

" How powerful is the shock of this electric prod? " I asked. " Put it on a bull's neck and it will knock him to the ground every time. The thinner animals are often knocked down as soon as it touches them."

When the space is filled the doors are dropped. The animals they had were often so large it was almost impossible to get four inside the two doors. A man who stood next to me must have been at least thirty seconds trying to get one animal under the door so he could drop it. The prod was held against him until he roared and bellowed and cried almost like a human being. At last, driven by that prod, he rammed his way in until he had shoved one of the others almost double at the further end.

Four animals were jammed in. The man who started at the head of the line struck the first animal three blows before he could even drop him to his knees. The first blow dropped the second one. The third one he struck twice. The fourth one, the first blow got him down. The first one got to his feet again. Already struck three blows with that great hammer as near the centre of the forehead as he could get, a final blow was struck which threw him on his knees.[1]

This description indicates the nature of the problem confronting humanitarians. This problem is further stated by Dr. Rowley as follows:

[1] *A. H. A., 44th Ann. Rpt.,* p. 33.

1. We kill for food in the United States so vast a number of animals as compared with other nations, that the elements of time and expense in our methods of slaughter present a problem other lands have scarcely to consider. In seeking our goal, not only must some device be found for the effective stunning of our food animals before bleeding, that can be operated with great rapidity, economical and safe, and demanding little delay to keep it in good order, but our great abattoirs must of necessity, change or rearrange certain of their present facilities for bringing their animals to the slaughtering pens, or introduce new facilities to make possible humane slaughter.

2. Again it must be acknowledged that the character of the cattle dealt with in our large abattoirs is very different from that of similar animals in European countries. Little is known in Europe of our wild, untamed, Western-range beef animals. The foreign slaughter houses have to deal with steers and cows and bulls which, with few exceptions, are more or less domesticated, used to daily contact with men, and used to being led or driven about the farm, or kept largely in the stable.

3. Still further, we have to remember that in all foreign countries with the exception of England, the great majority of the animals are killed at municipal abattoirs under the direct control of the city authorities. To these places, the individual butchers come not only to buy their animals but to have them slaughtered. Municipal abattoirs in all our larger cities and towns to which animals from the surrounding country could be brought, would eliminate no small part of the sufferings of our food animals now endured by reason of long shipments in trains often over-crowded, often side-tracked for other freight to pass, often subjected to climatic conditions which cause intense suffering, often enduring hunger, thirst, and exhausting weariness. None of us will dispute the statement that even when the best has been done that human genius can devise and humanity may dictate, the transportation and slaughter of our food animals will always, by the very nature of the business, involve more or less of suffering. To take from the ranch or the farm to the place of shipment, cattle, sheep, and swine; to

load and unload them; to bring into the slaughter pen amid unfamiliar scenes and odors, millions of creatures more or less frightened and incapable of reason and unable to understand what is wanted of them; to do this with a care and concern for their welfare that would prevent all suffering, would be to make the cost involved in the traffic absolutely prohibitive. This, however, must not for a moment stay us in our endeavor to better to the utmost limit of our power, the conditions which are responsible for this unavoidable suffering.[1]

After a recent study of European slaughter houses and abattoirs, Dr. W. Reid Blair concludes against the American method of stunning by a blow of the hammer. He says:

It is the unanimous opinion of all the directors of abattoirs with whom it has been my privilege to consult, that the only humane and practical method of producing insensibility in animals slaughtered for food, is by stunning or destroying the cerebrum or fore-brain. It has been repeatedly demonstrated that effective stunning acts as a perfect and instantaneous anaesthetic, and the stunned animal is lost in unconsciousness before there is time for the blow which produces it to be felt. . . . .

If the blow of the hammer was always accurately directed and with sufficient force, there would be no great objection to this method of stunning, but with butchers, as with all other men engaged in human endeavors, all are not equal in skill, strength or reliability in delivering the blow. To become an expert in stunning requires constant practice, and it is important to remember that these dumb creatures furnish the subjects for the practice. It is horrible to contemplate the sufferings of animals before the butchers become experts at proper stunning. In the case of thick-skulled bulls, often the blows of the hammer in the hands of even a skillful and strong man are not sufficient to cause even a temporary stunning, until the skull bones are broken through by repeated blows.[2]

[1] *The Charleston American*, April 8, 1923.
[2] *Amer. S. P. C. A., 57th Ann. Rpt.*, p. 104.

In line with these recommendations, the humane slaughter committee of the American Humane Association voted in 1922 for a publicity campaign and drew up the following model bill to be introduced into all state legislatures during the coming year:

Sec. 1. No animal shall be slaughtered for food or for rendering or other disposal unless such animal is first effectively stunned or otherwise deprived of sensation before being cut or bled; and such stunning or deprivation of sensation shall be done in as humane a manner as practicable, and so as not to cause such animal unnecessary pain or fright. No animal in the process of slaughter shall be caught up or hung up, by its hind legs, ears, tail, or otherwise, before it is so stunned or deprived of sensation. The word " animal " herein used shall not be deemed to include fish or fowl.[1]

To encourage progress along these lines, the American S. P. C. A. in the winter of 1922 offered two prizes: one of $5000 for the best acceptable device for casting animals previous to slaughter, and one of $10,000 for the best acceptable humane slaughtering device. No decision has as yet been rendered in this contest (November 1923) and the devices submitted will be put to extensive practical tests before final judgment is rendered.

The Jewish rite of kosher slaughtering precludes the possibility of stunning animals before slaughter, because the Rabbis believe such stunning prevents a complete draining of blood from the animal. The Massachusetts S. P. C. A. and the American Humane Education Society have been carrying on a campaign to prove by reference to adequate authorities that such is not the case in an endeavor to abolish the extreme cruelty of the rite.[2]

The western societies have been carrying on during the

[1] *National Humane Review*, vol. x, p. 1.

[2] *Vide* Francis H. Rowley, *Slaughter-House Reform in the United States and the Opposing Forces* (pamphlet, Boston, 1921), p. 9, *et seq.*

last few years a campaign directed towards the betterment of the conditions of the range stock in their states.[1]   All the plain and mountain states and a few of the Pacific and South Atlantic states—twenty-one or twenty-two in all— are considered range stock states.

It is reported that in one year 1,800,000 range cattle and sheep died from exposure.   In Colorado during the winter of 1916-1917, a particularly severe one, from 10 per cent to 35 per cent of the 1,680,197 range cattle and the 1,440,380 sheep in the state died.   There should be also taken into consideration the severe stunting of growth resulting to the survivors.   In the year ending March 1919, 900,000 head of cattle in the United States died of exposure.[2]

One of the biggest loss factors in this respect is the " shoe-stringer ".   He is the cattleman who operates without owning a foot of land and generally without credit or capital, taking his chances to make a winning on an open winter when his stock will get through without heavy losses.[3] The great cattle-range country is in a transition stage, Settlers are still crowding in and fencing in more and more land.   Large cattle companies — the best of them — have fenced lands and provide water, food and shelter.   They are crowding the " shoe-stringer " off the better lands, and as he is forced onto the poorer, his stock losses with all the animal suffering involved, are correspondingly higher.

Bona-fide cattlemen are as bitter against the " shoe-stringer " as are the anti-cruelty societies.   Through the efforts of western organizations of cattlemen and wool-growers, he is no longer granted leases to pasture his live-stock on the forest reserves, and these are granted now only to owners of cattle and sheep who are able to show owner-

---

[1] *Cf.* McCrea's account of his problem, *op. cit.*, p. 69.

[2] *National Humane Review*, vol. vii, p. 63.

    1915 circular of the Col. State Bur. of Child and Animal Protection.

ship of ranch lands and ability to take care of stock when it is taken off the reserve. They would gladly welcome a means whereby the " shoe-stringer " might be shut off from the state and federal range lands as he is also off the forest reserves.[1]

The owners of ranch lands, however, are not entirely free from charges of negligence and cruelty. They find it difficult to adapt themselves to the change from the earlier days when herds were smaller, ranges larger, and pasturage better. There is a reluctance to provide winter feed for their stock even in regions where dry farming is quite practicable and inexpensive. In addition to the western humane societies and state bureaus, the Red Star has devoted its attention to the relief of range stock. A broad publicity campaign was begun in 1918 and three special investigators as well as local volunteers began a thorough examination of range stock conditions. The representatives of the Red Star found the stock owners very ready to cooperate with them.[2] The measure of such support by the live stock associations may be gauged by the following letter of the Querno Verde Live Stock Association to the Wyoming State Board:

We are opposed to the grazing of live stock on the open range or forest reserve during the months of January, February and March. Each and every member of this association by these resolutions bind themselves to obey the above and exert every effort to gather all stock off the range at the beginning of the time mentioned each and every year.

We respectfully ask the State Humane Society to assist us by appointing one or more members of this association as humane officers to act within the boundaries of this association.[3]

[1] *Ibid.*

[2] *A. H. A., 43rd Ann. Rpt.*, pp. 4 and 15.

[3] *Wyoming State Board of Child and Animal Protection, Biennial Report of 1912*

In 1912 and 1913 inquiries were made into sheep-shearing conditions in several of the western states. It was found that grave abuses existed in Colorado, Wyoming and Oregon. California conditions were much better, whereas in Texas and Montana little information could be obtained. These six states constitute the principal sheep states in the United States.

The greatest abuse was the wounding of the animals through careless cutting. In the holding of the sheep, brutal methods such as stunning or undue pressure were sometimes employed. The sheepmen themselves were not responsible for these cruelties, for it was to their interest to have their sheep shorn as humanely as possible. The cruelties were perpetrated by irresponsible shearing crews. Consequently, the humane organizations were aided in their campaign by the National Wool Growers Association and by the various state and local sheepmen's associations.[1]

The form that the resulting campaign took is indicated by a report of the Wyoming State Board:

We sent out circulars to the sheep growers outlining our plan and requesting them to select discreet men in their employ to act as special agents under our appointment during the shearing season. In addition to this, we sent out our deputies to the largest shearing pens to report on conditions. Also a large linen poster was sent to each shearing station, giving the terms of the Wyoming laws in regard to cruelty to animals, and as warning to all persons violating the law, that they would be punished by fine or imprisonment or both.[2]

The campaign was successful in Wyoming and elsewhere.

During the same years, the western societies were active in discouraging the use of barbed wire fences in the cattle country and encouraging the substitution of smooth wire fences with moderate success.

[1] *National Humane Review*, vol. ii, p. 270.

[2] *Wyoming State Board of Child and Animal Protection, Biennial Report of 1916.*

CHAPTER VIII

HUMANE EDUCATION

IF the founding of animal welfare stations and animal hospitals is like the planting of healthy vegetation, and if the prosecution of cruelists is like the lopping off of the branches and twigs of a poisonous plant — similes often used by humanitarians — then humane education is a striking at the very root of that plant. If positive habits of kindness to animals can be implanted in children when they are young, they, as adults, will be the less likely to indulge in wanton cruelty. Moreover, as friends of animals, they will tend to spread further afield the doctrine of kindness. Hence, no small part of humane effort has been directed to this field.

During the last fifteen years there has been a growing movement to include humane education in school curricula, and to have it taught in an organized manner in the classroom. But before ever an attempt was made to bring the teaching of humaneness within school doors, there were societies and organizations already existing which were devoting their efforts to the training of children's minds in the direction of kindness to animals. The American Humane Education Society is the oldest and most active of these.

The American Humane Education Society was founded by George T. Angell to work in cooperation with the Massachusetts S. P. C. A., and was incorporated in 1889 by a special act of the Massachusetts Legislature.[1] In article

[1] *American Humane Education Society, 1921 Annual Report*, p. 21.

2 of its constitution, it stated its object — " to carry *Humane Education,* in all possible ways, into American schools and homes." [1]   In a recent report, the Society has explained its function more amply: " It is an organized effort to promote ' Peace on Earth ', ' Kindness, Justice, and Mercy to Every Living Creature ', by carrying humane education into all our American schools and homes, aiding humane societies and founding Bands of Mercy over the whole American continent." [2]

By 1910 it had grown to be a nation-wide organization. It employed humane workers in several western and southern states to carry on humane work and to assist in the promotion of humane education.   It had also representatives in several foreign countries, who headed movements for the formation of Bands of Mercy in those countries and facilitated the circulation of the Society's literature as translated into the languages of the countries.   It published and distributed at cost or less a number of books which taught the lesson of humaneness.   Of these the most important was *Black Beauty,* of which more than two and a half million copies had been circulated by 1910.   *The Strike at Shanes* and *Our Gold Mine at Hollyhurst* came next in popularity. In addition to subscribers and members, its organ *Our Dumb Animals* went every month to editors of newspapers and magazines in America north of Mexico, to the presidents of all American universities and colleges, and to members of Congress.

During 1910 a press-bureau was established at Palo Alto, California, to disseminate humane news to the press of the western states.[3]   A humane bulletin board was placed at Leland Stanford University and encouragement given to the

[1] This constitution is quoted in full in McCrea, *op. cit.,* pp. 218-220.

[2] *American Humane Education Society, 1921 Annual Report,* p. 21.

[3] *Cf. supra,* p. 88.

study of anti-cruelty subjects at the University. During this year the income of the Society was $31,656.83 and its expenses $26,545.21.

Each year since then, the work of the Society though not changing in character, has expanded. In 1914, for example, special attention was devoted to the southern states, and several new anti-cruelty societies were formed there with the cooperation of the Louisiana S. P. C. A. In 1917, in addition to establishing an eastern humane press bureau with headquarters at Boston, slides and lantern outfits were acquired and lecture courses projected. At this period was started the Jack London Club, which by March 1921 had a membership of 178,750. In this latter year, the Society made a new venture and filmed Longfellow's poem, *The Bell of Atri,* for the purpose of distributing it not only to regular moving-picture houses but to schools and churches on their request.

The Society has long ceased to be purely a national organization, but has taken upon itself an international character. It supervises the formation of Bands of Mercy, not only in the United States and in the countries of the North American continent, but in Turkey, in South Africa, in the Asiatic states. Its literature is translated into almost every language of the globe; Spanish translations intended for the Latin American countries predominate. Recently it has published *The Teacher's Helper in Humane Education,* an attractive booklet of thirty-two pages compiled to meet the needs of teachers wishing to introduce the study of human work into their courses. This pamphlet has been introduced not only into the schools in many of the states in this country, but has gone to the European countries, and in 1921 one order for 4,500 copies of it came from South Africa.[1]

American Humane Education Society, 1921 Annual Report, p. 23.

In addition to the American Humane Education Society, the American Humane Association *Annual Report* for 1922 notes seven other humane educational societies and three humane education committees attached to other anti-cruelty organizations.[1] Of these, however, only four answered a questionnaire sent to them in the autumn of 1922, and from other sources, two of those which did not reply were reported inactive.

One of the most active of the independent humane education societies is that of Rhode Island, organized in 1904. Unlike the American Humane Education Society, the Rhode Island society receives aid from the state; $375 in 1910, $2,500 in 1915 and each year since then. It divides its efforts between the distribution of humane literature and the organization of Bands of Mercy. In 1910, 34,820 pupils in the Rhode Island schools were enrolled in these Bands of Mercy.[2] It has each year made a practice of distributing art calendars which preach kindness to animals. For a time, the continuation of this practice was endangered by the increasing post-war cost of these calendars, which, while only $299.78 in 1910, had mounted to $1,053.20 in 1920.[3] Recent lower costs, however, have made it possible for the Society to continue their distribution. In 1921 the Society's income was $5,329.40 and the expenses $5,386.11.[4]

How little it is possible to judge of the activities of a society by its title, may be seen by comparison of the activities of the Chattanooga Humane Education Society and the Lehigh Humane Society. Earlier in its history the Chattanooga Society confined itself almost entirely to work

[1] *A. H. A., 46th Ann. Rpt.*, p. 64.

[2] *Rhode Island Humane Education Society, 6th Ann. Rpt.* (1910).

[3] *Cf. supra*, p. 58.

[4] *R. I. Humane Education Society, 17th Ann. Rpt.* (1921).

of an educational character; in 1912 it began a campaign of distributing literature and somewhat later, gave a series of lectures on humane topics. It held humane story contests in the schools of Hamilton County.[1] At present, however, it is becoming more and more an anti-cruelty organization, maintaining agents to seek out cases of cruelty and prosecuting offenders in court. In 1921 it investigated four hundred and fourteen cases involving five hundred and nine animals; in the course of the year, it examined nearly thirty-five hundred draught animals. It has added child and women protection to its schedule, attending to twenty-eight such cases during the year. In both fields it prosecuted thirty-seven cases, obtaining convictions in sixteen.[2] Its activities in the field of humane education have diminished rather than increased, although it has recently been publishing *The Humane Record* to encourage the establishment of humane education in the curricula of the schools of Tennessee.

On the other hand, the Lehigh Humane Society is listed in the American Humane Association reports as an anti-cruelty organization. Nevertheless, the greater part of its energies have gone into the field of humane education. In its 1921 *Report* the president writes: "The Society has during a period of fifteen years promoted an educational campaign, believing that the firmest foundation for the future is laid in the hearts and minds of the youth of the country; that education is the true preventive of cruelty to children and animals and the ultimate remedy for troubles to which law enforcement is now applied as a palliative."[3] There are several other anti-cruelty organizations which during recent years have been devoting more and more of their at-

[1] *The Humane Record*, vol. ii, no. 2.
[2] *Chattanooga Humane Education Society, Ann. Rpt. for 1921.*
Lehigh Humane Society, 15th Ann. Rpt. (1921).

tention to propaganda work and to labors amongst school children, so that they might now be considered more as educational than as prosecuting societies.

There are several large anti-cruelty societies which within the last few years have appointed special humane educational committees. It will be remembered that one of the original fields of interest of the Women's Auxiliary of the American S. P. C. A. as it was formed in 1906, was the formation of Young Defenders leagues and the interesting of the children of the city in humane work.[1] As the New York Women's League for Animals, this body continued its educational activities. However, when it became an independent organization, the American S. P. C. A. was left without any group or committee on humane education. This deficiency persisted until very recently.

Year by year the New York Women's League for Animals increased its educational program until this threatened to outrun its financial support. The American S. P. C. A. came to its assistance, and in 1920 formed the Department of Humane Education to cooperate with the League. The Department stated its purpose: " Our aim is not to *do* the humane education work in our schools, so much as to *stimulate* the work of the schools themselves."[2] A circular sent by the Department to all the district superintendents and principals of the New York schools assured them that the Department was " not for the purpose of enforcing the law which makes the teaching of humaneness compulsory, but to stimulate an interest in this feature of the curriculum ".[3]

In the schools of greater New York after the summer

[1] *Cf. supra*, p. 69.

[2] *Amer. S. P. C. A., 56th Ann. Rpt.* (1921), p. 15.

[3] *Ibid.*

vacation of 1921, the children were given essays to write on the topic " What I Did to Help the Animals This Summer ". The Department provided small medals as awards and a banner for the school in each district reporting unusual humane activity. During this same summer, the Department tried out an original scheme to test the effectiveness of its propaganda among the children of the lower East Side. Four of the school districts in that locality were asked to unite in relief work in behalf of animals. While the attitude of foreign-born adults was plainly one of indifference, the children of these same parents, inspired by school influence, became an army of welfare workers to rid the streets of homeless small animals. In order that this work might be done in a kindly and humane way, an instructive letter was read daily for two weeks in every schoolroom in these districts, as well as being posted in the libraries and playgrounds, the message reaching over eighty thousand children. The sympathy of the child and his sense of justice were appealed to, and it was plainly set forth that the ideal was not to collect as many animals as possible, but to confine activities to those that were homeless or stricken. It was suggested that their attention be given also to the sufferings of horses in hot weather by asking drivers if their horses had been given a drink, and directing them to the nearest fountain. Through the courtesy of the American S. P. C. 'A., temporary receiving stations were opened at desirable locations, with an attendant in charge of each. Fifteen thousand small animals were collected and brought to these stations and the Society humanely disposed of them.

In 1922 the Department repeated its activities of the preceding year, and expanded in some directions. Lecture courses with lantern slides and the distribution of literature were carried on in over three hundred schools. During " Be

Kind to Animals" Week, suitable slides were provided to all the largest moving-picture houses. In the late spring an extensive poster contest was conducted with the endorsement of the Board of Education and the Director of Art and Drawing of the elementary schools with schools in every borough participating. About three thousand posters were submited which represented several times that number drawn but not entered for the contest. Five hundred dollars was contributed by the New York Women's League for Animals, and was divided as follows: five prizes of ten dollars each, forty-seven prizes of five dollars each, thirty-six prizes of two dollars each, and one hundred and forty-three of one dollar each. The Department recommends that this feature be made an annual school event.

Apart from its work in New York City, the Department tries to keep in touch with educational headquarters at Albany and to supervise, as far as it is possible to do so, humane educational matters in the State. Normal schools are visited regularly in so far as this is possible. During 1922 the Department arranged for illustrated lectures before both teacher and civic groups in nine of the up-state cities.

In addition, the Department is ready to support any group of humane workers in the United States which is striving to further the cause of humane education in its own state. In the 1922 convention of the American Humane Association, there was hung a banner of the Department bearing the slogan "Humane Education in Every State by 1925". Letters were addressed to the commissioner of education in every state, offering the services of the Department in promoting humane education legislation.[1]

The Presbyterian Church of the United States has also

[1] *Amer. S. P. C. A., 57th Ann. Rpt.* (1922), pp. 11-19.

interested itself in humane education.   In 1920 it organized
as a part of its Board of Temperance and Moral Welfare,
a department of Humane Education.[1]   Its Director explained its purpose at the 1920 American Humane Association convention :

First of all, the Presbyterian Church does not propose to do
case work.   Our field is propaganda work.   We hope both in
spirit and method so to conduct this work that every humane
society, no matter how small or humble it may be, that every
individual worker, no matter how lonely and modest he may
be, will be stronger and more courageous and more enthusiastic
because of what we undertake to do.   It is to supplement and
not to supplant.   We hope the Humane Societies will find in
the Presbyterian and in other churches a more congenial at-
mosphere in which to carry on their activities.   Henceforth,
humane work is just as much a part of the program of the
Presbyterian Church as home or foreign missions, as Sunday
School, as education, as ministerial relief, or any other enter-
prise of the denomination, and will be supported in exactly
the same way.[2]

During the past three years, the Department of Humane
Education has labored to gain for the rights of animals
" that consideration which is scriptural, ethical and
humane ".[3]

At the annual meeting of the Executive Committee of
the Federal Council of the Churches of Christ in America
held in December 1921, the following resolution was voted :
" That the Executive Committee approves a recommenda-

---

[1] *Minutes of the General Assembly of the Presbyterian Church of the
U. S. A.* (1920), pt. ii, sec. 9, p. 12.

[2] *A. H. A., 44th Ann. Rpt.* (1920), p. 15; *cf. Amer. S. P. C. A., 56th
Ann. Rpt.*

[3] *Minutes of the General Assembly of the Presbyterian Church in the
U. S. A.* (1923), pt. ii, sec. 9, p. 10.

tion of the Board of Temperance and Moral Welfare of the Presbyterian Church in the U. S. A. that a committee be formed in the Commission on Church and Social Service, ' On Kindness to Animals ' or some other appropriate title; and that the committee bring together the responsible officials of the denominations affiliated with the Federal Council, to consider appropriate educational effort in this field." [1]

One of the principal agencies of humane education work among children is the Bands of Mercy movement. The first Band of Mercy was formed in Boston on July 28th, 1882, through the efforts of George T. Angell and of an English clergyman, the Rev. Thomas Simmons. Their models were the English Band of Mercy societies, the first one of which was established in 1875. The spread and growth in popularity of these Bands have been very great, and on July 1st, 1923, there were over 140,000 Bands of Mercy in the country with no less than 4,000,000 members. [2]

These Bands of Mercy, or as they are now sometimes called, Junior Humane Leagues, are formed in schools of all grades, and in Sunday Schools of all denominations, Protestant and Roman Catholic, under the auspices of the American Humane Education Society or other anti-cruelty organizations. They pledge their members " to Kindness and Justice to All Living Creatures (both dumb and human)".

The beneficial influence of the Bands of Mercy is not to be questioned. Note should be taken, however, of its transitory character unless each individual Band is followed up by some responsible organization. In a school in which executives and teachers are heartily in sympathy with the

[1] *Ibid.* (1922), pt. ii, sec. 9, p. 13; *cf. National Humane Review*, vol. x, p. 50.

[2] Pamphlet issued by the American Humane Education Society, February, 1923.

movement, the children can be encouraged to take a really astonishing interest in humane work. Where, however, the Bands are formed half-heartedly and no attempt is made to encourage them, they soon dissolve, leaving little or no effect upon the children's characters.

This phenomenon was brought acutely to the attention of the Louisiana S. P. C. A. in 1915. During the previous year, the funds of the Society had run low. It was forced to contract its work and it lost touch with the Bands of Mercy it had founded throughout the state. When it found it possible to resume this work in 1915, there was scarcely any trace of its earlier activities. The previous Band of Mercy membership had vanished. The children had lost their buttons, their interest in the organization had fled, and they had forgotten their pledges.

The Society decided upon a new policy. No attempt would be made to organize as many Bands as before, but a closer grip was to be kept on each. The members were now furnished with buttons that had safety clips, and had to promise to wear them at least a part of every day. The Society planned a program of excursions and movie entertainments for the Bands, and each was encouraged to keep and care for a pet. It was also planned to hold annual mass meetings, when a medal would be given to the Band which had done most to help animals during the year. In the carrying out of this plan, the Louisiana Society organized only forty-two Bands during 1915.[1]

The Salvation Army, before its attention was so largely occupied by war needs, organized Bands of Love for children between the ages of six and fourteen. Part of the pledge of these Bands of Love was to " love and be kind to animals ". In 1914 these Bands of Love numbered seven thousand members. During the War they were necessarily

[1] *Louisiana S. P. C. A., 41st Ann. Rpt.* (1915), p. 11.

neglected. Since 1918 the lost ground has not only been recovered, but new Bands have been formed throughout the United States. By the close of 1922 the membership of these Bands numbered 7,561.[1]

The Boy Scouts of America likewise include kindness to animals among their obligations of scouthood. Scout Rule No. 6 reads: " A Scout is kind. He is a friend to animals. He will not kill or hurt any living creature needlessly, but will strive to save and protect all harmless life ". One of the Scout Merit Badge subjects is First Aid to Animals. To obtain this Merit Badge a scout must have passed his tender-foot, second class and first class examinations; he must have a general knowledge of domestic and farm animals; he must be able to treat a horse for colic and describe symptoms and give treatment for the following—wounds, fractures, sprains, exhaustion, choking and lameness; he must know what to do for horses in harness when they fall on the street and what to do when animals are being cruelly mistreated.[2] Scout Rule No. 6 of the Girl Scouts establishes the same standard of kindness to animals in that organization.[3]

Many newspapers include children's departments as a regular feature of their daily issues. Quite a few of these papers organize their child readers into junior humane clubs. The scope of the activities of these organizations is limited, but by encouraging the children to write their experiences in helping animals and publishing these accounts, they maintain the children's interest in humaneness. Very significant is the development of the " Bed Time Story " section of many evening papers. These stories, best re-

---

[1] Manuscript letter of December 1, 1923, from Col. J. E. Margetts of the Eastern Territory of the Salvation Army.

[2] *Scout Manual*, official handbook of the Boy Scouts of America.

[3] *Scouting for Girls*, official handbook of the Girl Scouts of America.

presented by the Uncle Remus and Uncle Wiggely tales, arouse in their young readers the sense of brotherhood with the brute creation.   Their inclusion in radio programs gives them a still wider audience.

The Jack London Club was formed a few years ago for a specific humane purpose.   In 1916 Jack London published *Jerry of the Islands,* a dog story which detailed the horrors that formed a part of the training of animals for the stage.   In his preface, he appealed to his readers to co-operate in stamping out this abuse.   He wrote:

It is so easy.   We will not have to think of dues or corresponding secretaries.   We will not have to think of anything save when, in any theatre or place or entertainment, a trained animal turn is presented before us.   Then, without premeditation, we may express our disapproval of such a turn by getting up from our seats and leaving the theatre for a promenade and a breath of fresh air outside, coming back when the turn is over, to enjoy the rest of the program.   All we have to do is just that to eliminate the trained animal turn from all public places of entertainment.   Show the management that such turns are unpopular, and in a day, in an instant, the management will cease catering such turns to its audiences.

Dr. Francis H. Rowley, president of the American Humane Education Society, had both book and preface called to his attention and decided to carry out Jack London's suggestion.   The Jack Lnodon club was organized, unique in having no officers, nor fees, nor dues.   All that was asked of its members was: first, if they cared to, to distribute anti-cruelty literature outside music halls where animal turns were on; second, to express disapproval by hissing cruel turns, or leaving their seats while that part of the performance lasted; third, to write to the theatre manager to express disapproval; fourth, to write letters to the press when such performances occurred in their neighborhoods, avoiding, however, any mention of individuals which might be considered libelous; fifth, to send to the American Humane Education Society the names and addresses of persons likely to be willing to help.[1]

In 1910 the annual conference of the American Humane Association resolved that the humane societies of the country should " use their best efforts to have the clergy in their respective districts set apart some Sunday in each year, in May if possible, which shall be called ' Mercy Sunday ', and which shall be devoted to the teaching of humane principles ".[2] No action was taken on this resolution until 1913. In that year the conference passed a similar resolution and a committee on the subject was appointed. It consisted of a chairman and secretary, and forty-two state chairmen. Owing to delay in getting work under way, many of the state chairmen found that they did not have sufficient time to develop the work to their complete satisfaction. The following year, chairmen in twenty-one states sent reports of sermons preached, and clergymen to the number of seven hundred and seventy-three from thirty-six states wrote for special literature.[3]

Since then Mercy Sunday with its attendant feature, " Be Kind to Animals " Week, has gained popularity with each succeeding year. One interesting and valuable feature of the Humane Sundays during the past five years has been the " Be Kind to Animals " supplement of the *Charleston (S. C.) American* published on those days. This twenty-page supplement is paid for by one of the prominent humanitarians of that city. It contains articles by noted humanitarians, often of more than transitory value.[4]

[1] Pamphlet of the American Humane Education Society, 1923.

[2] *A. H. A., 34th Ann. Rpt.*, p. 148.

[3] *A. H. A., 38th Ann. Rpt.*, p. 14.

[4] *Cf. supra*, p. 116, quotations from an article by Dr. Rowley on animal transportation, contained in the 1923 supplement.

The periodicals published by various humane associations provide a very important means of humane education. The most important of these is the *National Humane Review,* published by the American Humane Association. At the 1911 conference of the Association, its president stated as one of its most vital needs, a national humane magazine. [1] The previous conference had already passed a resolution that a committee be appointed for the establishment of such a humane monthly.[2] Not until 1913 was this periodical established. The *National Humane Review* has been for the past decade a storehouse of valuable information on the history of the humane movement. Theoretically devoted to both child and animal protection, the greater part of its space has been given to animal welfare. It serves the dual purpose of a propaganda organ and an informational periodical.

Of other humane publications, *Our Dumb Animals* published by the American Humane Education Society is the most valuable. Its purpose is frankly propaganda, but it often contains articles of more than passing interest. Other humane publications range in size down to small two-page sheets issued by struggling rural societies.

Humanitarians have long felt that the inculcating of humane doctrine in the minds of the children should be a part of the public school program. The St. Augustine conference of the American Humane Association held in November 1915 adopted a resolution, " that the American Humane Association places itself on record as being in favor of a law to establish compulsory education in each of the states, and that humane education be made a part of

[1] *A. H. A., 35th Ann. Rpt.,* p. 12.
   A. H. A., 34th Ann. Rpt., p. 146.

that system." [1]   The Illinois law of 1909 [2] providing for humane education was selected as a model, and all societies were urged to work for the passage of such a law. [3]

Illinois was not the first state to provide for humane education, but the 1909 law was the most practicable so far passed in that it penalized non-observance of the act and provided that instruction on the subject be given in the normal schools.   At the time, twelve other states made more or less provision for the teaching of humaneness, the acts ranging in definite provisions from the Texas requirement of " once a week ", [4] and New Hampshire's " prescribed reading course ", [5] to Oklahoma's " not less than one half hour per week ". [6]   Nearly all the states were indefinite as to the time allowed for such teaching.   Maine authorized " not less than ten minutes per week ". [7]   Washington allowed just ten minutes each week. [8]   Three states divided the time into two periods of ten or more minutes each week. [9]

With the exception of the Illinois statute, these laws were not successful.   In the first place they made no provision for their enforcement and unfriendly superintendents and teachers ignored them with impunity.   Where teachers expressed willingness to carry out the statutes, they found themselves without suitable texts, or syllabi of materials for this purpose.

[1] *A. H. A., 39th Ann. Rpt.*

[2] *Vide* appendix iv.

[3] *National Humane Review*, vol. iv, p. 48.

[4] *Tex. Sess. Laws*, 1907, ch. 169.

[5] *N. H. Sess. Laws*, 1909, ch. 49.

[6] *Okla. G. S.*, secs. 6663-6664.

[7] *Me. R. S.*, ch. 15, sec. 86.

[8] *Wash. Sess. Laws*, 1909, ch. 97, title ii, sec. 2.

[9] *Col. Mills Supp.*, sec. 4043 (*Sess. Laws*, 1909, ch. 216, amended this to " a portion of time in all public schools "); *N. D. Sess. Laws*, 1905, ch. 108; *Wyo. Sess. Laws*, 1901, ch. 8.

The American Humane Association concentrated attention on the subject. The Illinois statute was held up as an
example of what could be accomplished by effective provision. A Chicago teacher commented on its operation in
1917 as follows:

The method of instruction is generally through indirect means
rather than formal lessons, and is left largely to the judgment
of the principals and teachers. It is difficult to formulate rules
by which the doctrine of kindness may be taught. For that
reason, more depends upon the school life, and the character and
influence of the teacher, than upon any outlined plan. The
teacher must be imbued with the spirit of her task and interested enough to devise ways and means to teach honesty, obedi-
ence, self-control, interest in humanity and regard for the
rights of all living creatures. . . .
The textbooks which are now being introduced into the
schools of Chicago have been planned to meet the needs of the
Humane Education law, and contain many valuable lessons that
will assist very materially in carrying out its principles. The
schools throughout the city have generally cooperated in this
work, and many have organized Bands of Mercy with splendid
results.[1]

During the past decade, there has been a satisfactory advance in the legislation passed providing for humane education. By 1922 twenty states had humane education
laws. Three, New York, Oklahoma and Illinois, provided
penalties for non-observance of the act by withholding the
teachers' salaries or public money from the schools. Nine
states specify minimum lengths of time to be devoted—thirty
minutes in Illinois, Kentucky, Maine, Oklahoma and Pennsylvania; twenty minutes in Colorado, North Dakota and
Wyoming; ten minutes in Washington. Five states, Alabama, Illinois, Kentucky, Michigan and Pennsylvania, require teachers to report monthly concerning their obser-

[1] *A. H. A., 41st Ann. Rpt.*, p. 69.

vance of the law.   Three states, Alabama, Illinois and New
York, provide that humane education shall be included upon
the programs of the teachers' institutes.

It is evident that much is yet to be accomplished in order
to secure a higher standard of humane education laws and
their adoption in states which at present possess none.
The requirements of an ideal humane education act have
been stated by Mr. Sydney H. Coleman as follows:

I. What is to be taught must be specifically defined.

II. A clear explanation of how this teaching is to be carried
out.

III. A minimum time of not less than thirty minutes per
week.

IV. A money forfeiture for non-observance (applicable to
individual school teachers and school districts).

V. Responsibility for enforcement must rest on the state
superintendent of public education.

VI. It must be on the programs of state teachers' meetings
and teachers' institutes.

VII. It must be a required subject in all normal schools,
training classes and colleges.[1]

Opinions are divided among humanitarians as to whether
humane education acts should specify the time in each week
or month to be devoted to the subject, or whether they
should copy the New York law, which reads: " Such instruction shall be for such period of time as the Board of
Regents may prescribe ".[2]   The New York and Pennsylvania acts are also unique in that they are amendments to
the general education law of the states instead of being independent legislation.   The defenders of the New York
act claim that it fits into the scheme of instruction in a more

[1] *National Humane Review*, vol. iv, p. 71.

N. Y. Sess. Laws, 1907, ch. 102.

practical way and is less apt to arouse opposition in the school system. [1]

The 1920 convention of the American Humane Association provided for a committee to draw up a model humane education act. In the 1921 convention, two were reported, the first a proposal to amend the general education law; the second a special act. The first amends the general education act of any state to read as follows: " In every elementary public and private school established and maintained in this commonwealth, the following subjects shall be taught in the English language and in English texts, (here follows a list of the usual school subjects), including . . . . *the mane treatment of birds and animals."* [2]

The second proposed special act read as follows:

Section 1. The officer, board or commission authorized or required to prescribe courses of instruction shall cause instruction to be given in every elementary school, under state control or supported wholly or partly by public money of the state, in the humane treatment and protection of animals and birds and the importance of the part they play in the economy of nature.

Section 2. Such instruction shall be for such period of time during each school year as the proper school authority shall proscribe and may be joined with work in literature, reading, language or nature study. A school district shall not be entitled to participate in the public school money on account of any school or the attendance at any school subject to the provisions of this section, if the instruction required hereby is not given therein.

Section 3. The proper school authority shall, and at such time as the proper authorities may prescribe, pursuant to this act, cause the consideration of the humane treatment of animals and birds to be included in the program of teachers' institutes.

[1] *A. H. A., 44th Ann., Rpt.,* p. 29.
National Humane Review, vol. x, p. 13.

Section 4. All acts or parts of acts inconsistent herewith be and the same are hereby repealed.[1]

There can be no question that the progress made in humane education has been the most important development in animal welfare since 1910.   In that year it was still in the experimental stage.   The American Humane Education Society was doing pioneer work in its field, other organizations like the Rhode Island Humane Education Society still having to struggle to maintain themselves.   The larger S. P. C. A.s were interested in humane education and were making tentative efforts along this line, but as yet they were hardly applying themselves seriously to its problems.

Twelve years later we find a marked advance.   The original humane education societies have increased their sphere of activities, and they are assisted by a number of other agencies which have interested themselves in the subject— the humane education committees of the larger S. P. C. A.s, the Presbyterian Church through its Board of Temperance and Moral Welfare, Humane Sunday, the Jack London Club, the Bands of Love of the Salvation Army, etc. Children and adults are impressed with the significance of animal life; the tendency to be cruel is nipped in the bud.

There has also been a great development in the teaching of humaneness in the schools.   In 1910 the Illinois statute was the only one which successfully met the problems of humane education, and Chicago teachers were experimenting with texts and curriculum arrangements.   By 1922 twenty states had humane education laws and several prominent humane education organizations looked forward to having such laws upon the statute books of every state by 1925 or 1926.   Many of the best features of the Illinois and the New York laws had been copied by other states.   In some, humane education had found a place upon the schedules of teachers' training schools.

[1]*A. H. A., 45th Ann. Rpt.*, p. 18.

CHAPTER IX

ANTI-VIVISECTION

THE anti-vivisectionist movement opposing the use of animals in medical experimentation, owes its beginning in this country, like the animal and child protective movements, to Mr. Henry Bergh. The first attack upon this practice was made by him and opposed by the New York State Medical Society in 1867. In that year Mr. Bergh introduced and obtained the passage of an anti-cruelty act by the New York legislature.[1] The annual convention of the Medical Society of the State of New York was being held at the time when the act came up before the legislature for discussion. Through the influence of the convention, a provision permitting animal experimentation was included, despite the very vigorous opposition and much to the disappointment of Mr. Bergh.[2] This provision was incorporated in the final clause of the act and read: " nothing in this act shall be construed to prohibit or interfere with any properly conducted scientific experiments or investigations, which experiments shall be performed under the authority of the faculty of some regularly incorporated medical college or university of the State of New York."

During the next few years Mr. Bergh's time and attention were taken up with the work of organizing the American S. P. C. A. and nursing its early development. In 1874, however, he reopened the campaign against vivisection, seek-

[1] *N. Y. Sess. Laws*, 1867, sec. 95.

[2] *New York Evening Post*, Sept. 4, 1874.

y

b
141]   141

ing to bring the American S. P. C. A. with its growing influence to the support of his new project. He carried on an educational propaganda during the next six years, and on January 21, 1880, he introduced into the New York legislature, the first American anti-vivisection bill. It read:

Sec. 1. Every person who shall perform, or cause to be performed, or assist in performing, in or upon any living animal, an act of vivisection, shall be guilty of a misdemeanor.

Sec. 2. The term "vivisection" used in this Act shall include every investigation, experiment, or demonstration, producing, or of a nature to produce, pain or disease in any living animal, including the cutting, wounding, or poisoning thereof, except when the same is for the purpose of curing or alleviating some physical suffering or disease in such living animal, or in order to deprive it of life when incurable.[1]

The medical organizations, not only of New York state, but also of the other states, protested and sent memorials to the New York legislature. The bill was adversely reported in the assembly committee and never came to a vote.[2]

As may be noted in the bill introduced by Mr. Bergh, the term "vivisection", originally implying merely the cutting of a living animal by way of experiment, had come by 1880 to include all scientific investigations upon animals whatsoever, even when such researches or demonstrations involved no surgery of any kind. Since then, the term has acquired a still wider connotation, and the definition of " vivisection " given by one of its recent and most scholarly opponents is "the exploitation of living animals for experiments concerning the phenomena of life".[3]

[1] Medical Record, January 31, 1880.

[2] Ibid., March 31, 1880.

[3] Dr. Albert Leffingwell, An Ethical Problem (2nd edition, New York, 1916), p. 2.

The most natural objection to the practice of vivisection is the pain thereby caused to the animals which are the subjects of experiment. The extreme anti-vivisectionists have long accused medical practitioners of taking a more or less fiendish delight in the sufferings of the animals in their power, and have asserted that their familiarity with the instruments and routine of surgery has obliterated all feelings of sympathy. Moderate opponents of vivisection, passing over such charges as these, point out that there is a necessary minimum of suffering that must be borne by the animals, and which all too often is increased by carelessness and thoughtlessness, rather than viciousness.

Against this necessary and doubtless irreducible animal suffering, defenders of vivisection have placed the benefits accruing to mankind in the perfecting of surgical practice and the greater knowledge of the nature and cures of various diseases. The anti-vivisectionists' retort to this defense has been two-fold. Some question outright whether human beings have the moral right to gain health and freedom from certain physical ailments at the cost of any suffering to animals, no matter how slight the extent of such suffering.[1] This " ethical problem " has been stated; " Is it right to do an evil and abominable thing, fouling our best nature, and degrading us below the level of the beasts of the jungle, ' red in tooth and claw ', that we may save our skins for a while? "[2]

In the second place, anti-vivisectionists deny that benefits have accrued to medical science through animal experimentation. In support of this assertion, they quote various

[1] *Vide* testimony of Dr. Hadwin before the subcommittee of the U. S. Senate Judiciary Committee (1921), 62nd Congress, 1st Session, *Hearings on S. 758*, p. 4, *et seq.*

[2] *New England Anti-Vivisection Society, Ann. Rpt. for 1919-1920*, p. 15.

medical authorities during the past two centuries.[1]   Special protest is made against the practice of vivisection in demonstrations in medical colleges in connection with teaching.

There are not a few anti-vivisectionists who base their denial of the benefits of vivisection on a repudiation of the germ theory of disease.   To the doctors' claim that animal experimentation has enabled them to isolate the germs of several diseases and to discover their cures, these opponents reply that the entire germ theory is false and therefore all the animals used in the experimentation had to suffer for a medical delusion.[2]   The president of one of the most important anti-vivisection societies quotes with approval the following excerpt from the speech of an anti-vivisectionist medical practitioner: " The germ theory, which has been worked out by the most refined and long-drawn-out cruelty to sentient animals that has ever disgraced the name of science, is opposed to all of Nature's laws and teachings. It is but a fashion of thinking—first among theorists, and now among the millions of ignorant and misled." [3]

Anti-vivisectionists are likewise opposed to the use of anti-toxins and serums obtained from animals.   They point to the undoubted pain that the processes for obtaining some serums must cause the animals used.   In addition, those who deny the germ theory insist that this pain is suffered for a delusory cause and some make the additional charge that the whole doctrine of innoculation and vaccination is propagated by commercial organizations interested in producing these serums for financial gain.   Henry Bergh was the first American anti-vivisection protagonist of the anti-

[1] Cf. Medical Opinions Against Vivisection, pamphlet issued by the N. Y. Anti-Vivisection Society.

[2] Vide testimony of Dr. Hadwin, cit. supra, p. 20.

[3] New England Anti-Vivisection Society, Ann. Rpt. for 1919-1920, p. 16.

vaccination movement.[1]   A recent pamphlet of the Maryland Anti-Vivisection Society states that

eminent authorities warn us that all serums and vaccines
are a danger to health and not infrequently to life itself.   The
persistent continuance of this revolting practice can only be
explained by the rank commercialism associated therewith and
it is beyond dispute that but for *commercialism* and the *super-
stition* of the uninformed, the whole system of inoculating
diseased animal matter into the human organism would collapse.
The gross selfishness that tempts believers to gain supposed
profit for themselves either as a prevention of or cure of disease at the cost of such intense suffering to a sentient being,
gagged, bound down, and helpless—indicates the moral depravity inherent among us.

The president of the New York Anti-Vivisection Society
said at the London Anti-Vivisection Congress in 1909:

What is the way of salvation?   It seems to me that the only
real way to freedom, not only for the sub-human but for the
human as well, lies in getting away from the unfortunate and
mistaken idea of the germ theory of disease, with its filthy
inoculations of poison into healthy blood and tissue.   Fundamentally, our work and our battle are there.   The insanity of
serum therapy is increasing so rapidly that soon no one will
be safe from the infection of any and every kind of disease;
the blood of the children will be impure from the hour of their
birth, and the certain sure retrogression of the race is bound
to follow, since all these results from serum therapy are cumulative, and we have reached the natural but inevitable result of
blood pollution by serum therapy, *i. e.*, a degenerated race.

Just as the attacks upon animal experimentation range
from moderate accusations to most radical charges, so do
the solutions of the controversy proposed by anti-vivisec-

[1] *Vide* his interesting letter to the *New York Tribune*, December 18, 1881.

[2] *New York Herald*, July 8, 1909.

tionists. On the one hand is the conservative program suggested by Dr. Leffingwell: "First of all, public opinion
should be aroused, not so much to condemn all experimentation upon animals, as to know with certainty the facts
about them . . . . then a campaign should be waged to
register all laboratories and experimentors and to provide
that all animals used and experiments made be duly reported on ".[1] On the other hand, several anti-vivisection
societies desire the total prohibition of animal experimentation and the discontinuance of vaccination under heavy
penalties.

The first society opposed to animal experimentation—the
American Anti-Vivisection Society—was founded at Philadelphia in 1883. Its object was "the restriction of the
practice of vivisection within proper limits, and the prevention of the injudicious and needless infliction of sufferings upon animals under the pretense of medical or scientific
research ".[2] In 1887 it announced its purpose as the total
elimination of all forms of animal experimentation.

The American Society for the Regulation of Vivisection
was formed in 1896, and devoted itself to the distribution
of anti-vivisection literature. In 1903 this society was
merged with the Vivisection Reform Society of Chicago,
then incorporated. This compound organization likewise
devoted itself almost exclusively to propaganda. At a later
period it was merged with the National Society for the
Humane Regulation of Vivisection. It stated in its program:

To critics we answer that we realize that vivisection cannot be
prohibited at this time. We believe the day will come when
science will find a way to do all that is now accomplished by
this means, and to do it without recourse to cruelty. In the

[1] Leffingwell, op. cit., p. 203.
[2] Leffingwell, op. cit., p. 216.

meantime, we do believe that it is possible to overwhelmingly reduce the number of victims sacrificed by very unscientific experimentors and to insist on the use of such anaesthetics as shall prevent suffering, and that, having served its purpose, the subject shall be put to death painlessly, instead of being allowed to drag out a wretched existence.[1]

In 1898 the Anti-Vivisection Society of Maryland was formed. Its charter was amended in June 1911 and it was reentitled the Maryland Anti-Vivisection Society. Its purpose was now stated as " the protection of animals and human beings from vivisection, inoculation, and cruel and unnecessary experiments for scientific research or for any other reason, and to ascertain the relation of vivisection and experiments upon animals and human beings to science and also its effect upon the character and morals of those who experiment in such ways, and the known deleterious as against the claimed good effects of such practice generally ".

In 1907 the Society for the Prevention of Abuse in Animal Experimentation was organized in Brooklyn.[2] During its existence, this society, together with the New York Anti-Vivisection Society, waged a steady fight to have an anti-vivisection bill passed by the New York legislature. The first of this series of bills was the Francis Bill introduced in 1907 " to prevent cruelty by regulation of experiments on living animals ". Its requirements were: first, institutions conducting experiments must be licensed by the State Board of Health, must be open for inspection, and issue semi-annual reports; secondly, that such experiments must not be for demonstration of fact, must be conducted under general anaesthetic, and the animal must be killed immediately after. In 1908 two similar bills were introduced into the New York assembly. The opposition

[1] *Mercy and Truth*, vol. i, no. 14.

[2] Leffingwell, *op. cit.*, p. 219.

to these bills was most bitter. The medical associations under the leadership of the Medical Society of the State of New York combated all three bills. The newspapers took up the fight, the *New York Herald* supporting the anti-vivisectionists, and most of the other papers ranged against them.

The next few years saw a vigorous growth of the antivivisection movement and likewise the beginning of organization on the part of the medical fraternity to oppose it. The Washington Anti-Vivisection Society was organized in 1908, and began a campaign for anti-vivisection laws in Washington, D. C. The California Anti-Vivisection Society was organized in Los Angeles in the same year. The New York Anti-Vivisection Society and the International Anti-Vivisection Union had amalgamated for better cooperation a few months earlier.

At the annual meeting of the American Medical Association, held in Chicago in June 1908, the subject of attempted restriction was discussed, and a committee of seven was appointed for the defense of freedom in experimentation.[1] During the next few years, under the auspices of this committee a series of " Defense of Medical Research " pamphlets was issued, thirty in all. By far the larger number of these were devoted to showing the benefits accruing from experimentation in certain fields of medicine and the prevention of disease. A few of them were direct attacks upon the methods and charges of certain anti-vivsection organizations. The Medical Society of the State of New York appointed a committee on Experimental Medicine which likewise issued a series of controversial pamphlets. In defense of their position, the doctors asserted that if there was an ethical problem involved, it was not that humans had no right to benefit from the sufferings of animals, but that

[1] McCrea, *op. cit.*, p. 123.

I. Scientific men are under definite obligation to experiment upon animals so far as that is the alternative to random and possibly harmful experimentation upon human beings, and so far as such experimentation is a means of saving human life, and of increasing human vigor and efficiency. II. The community at large is under definite obligation to see to it that physicians and scientific men are not needlessly hampered in carrying on the inquiries necessary for an adequate performance of their important social office of sustaining human life and vigor.[1]

Direct attacks were made upon the programs and controversial methods of the anti-vivisection societies themselves. They were accused of "exaggerated statements, repetition of allegations of cruelty which have never been proved or even examined, use of sporadic cases of cruelty to animals in Europe a generation or two ago as if they were typical of the practice in the United States today, refusal to accept the testimony of reputable scientific men regarding either their own procedure, or the benefits that have accrued to humanity and to the brute kingdom itself from animal experimentation, uncharitable judgment varying from vague insinuation to downright aspersion ".[2] It was claimed that a study of the medical authorities quoted by the anti-vivisectionists showed few of them to be established practicing physicians or surgeons, nor fully competent to set themselves up as authorities, and that many of the authorities they quoted had been dead for periods ranging from a few years to a century. More serious were the charges that statements used were misquoted and that when their authors called the attention of the anti-vivisection organizations to this, no change was made, nor were the statements

[1] John Dewey, *The Ethics of Animal Experimentation* (Pamphlet issued by Committee on Experimental Medicine of the Medical Society of the State of New York, 1909).

[2] *Ibid.*

withdrawn from circulation. Also it was charged that qualifying statements in the description of experiments (such as the fact that an anaesthetic was used) were suppressed. The anti-vivisectionists were challenged for appealing to the emotions instead of to the intellect.

The doctors made direct statement of their own position:

In the first place, the investigators object to any step tending to check the use of animals for medical research. They maintain that such interference is not justified by the present treatment of the experimental animal. They declare that the imagined horrors of medical research do not exist. The insane lust for blood, the callousness to the infliction of pain, which are attributed to the experimentors, they resent as most absurd and unjust accusations. Only the moral degenerate is capable of inflicting the torment that the anti-vivisectionists imagine. No one who is acquainted with the leaders in medical research, who are responsible for the work done in the laboratories, can believe for a moment that they are moral degenerates. The medical investigators further maintain that judgment should be based on knowledge, not ignorance. They rightly insist that their critics are ignorant—ignorant of the conditions of medical research and ignorant of the complex relations of the medical sciences to medical and surgical practice, and they contend that these critics in their ignorance are endeavoring to stop that experimental study of physiology and pathology.[1]

In reply to the demand that experimental laboratories be opened to investigation, direct refusal was made, the doctors insisting that inspection of laboratories would not satisfy the anti-vivisectionists, who looked upon this as the first step towards complete prohibition of the practice. The representatives of anti-vivisection societies who conducted such inspection would be untrained, and would feel it their

[1] Dr. W. B. Cannon in the *Journal of the American Medical Association*, vol. li, pp. 635-640 (1908).

duty to find "horrors" where such did not exist.[1] As proof of good will, however, and to defend the medical profession against the charges of the anti-vivisectionists, the Committee on Protection of Medical Research of the American Medical Association formulated a code of laboratory procedure which was formally adopted by medical schools, research institutes and health laboratories and posted so as to be visible to all workers in the laboratories.[2]

[1] Dr. W. B. Cannon in *Defense of Medical Research* pamphlet no. xvi (1909).

[2] "I. Vagrant dogs and cats brought to this laboratory and purchased here shall be held at least as long as at the city pound, and shall be returned to their owners if claimed and identified.

II. Animals in the Laboratory shall receive every consideration for their bodily comfort; they shall be kindly treated, properly fed, and their surroundings kept in the best possible sanitary condition.

III. No operations on animals shall be made except with the sanction of the Director of the Laboratory, who holds himself responsible for the importance of the problems studied and for the propriety of the procedures used in the solution of these problems.

IV. In any operation likely to cause greater discomfort than that attending anaesthetization, the animal shall first be rendered incapable of perceiving pain and shall be maintained in that condition until the operation is ended. Exceptions to this rule will be made by the Director alone and then only when anaesthesia would defeat the object of the experiment. In such cases an anaesthetic shall be used so far as possible and may be discontinued only so long as is absolutely essential for the necessary observations.

V. At the conclusion of the experiment the animal shall be killed painlessly. Exceptions to this rule will be made only when continuance of the animal's life is necessary to determine the result of the experiment. In that case, the same aseptic precautions shall be observed during the operation and so far as possible the same care shall be taken to minimize discomforts during the convalescence as in a hospital for human beings."

The deans and directors of the laboratories also consented at the same time to admit at all times officials of humane societies in order that the latter might acquaint themselves with the actual conditions under which animal experimentation is being conducted. (The anti-vivisectionists claim that the spirit of this agreement has not been lived up to.)

Cf. The First Public Declaration of the Open Door in Laboratories for Animal Experimentation (1922) published by the Blue Cross Society of Springfield, Mass. *Cf.* also editorial in *Journal of the American Medical Association*, June 10, 1922.

In some cases active steps were taken to combat the propaganda of the anti-vivisection societies. In New York in February 1914, the anti-vivisection booth was excluded from the Women's Industrial Exhibition in the Grand Central Palace upon the protest of several medical organizations, although it had been permitted in former years.[1] Similar exclusions were made at other exhibits.

This opposition added to the ardor of the anti-vivisectionists. Under the influence of Mr. Stephen Coleridge, an English anti-vivisectionist who visited this country in 1910, American opponents of animal experimentation swung from the advocacy of regulation to abolition. In the winter of 1909 the *New York Herald* published a series of revelations of former employees of the Rockefeller Institute relative to horrors which they asserted were perpetrated there. On the crest of this wave of excitement, the New York Anti-Vivisection Society announced its 1910 bill to be introduced into the New York legislature.

The year before, the Murray-Brough Bill had introduced an innovation by providing for a board of inspection whose members should be chosen by anti-vivisection societies and appointed by the State Board of Regents. This was the bill reintroduced in 1910 by the New York Anti-Vivisection Society. At the same session, the Goodspeed-Bayne bill was introduced, providing also for an inspection commission, whose membership in this case specifically included two scientists, two anti-vivisectionists, two lawyers and one member at large, all to serve without compensation. Both bills were actively opposed by the state medical association and were defeated.

In 1911 both of the 1910 bills were reintroduced. To these a third was added, the Griffin Bill, which provided for an amendment to Section 185 of the Penal Code (pun-

[1] *New York Herald*, February 6, 1914.

ishing cruelty to animals) to read: " In all cases where animals are subjected to operation, mutilation, experimentation, treatment or tests involving pain, which, were the operation, experiment, or test performed on human beings, anaesthetics would be administered, the animal shall first be properly and fully anaesthetized, and if, when the operation is completed, its further existence would entail pain and suffering, it shall forthwith be put to death." All three bills failed to pass.

From 1911 to 1923, one or more of these three bills has been introduced into each session of the New York legislature. Some of these have contained slight variations from the types noted: the McClellan Bill of 1913, similar in other respects to the Goodspeed-Bayne measure, provided for a commission of only five members; the Herrick Bill of 1914 provided that a commission of seven should investigate experimentation upon children as well as upon animals; the Boylan Bill of 1920, modeled upon the already-mentioned Griffen Act, prohibited experiments upon living dogs. During the last three years, the Boylan Bill has been introduced into each session. A bill introduced by Senator Cotillo in 1923 modeled on the Boylan Bill prohibited experiments on children. All of these bills were defeated in committee, except one or two of the earlier ones which were killed by legislative vote.

In 1909 the first anti-vivisection exhibit was held in July at Atlantic City. The exhibit consisted of stuffed animals represented as undergoing various types of torture under the surgeon's knife, and pain-producing apparatus reputed to be used in the course of experiments. The exhibition was repeated in New York in November of the same year under the auspices of the New York Anti-Vivisection Society. In 1910 it was held in Baltimore; in 1911 in Boston, Philadelphia and Los Angeles; and since then it has been repeated in many of the large cities.

In 1910 anti-vivisection became an issue in the American
S. P. C. A.   In that year the board of managers declared it
the duty of the Society to draw public attention to vivisection, to cause state authorities to investigate, " and here-
after, to try to secure the passage of legislation which, while
not prohibiting entirely such animal experimentation, will
penalize all acts which are properly characterized as cruel ",
and to limit the practice and to place it under the supervision
and control of the State.[1]   The Society supported the
Murray-Brough and the Goodspeed-Bayne bills of 1910,
1911 and 1912.   Since then, however, the American S. P.
C. A. has confined itself to enforcing the statute against
unauthorized animal experimentation (not under the supervision of some medical college or foundation), feeling that
any campaign for further restriction can best be left to
anti-vivisection societies specifically incorporated for that
purpose.

In 1911 there occurred an epidemic of charges by the
anti-vivisection societies that colleges were stealing animal
pets or paying for stolen animals to be used in their laboratories.   Accusations were made against Harvard, Welles-
ley, Vassar and Barnard among others.   Several newspapers and magazines now actively championed the cause
of anti-vivisection.   The *New York Herald* stood foremost
among the daily papers which gave wide publicity to these
charges.   The *Boston Post* and the *New York Globe* were
very sympathetic.   *Life* and *Vogue* among the magazines
were favorably inclined.

In 1912 the Vivisection Investigation League made public
a report [2] which accused doctors of the Rockefeller Institute

[1] This announcement, published in all the New York papers, was not included in the *45th Annual Report* (1910) of the Society.

[2] *What Vivisection Inevitably Leads To*, pamphlet published by the
Vivisection Investigation League, New York.

of infecting one hundred and forty-six persons of pure blood, "many of them children between the ages of two and eighteen years", with the virus of syphilis. This charge was too serious to go uninvestigated and President John D. Lindsay of the New York S. P. C. C. called it to the attention of District Attorney Charles Whitman of New York City. After consultation with the doctors of the Institute and an investigation into the nature of the experiment, the District Attorney's office issued a statement that the inoculations for the purpose of testing for the presence of the disease were "rendered absolutely innocuous by treatment", and that it was certain that no person had been harmed by them.[1]

This controversy raised the whole question of "human vivisection", which until then had received little attention from either the public or the anti-vivisectionists. In the term "human vivisection" the anti-vivisectionists included "every experiment upon a living human being for any other purpose than his individual benefit, unless such experiment is positively known to be free from discomfort, distress, pain or danger to health or life; or unless it is made with the full and intelligent consent of the person experimented upon".[2]

Four groups of cases are included in the anti-vivisectionists' charges of human vivisection. The most important are those against the Rockefeller institute mentioned above.[3] Reference is also made to two sets of experiments made in 1908 and 1910 in the use of tuberculin tests for the pre-

[1] *New York Times*, May 21, 1912.

[2] J. S. Codman, *Human Vivisection and the American Medical Association* (Boston, 1923), p. 4.

[3] The report of District Attorney Whitman has never been accepted by the anti-vivisectionists, and the Vivisection Investigation League still publishes the original account of the Rockefeller Institute experiments which it issued in 1912.

sence of tuberculosis.   Lumbar-puncture tests made in 1896 which determine the efficacy of the anti-menigitis serum are also used as illustrations, and finally, the " Rafferty case " —a series of experiments made in 1874 upon the brain of an Irish servant girl—is pointed to.[1]

Discussion of these charges of human vivisection gave impetus to the formation of the Interstate Conference for the Investigation of Vivisection, created in 1912 to give the anti-vivisection movement a national character.   The groups that organized it were the Society for the Humane Regulation of Vivisection (Washington, D. C.), the American Anti-Vivisection Society (Philadelphia), the New England Anti-Vivisection Society (Boston), the Society for the Prevention of Abuse in Animal Experimentation (Brooklyn), the New York Theosophical Anti-Vivisection Society (New York) and the Vivisection Investigation League (New York).   Shortly after, the Convention was joined by the New Jersey Vivisection Investigation Society (Newark) and the Maryland Anti-Vivisection Society (Baltimore). The federation was composed of " societies, either opposed to vivisection or any cruelty in the practice thereof, which shall meet tri-yearly, or at such other intervals as may prove desirable, for the purpose of discussing methods and results, or to take such action as is deemed advisable ". The Interstate Conference has grown in adherents during the past decade and now is supported by thirty-two societies, and also by a limited individual membership of its own. It follows an opportunist program for the amelioration of animal experimental conditions, studies the reports of hospitals and medical examinations, and sends excerpts of these to different anti-vivisection and animal protective societies.

---

[1] Full accounts of these cases appear in the *Human Vivisection* series of pamphlets published by the Vivisection Investigation League (New York).

In 1913 a bill came up in the Pennsylvania legislature providing that any official of a dog pound refusing to sell unclaimed animals to medical schools or institutions, should be guilty of a misdemeanor. The Pennsylvania humane societies opposed the bill, the state federation making a special issue of it. It was killed by amendment. On the strength of this, the American Anti-Vivisection Society the next day introduced a house bill to prohibit animal vivisection and a senate bill to prevent " human vivisection ". Both bills were killed in committee.

Following this failure, the Pennsylvania anti-vivisectionists brought charges of cruelty against members of the medical staff of the University of Pennsylvania, and obtained indictments against five. The trial was concluded in April 1914, the jury disagreeing. Thereupon the anti-vivsection societies of the country made plans to bring cruelty charges against all prominent surgeons who engaged in experimentation. This program was never carried through. Until this period the Pennsylvania anti-cruelty societies and the American Anti-Vivisection Society had worked in cooperation. The trial of the University of Pennsylvania surgeons brought about a split between them which has never been healed.

In 1914 the New Jersey Vivisection Investigation Society succeeded in preventing the establishment of a Rockefeller Foundation research institute in that state. The next year a bill authorizing the establishment of the institution was passed over the protest of the anti-vivisectionists.

In 1915 the California Anti-Vivisection Society obtained the passage of a bill to prohibit experimentation in schools below a certain grade and to provide for the right of search and inspection of experimental laboratories. The attorney-general and a committee of lawyers assured the governor that it would be unconstitutional and he killed it with a pocket veto.

In 1916 a bill was introduced into the national congress directing the Secretary of Agriculture to " examine into the extent and conditions of the practice of experimentation on living animals in laboratories for research and in hospitals and other establishments, and in the commercial production of serums and vaccines for sale, for the purpose of ascertaining whether such experiments and practices are attended with unnecessary and preventable suffering arising from useless repetitions of experiments, want of proper skill in the experimenters, non-use of anaesthetics, and the absence of proper care of the animals upon which such experiments or operations are conducted "; the bill perished in committee.   This was not the first anti-vivisectionist measure to be introduced into the National Congress.   In 1900, hearings were held before the Senate Committee on the District of Columbia on a bill [1] to prohibit animal experimentation in the District; no action was taken.   In 1920 still another such bill [2] was introduced " to prohibit experiments upon living dogs in the District of Columbia or in any of the Territorial or insular possessions of the United States and providing a penalty for the violation thereof "; this bill likewise died in committee.

With the entry of the United States into the World war and the concentration of troops in the training camps, the anti-vivisection societies protested against the compulsory inoculation of the soldiers, alleging that the training-camp mortality was due to this cause.   In February 1918 the New York Anti-Vivisection Society submitted a request to Secretary of War Baker " that the present medical rule of compulsory inoculation be rescinded, and that it be left to the free will of each soldier as to whether his health and life shall be endangered by an operation, which, in actual

[1] 56th Cong., 1st Sess., S. 34; hearings published as *Sen. Doc. 337.*
[2] 66th Cong., 1st Sess., S. 1258.

experience, has resulted in deplorably affecting the strength and availability of our national army, and occasioned unnecessary loss to thousands of American families, who have bravely offered their young manhood to our beloved country." [1]

In the winter of 1917 the National Red Cross announced that it had been requested by the U. S. War Department to make investigations into the nature and prevention of trench fever. For this purpose it proposed to set aside $100,000 of its general fund. As this investigation would avowedly necessitate experiments on animals, the anti-vivisection societies, with the *Christian Science Monitor* as their most active organ, protested. A special fund was contributed by interested persons to make the necessary investigations, and thus the need to draw upon the general funds of the organization was obviated.

Since the War the anti-vivisection movement has gained strength in the West. The Minnesota Anti-Vivisection League was organized in November 1918. The next year the California Federation of Anti-Vivisection Societies was formed, composed of the California Anti-Vivisection Society of Los Angeles, the San Francisco Anti-Vivisection Society and the Alameda County Anti-Vivisection Society. They introduced an anti-vivisection bill as a referendum measure in the elections of 1920. It failed as did a similar measure in 1922.

In 1921 the Washington Humane Education and Anti-Vivisection Society was organized; in its by-laws it stated that a part of its purpose was " to study the practice of vivisection, its relation to science, and its effect upon those who practice it and upon society; to expose and oppose secret or painful experiments upon living animals, inmates of charity hospitals, foundling institutions, asylums." [2]

[1] *Christian Science Monitor*, Feb. 17, 1918.

[2] *Washington Humane Education and Anti-Vivisection Society, 1st Ann. Rpt.* (1922).

Referendum measures similar to those of California failed in Colorado and Louisiana in 1921.

Recently there has been strong opposition in some quarters to the activities of the anti-vivisection organizations. The Blue Cross Society of Springfield, Mass., while campaigning for the "Open Door" in laboratories, has been far more severe in its criticism of anti-vivisectionist tactics than of the practices of animal experimentors. Its publication, *The First Public Declaration of the Open Door in Laboratories for Animal Experimentation (1922)*, containing letters from directors of the medical schools and experimental foundations assuring their adherence to the policy of the Open Door, amounts to a refutation of many of the accusations of more radical anti-vivisection organizations.

In the July 1921 number of the *Woman's Home Companion*, there appeared an article entitled "The Truth About Vivisection" by Ernest Harold Baynes criticising the anti-vivisection literature and defending the work of animal experimentors. Later in the year, after an address by Mr. Baynes in Boston which was highly critical of anti-vivisectionist activities, an organization for the defence of animal experimentation was formed. This remained in a rudimentary form until 1923 when it incorporated in Massachusetts as "The Society of Friends of Medical Progress". It gave as its purposes:

(1) To encourage and aid all research and humane experimentation for the advancement of medical science; (2) To inform the public of the truth concerning the value of scientific medicine to humanity and to animals; (3) To resist the efforts of the ignorant or fanatical persons or societies constantly urging legislation dangerous to the health and well-being of the American people.[1]

[1] *The Society of Friends of Medical Progress, Why It Was Founded* (1923).

The organization proposes to issue pamphlets and literature to confute anti-vivisectionist claims, and to oppose the
efforts of anti-vivisection societies to obtain legislation re-
stricting animal experimentation.

The vehemence with which the anti-vivisection organizations have directed their charges against animal experimentors, and the bitterness of the retorts of the latter, have given
the controversy the appearance of greater importance than
it deserves; there can be no question of the sincerity of the
anti-vivisectionists, though intemperance of language and
acts must often be deplored. Nevertheless they have not
accomplished the objects they originally aimed at—not
even during the past decade when their activity has been at
its highest—although they must be credited with having
aroused great interest in a subject previously ignored by lay-
men.

The anti-vivisection controversy, by bringing forward the
ethical issue in animal experimentation, has aroused a not inconsiderable minority against the practice. But this anti-
vivisectionist support has not proved sufficient to cause the
passage of legislation specifically to limit the practice.
State legislatures have consistently refused to take any steps
to this end, and in the few cases where the issue has come up
for popular decision, the verdict has each time been against
the anti-vivisectionists.

Against these negative accomplishments of the anti-vivisectionist campaign must be set the fact that not only have
medical organizations been goaded to retaliatory efforts, but
non-professional organizations have joined with them in
combating the propaganda of anti-vivisection. Some of
the larger life-insurance companies have contributed both
money and efforts to defeat anti-vivisection measures before
various legislatures and in the national Congress. Finally,
the new organization, the " Society of the Friends of Medical Progress ", represents a growing disapproval, if not of
the aims, then of the methods of anti-vivisectionism.

CHAPTER X

ORGANIZATIONS FOR CHILD PROTECTION

IN 1922 there were fifty-seven societies for the prevention of cruelty to children, and of the three hundred and seven humane societies combining child and animal work, a few, like the Ohio Humane Society, devoted themselves almost exclusively to child protection. In general, the distribution of child protective societies is the same as that of the animal protective organizations. Perhaps they are slightly more concentrated in proportion to their number in the Atlantic States where the greater density of population makes child problems more acute.

In New York State there has been a regional organization of child protective activities similar to that for animal protection. New York City is served by the New York S. P. **C. C. together with the Brooklyn, Bronx County, Queens and Richmond S.P.C.C.s in their respective boroughs. The central part of New York State is covered in its child work by the Mohawk and Hudson River Humane Society with its branch organizations. A number of small independent S.P.C.C.s and humane societies fill in the interstices.**

The New York S. P. C. C. was organized in December 1874, upon the initiative of Mr. Henry Bergh and his counsel Mr. Elbridge T. Gerry, after the "Mary Ellen case" had drawn their attention to the cruelties being practiced on children.[1] At the organization meeting, the purposes of the Society were stated " to seek out and to rescue from the dens and slums of the city those little unfortunates whose childish lives are rendered miserable by the constant abuse and cruelties practised on them by the human brutes who

[1] McCrea, *op. cit.*, p. 135.

happen to possess the custody or control of them " and " to
enforce by lawful means and with energy the laws referred
to (for the protection of children), and secure in like manner the prompt conviction and punishment of every violator
of any of these laws." [1]

In April 1875 the Society was incorporated by a special
act.[2]   It was empowered to " prefer a complaint before any
court or magistrate . . . . for the violation of any law
relating to or affecting children " and " to aid in bringing
the facts before such court or magistrate."   It was assured
the assistance of all municipal and state police officers in
enforcing the law.

In May 1875 the Society prosecuted its first case.   By
the end of the year sixty-eight prosecutions had resulted
from over three hundred complaints, and seventy-two children had been rescued and provided for at the Society's in-
terposition.[3]   Thus was marked out the New York S.P.C.C.'s
primary field of activity.

In the following year the Society introduced into the
New York Legislature an act " to Prevent and Punish
Wrongs to Children " which was passed on April 14.[4]   This
was only the first of such measures introduced by the
Society.   In 1883 was submitted an act " to Prevent Baby-
Farming ".[5]   In the following year, President Gerry
brought about the codification of existing child-protective

[1] *New York S. P. C. C., First Annual Report* (1875).

[2] *N. Y. Sess. Laws*, 1875, ch. 130.

[3] Unless otherwise indicated, the details of this account of the New
York S. P. C. C. have been drawn from its annual reports, from a printed
Memorandum submitted by the Society in November 1923 to the New
York State Commission to Examine Laws Relating to Child Welfare,
and from the historical account of the Society which was placed in the
cornerstone of its new building and of which a copy was furnished through
the courtesy of the Society's officers.

[4] *New York Sess. Laws*, 1876, ch. 122.

[5] *N. Y. Sess. Laws*, 1883, ch. 40.

laws in New York State.[1]   Numerous child-protective acts
have since then been sponsored by the Society.

From the very beginning of its prosecuting activities,
the Society had felt the need of a shelter to house the children who came under its supervision.   During its early years
it made arrangements with the matron at Police Headquarters to care for children temporarily in the Society's custody.
In 1880, after it had secured permanent quarters for itself,
it was able to maintain a children's shelter in the floor-space
of its own building.   In this year, also, a method was established by the city magistrates to make all orders requiring
the payment by parents of moneys toward the support of
committed children payable at the office of the Society.   The
Society gladly undertook the labor of collecting these funds,
performing this function without charge to the city or to
the individuals concerned.

The great value of the Society's services and the unquestioned need for them—the greater in New York City
because of the large foreign population with its Old World
conceptions of the rights of children—resulted in a rapid
and sound growth of the organization.   In 1876 there were
348 members; by 1910 the number had risen to 503 annual
members and 484 life members.   By this year the Society
enjoyed a total income of $116,994.92; from members it
received donations and subscription dues amounting to
$39,176.33, it received an annual appropriation of $60,000
from New York City, and from invested legacies it received
$3,000.00.   During the year, it received an additional
$8,617.42 in legacies which it added to its investment fund.[2]

During 1910 it investigated 18,541 complaints involving
the welfare of 51,000 child victims of neglect or abuse which
were brought to its attention.   It prosecuted 541 adult of-

[1] *N. Y. Sess. Laws*, 1884, ch. ii, secs. 278-293; now comprised in *N. Y. Code of 1909*, art. 44, secs. 480-494.
[2] *New York S. P. C. C., 36th Ann. Rpt.* (1910), p. 12.

fenders against children, and appeared in 7947 cases involving children in the Children's Court.[1]

At this time the Children's Court of New York City had no parole officers attached to it. This labor was shared by a group of child-aid organizations of which the New York S. P. C. C. was one of the most important. However, in 1912 this not entirely satisfactory situation was remedied, appropriations for probation officers were voted by the City, and the Society relinquished its share in this work. It now confined itself to the maintenance of records for all children passing through the Court, and to receiving the custody of the children for shelter during case procedure.

Of the three types of child cases involving Children's Court action—juvenile delinquency, ungovernable and disorderly children and improper guardianship and neglect— only the third to any great extent concerns the New York S. P. C. C. On occasion, S. P. C. C. agents are involved as witnesses in juvenile delinquency cases or are instrumental in bringing them to court, but this is usually accomplished through other channels. Of course, it often happens that such children are remanded to the Society for temporary shelter. The ungovernable, disorderly child is likewise outside the Society's sphere. On the other hand, the Society is the usual agent for handling cases of improper guardianship and neglect, and almost the sole agency for prosecuting outright offenders against childhood whose cases are dwelt with in Magistrates' Court, the Court of Special Sessions and the Court of General Sessions.

Feeling that a great moral danger existed in the illegal admission of children into moving-picture houses, the Society devoted special attention to this matter during 1910, and brought 87 such cases to court during the year. Its list of cases prosecuted covered misdemeanors such as buying junk from minors and general neglect, and felonies including

[1] *Ibid.*, p. 57.

abduction and criminal assault. It investigated 5,308 charges of improper guardianship and dealt with 95 theatrical investigations.

One significant feature of its work during the year was the investigation of 1,930 applications for baby-farm permits. In 1880 the Society had prosecuted one Edward Crowley who had conducted a baby-farm and maltreated his charges. Three years later it induced the New York legislature to pass an act to control baby-farming [1] Thereafter it made it a part of its duty to investigate all applications from such institutions.

During 1910 it collected $26,424.55 from parents under order of court to pay the board of their children maintained in institutions. This feature of its work was also begun in 1880 by arrangement between the Society and the city magistrates.

The importance of the Society's shelter work had increased year by year. It was enabled to meet the demands made upon it in this respect through the facilities of its building which it had erected in 1893. During 1910 it accomodated 7,899 children in its rooms. These children had either been rescued by the Society from cruel surroundings and were retained in its custody until the date of their trial, or else were juvenile delinquents who had temporarily been placed under the supervision of the Society while under the control of the Children's Court. The expenses of the shelter during 1910 occupied, as in every year, an important position in the Society's schedule of disbursements. Apart from the overhead expenses, the cost of the children in the Society's custody during the year was $7,771.21 and $1,498.75 was expended for their medical attendance.

In 1915 the New York S. P. C. C. helped to establish a sister society in Bronx County. This was the third such society founded by it in the metropolitan district. The two

[1] *N. Y. Sess. Laws*, 1883, ch. 40.

earlier organizations were the Brooklyn and Richmond County societies. The New York S. P. C. C. did not establish these new societies as branch organizations dependent upon the parent body; but from the very beginning they developed as full-fledged, independent child-protective societies. It was felt that in this way the local community pride of the counties concerned would be awakened and would come to the support of the organizations. The existence of these younger organizations has enabled the New York society to concentrate its efforts entirely in the county of New York. Thus the superintendent's report for 1916 showed that in that year, after the Bronx County Society had taken over the jurisdiction of its district, there was an increase of 1,185 cases over the number handled by the New York Society in the previous year.

1920 was a significant year for the Society. An appeal made by the Society to Mr. August Heckscher for a motorbus brought the response from him of an offer of a $1,500,-000 building for the Society with a large endowment to enable the Society to fulfill its functions better. The directors of the Society felt that the acceptance of this offer would involve it in *child welfare* work of a nature foreign to its purpose. As a result, Mr. Heckscher altered his gift, and established the Heckscher Foundation for Children. A $1,650,000 building was constructed in which both the Foundation and the New York S. P. C. C. would be housed. The Society agreed in 1921 and contributed $350,000 towards the construction of its wing of the edifice (this fund was derived from the sale of its former home). It entered upon its new home in 1922.

The accompanying figures indicate the development of the Society's finances and the extent of its major activities during the period from 1910 to 1922. (The form in which the Society presented some of its statistics prior to 1914 makes their inclusion in this tabulation impossible).

	Members' dues, donations and special contributions	Income from investments and rents	Fines and grants from New York City	Total net income exclusive of bequests	Bequests	Salaries, executive and service departments
1910..	$39,189.55	$13,145.37	$64,660.00	$116,994.92	$23,857.08	$64,306.08
1911..	35,294.24	14,093.75	62,675.00	112,062.99	41,281.72	66,889.66
1912..	30,889.00	15,536.26	88,595.00	135,022.26	29,089.59	76,332.33
1913..	31,730.35	16,199.25	81,085.00	129,151.29	20,172.70	82,551.84
1914..	32,006.87	16,598.71	87,670.00	136,429.54	9,025.00	79,972.39
1915..	37,159.00	18,786.45	90,050.00	154,795.45	15,904.55	85,870.89
1916[1].	31,711.81	19,724.57	78,690.00	130,126.38	12,241.99	81,179.33
1917..	30,817.85	22,195.76	89,720.00	142,733.61	7,059.31	85,106.79
1918..	41,830.05	23,322.17	104,385.00	169,637.22	11,681.46	86,767.13
1919..	46,607.76	24,640.83	103,435.00	174,683.59	18,104.37	95,740.75
1920..	29,705.25	49,594.38	128,700.00	206,899.63	179,804.50	125,756.37
1921..	25,918.33	35,508.11	140,100.00	201,526.44	7,090.34	132,530.40
1922..	36,806.62	34,553.92	153,010.00	234,570.34[2]	42,128.17	127,925.58

Throughout this period, the figures for the total income
of the Society show an increase from $116,994.92 in 1910
to $234,570.34 in 1922. Examination shows, however, that
none of this increase may be attributed to growth of membership or increased contributions from members. While
the figures for the membership of the Society during this
period are not available, it is possible to weigh the importance of this factor by the figures for the combined income
from membership dues and donations. In 1910 the income
from these sources was $39,189.55; by 1913 it had fallen to
$31,730.35. By 1915 it had increased to $37,159.00. The
establishment of the Bronx County S. P. C. C. drew some
support from the New York organization during the following year. By 1919, however, the income from this

[1] Bronx Co. S. P. C. C. established.

[2] Including $10,000 allowance by Heckscher Foundation from Endow-
ment Fund.

S. P. C. C., 1910-1922

Shelter expenses	New and old complaints affecting children investigated	Adults arrested for offenses against children	Children's cases necessitating court action by the Society	Children passing through the shelter during the year	Number of meals served during year	Money collected from parents to pay board of children in institutions
$11,112.81	....	.. .	....	7,817	......	$26,424.55
12,400.87	....	....	....	9,812	......	23,919.38
21,493.96	....	....	....	10,775	......	25,116.09
24,537.36	....	....	....	10,550	......	14,614.74
24,674.54	5,001	785	2,283	10,783	133,625	22,624.25
27,648.29	5,350	1,003	2,489	7,997	148,742	19,902.12
26,638.57[1]	7,848	830	2,013	5,888	117,168	22,275.00
31,167.32	9,204	927	2,718	8,409	153,999	34,747.70
21,421.54	8,410	827	2,477	9,087	147,793	54,643.63
22,068.81	7,810	781	2,071	8,862	156,124	70,576.62
25,654.90	9,083	748	1,643	8,225	156,212	76,971.30
20,386.32	8,428	789	1,375	6,335	154,177	68,447.92
55,466.71[2]	9,255	701	1,140	6,364	168,630	67,016.39

source had increased to $46,607.76. The next two years
of industrial depression saw a decrease to $25,918.33. Re-
covery began again in 1922.

Since 1907 the New York S. P. C. C. has maintained the
general principle of investing all unrestricted cash bequests.
The only exceptions to this rule have been for the purpose
of canceling floating indebtedness. Hence there has been
a steady increase in the income from invested funds. In
1910, $13,145.37 was received from rents and investments;
by 1923 this had increased to $34,553.92.

The most important source of the New York S. P. C. C.'s
income is the City of New York. Of the total income
from this source, fines paid to the Society represent an
inconsiderable fraction, usually averaging two or three

[1] Including extra expense of maintaining a separate shelter during the
epidemic of infantile paralysis.

[2] Including $24,985.93 for care of the Society's children by Heckscher
Foundation, Aug. 28 to Dec. 31, 1922.

thousand dollars annually. On the other hand, the annual appropriation by the City of New York to the Society has increased from $60,000 in 1910 to $150,000 in 1922, and during the past ten years has represented the major portion of the Society's total net income.[1]

Although the expenditures of the Society for items such as printing and stationary, legal expenses, telephone calls, gas and fuel, etc., are always of considerable amount, the main items of expense are salaries and shelter upkeep. Moreover, these two have expanded more rapidly than the others during the period studied. This is accounted for by two factors. There has been a slight increase in the number of the salaried staff — the force of agents has grown— and there has likewise been an increase in the shelter work undertaken. In addition, during the period from 1914 to 1920, the rapid rise of prices necessitated corresponding wage increases on the part of the Society; otherwise it faced the risk of having its employees attracted to other occupations. The rise in prices also added to the costs of the shelter work.

The figures for the Society's accomplishments indicate a perceptible though irregular increase. The Society investigates applications for infant boarding-house permits and supervises the appearance of children on the stage or in moving pictures. These and applications for aid and advice are largely routine matters and make little demand upon the Society's initiative. A truer indication of this is to be found in the investigations it makes of complaints— complaints of the neglect, abuse or exposure of children; complaints against individuals, against candy-stores, moving-picture houses and junk shops. Every year there are new investigations made or old cases reinvestigated. In addition, there are special investigations undertaken every

---

[1] *Cf. Memorandum, cit. supra,* exhibit A, p. 34.

year upon request of the District Attorney or of other child protective societies. In 1914 these investigations totaled 5,001. By 1917 they had increased (excluding Bronx County in this year) to 9,204. Thereafter, there is a sharp decrease and not until 1922 is this previous total bettered.

One of the most significant indexes of the Society's accomplishments, the annual total of adults arrested for offenses against children, shows a marked decrease, from 1,003 in 1915 to 701 in 1922. In part, this may be accounted for by the giving of jurisdiction in Bronx County to the new society there in 1916. But since 1917 there has been a decrease in the figures for New York County alone. Officials of the New York S. P. C. C. do not interpret this as a weakening in the Society's efforts, but rather as an indication of the success of its work, in that cruelists are more and more deterred from the commission of offenses by fear of immediate retribution; they point out also that prosperous times during the war years and after, better living conditions and prohibition made their influence towards the reduction of crime felt. There has been a similar falling-off of child cases, including improper guardianship and neglect, offenses against childhood, cases of juvenile delinquency and ungovernable children that come to the Society's attention, necessitating court action.

On the other hand, the shelter work of the Society has expanded. This is not at first evident if we consider only the figures for the number of children who annually pass through the shelter. There were 7,818 in 1910, 10,775 in 1912, 9,087 in 1918, and only 6,364 in 1922. But in 1910 the average time spent by a child in the shelter was less than three days; at present it is more than nine. Consequently there has been a real growth in the shelter work. This is indicated by the figures for the number of meals served per year—133,625 in 1914 and 168,630 in 1922.

The state of Massachusetts presents an organization of child protective work radically different from that of New York. Instead of a scattered number of societies, each serving its limited locality and united in cooperation only by a state humane association, Massachusetts is served by a single state-wide Society for the Prevention of Cruelty to Children, which, with its headquarters at Boston, covers the state through its branch organizations.[1]

The Massachusetts S. P. C. C. was organized in 1878, and from that time until 1907 devoted itself almost exclusively to the city of Boston. Its policy, like that of the New York society, was conservative. It confined itself more or less to being " the arm of the law ", protecting children from active forms of cruelty and prosecuting the offenders; and by keeping its expenses always within its income by investing all bequests, it built up a very strong endowment. In 1907 under the influence of its secretary, Mr. C. C. Carstens, it entered upon a new policy. It interested itself in many forms of child welfare which it had previously considered outside of its sphere and it decided to become, as its charter provided, a state organization.

It was realized that such an expansion would prove a heavy drain upon the Society's resources. Almost certainly the mounting expenses would very soon pass the figure of the annual income. The directors of the Society decided to shoulder the responsibility for this radical step, and later explained the problem they faced and its solution:

whether unrestricted bequests should be used to build up a fund, the income of which only could be used, or whether these bequests should be applied to our current needs. We have

[1] Exception must be made of the city of Lowell whose humane society had taken upon itself, as a share of its duty, the protection of children at an early period and which at present cooperates to a limited extent with the Massachusetts S. P. C. C.

decided that the yearly deficiency should be made up from these unrestricted bequests on the theory that we cannot allow the present work of the Society to be hampered for the sake of accumulating a large reserve fund.[1]

As resources permitted, branch societies were now established in the surrounding cities and towns. By 1910 four of these had been formed—in Beverly, Brockton, New Bedford and Northampton. These branches were nominally an added expense. Nevertheless, it was expected that they would to a greater or lesser degree pay their own way. The annual report of this year said: "Wherever the Society has begun systematic local work, it has asked for local financial support as soon as it was able to show what it had accomplished during a probationary period and what its plans for the future were. Some financial support has come from all the new fields after a reasonable time. We believe that local self-support will gradually come about." [2]

One of the most important elements in attaining the desired financial independence of each branch would be the appeal to the local community pride of the district where it was established. For this reason, the mother society considered it desirable to make no attempt to assert absolute authority over the branch organizations, but rather to develop independent action upon their part insofar as could wisely be done. A few years later the president of the Society made the suggestion that at least one representative from each branch organization be elected to the board of directors, instead of composing it entirely of residents of the city of Boston as had been the case in the past. This suggestion was carried out.[3] The Society has found it advisable to assert its authority over the branches only in

---

[1] *Mass. S. P. C. C., 35th Ann. Rpt.* (1915), p. 10.
[2] *Mass. S. P. C. C., 30th Ann. Rpt.* (1910), p. 20.
[3] *Mass. S. P. C. C., 35th Ann. Rpt.*, p. 20.

the matter of the appointment of agents and in a few cases, of expenditures of money for special purposes.

Each branch organization has been encouraged to meet its local problems in the way it considers best, and each branch organization has, since its founding, issued an annual report either as a part of the report of the mother organization or as a separate pamphlet. In 1910 the New Bedford branch, the oldest, announced a program of " emphasis upon the supervision of children in their own homes and the discipline of negligent parents whenever the welfare of the children permitted that they be left at home ".[1] It submitted a report in cooperation with the Charity Organization Society of the town to the superintendent of schools on the extent of defective eye-sight, adenoids, tonsils and bad teeth among the school children and advocated a school nurse. It prosecuted cases of illegal employment of minors under fourteen on milk-wagons in the early morning. As preparation for more extended work in the future, it made an investigation of birth registration and infant mortality in the New Bedford district, and made maps of the distribution of neglected children, delinquent children, infant mortality and tuberculosis cases.

The Brockton branch during the same year stated its intention " to attack as many as possible of the problems of neglect before the children become delinquent, and to make all possible effort to bring neglecting parents to realize and assume their true responsibilities. We are also trying to establish in our office a bureau of cooperative registration and confidential exchange of information." [2]

The Hampshire branch founded in March 1910, also announced a plan for a " confidential exchange " for all charitable societies in the district; this would be accomplished

[1] *Mass. S. P. C. C., 30th Ann. Rpt.*, p. 29.
[2] *Ibid.*, p. 30.

by a committee of three and an auxiliary committee made up by different organizations using the exchange. Later in the year, a temporary home being desired, the Children's Home Association was formed as a separate organization closely affiliated with the Hampshire branch, and a home was bought.[1]

In the city of Boston during 1910 the mother society carried on a vigorous prosecution of causes of carnal abuse of young girls, a matter to which it had devoted attention during the past two years. Eighty-five cases came to the notice of the Society. Of other types of cruelty, 3,522 cases involving 7,213 different children were attended to.

No new lines of work were begun in 1911, but in the following year, the mother society organized the Children's Welfare League of Roxbury. This was to be, according to the Society's plans, the first of a series of such Leagues in the city of Boston. Preparatory to its foundation, a survey of the disposition of cases of juvenile delinquency was made, which showed that Roxbury was the worst district of Boston in this respect. In January 1912 the Welfare League was organized to draw together the thirty-five children's agencies serving the district of Roxbury and to develop a common program to which schools, settlements, relief societies, children's agencies and all welfare institutions, public and private, might contribute. One committee of the League that the Massachusetts S. P. C. C. considered highly important because it dealt not solely with socially defective children but helped all boys and girls who might choose to benefit by its services, was the Placement Bureau. Through it the pupil leaving school was carefully placed in a suitable position and his business career followed until there was reasonable assurance of his having found a place of employment fitted to his capabilities. This bureau became

[1] *Ibid.*, p. 38.

city-wide by 1915 and cooperated with the Boston School Committee.

The original intention of the Massachusetts S. P. C. C. was that the Welfare League should be as largely as possible a local movement, having the moral and financial backing of the district, and independent of supervision or direction from any outside source. Consequently, in November 1912, when it was apparent that the League was firmly established, the Society withdrew its financial support, though continuing in the closest of friendly relations.[1]

In 1913, pursuing this policy of encouraging cooperation among the many child-welfare organizations in the city of Boston, the Society formed a confidential exchange, enlarging upon the model created by its Hampshire branch in 1910.[2]

As the resources of the Society permitted, new branches were being established during this period. In 1915 a branch was formed at Hyannis on Cape Cod, and by means of rural agents work was extended to Newburyport, Framingham, Gloucester and Salem. The following year a new district office was opened at Lynn and new branch offices in Waltham, Athol, Orange, North Adams, Taunton and Attleboro. By this time twelve district offices and fourteen branches had been established.[3]

In 1917 the mother society began a campaign for state action on illegitimacy. Legislation in this field in Ohio and Minnesota was held up as a model. This year also witnessed a most encouraging development for the Society. The New Bedford district branch announced that it felt ready to enter upon a more independent existence. The Society willingly granted the request for autonomy. Re-

---

[1] *Mass. S. P. C. C., 35th Ann. Rpt.*, p. 21.

[2] *Mass. S. P. C. C., 33rd Ann. Rpt.* (1913).

[3] *Mass. S. P. C. C., 35th Ann. Rpt.* (1915), p. 23.

sponsibility for the conduct of the branch was now placed entirely upon its own board of directors. The only limitations were that the agents should be appointed by the central office and that the schedule of the branch society's salaries should conform to that of the mother society. In return the central office agreed during the first year to meet any deficit of the New Bedford branch up to a certain amount.[1]

In 1918, in addition to its usual routine, the Society took upon itself to patrol the neighborhoods of the military and naval cantonments near Boston for the double purpose of protecting the soldiers and sailors from intercourse with vicious girls and to protect young girls from the advances of the service men. In performing this office, the agent of the Society, then as now without police power, often usurped such power in making arrests. Under the stress of war-time needs, this was condoned by the Massachusetts courts.

In this year a district office was established in Springfield and a branch in Holyoke. This completed the Society's program of expansion, for, except in Lowell, where the Lowell Humane Society was active in child protective work, the entire state was now served by the district and branch organizations. The president of the Society announced: "We have accomplished what we set out to do a number of years ago, and the state is now virtually covered by our agencies."[2]

The financing of this expansion makes an interesting history. The income of the Society may be divided into three classes—that from subscriptions and donations, the income from investments, and the accidental income arising from bequests restricted or unrestricted in character. In addi-

[1] *Mass. S. P. C. C., 37th Ann. Rpt.* (1917), p. 26.
   Mass. S. P. C. C., 38th Ann. Rpt. (1918), p. 17.

tion, the incomes of all the non-independent branches of the Society have been entered upon its books as an independent source of income. On the other hand, the Society has followed the policy of not including the unrestricted bequests received during the year as a part of its income, balancing off against them any annual deficits that arise and adding or subtracting the remainder from the total invested wealth of the Society. Keeping this in mind, let us examine the financial statements for the period from 1910 to the completion of growth in 1918.

In 1910 the income from subscriptions and donations was $23,309.86, from investments $8,462.25, and from the seven branch organizations which existed by the end of the year $1,850. The addition of income from other minor sources brought the total net income to $41,414.69. In this year the expenses of the branch offices were $4,179.25 out of a total of $38,527.23. Thus, although the expenses of the branch organizations exceeded the income from them by nearly $2500, the Society had no deficit to meet, but instead a surplus income of $2,887.46 to be added to the $12,274.11 of unrestricted bequests, both of which sums went into the reserve the Society was building up against probable excesses of expenditure in future years.

In 1913 the income from the branch organizations had risen to $9,031.43, while the income from subscriptions, drawn, it must be remembered, almost exclusively from residents of the city of Boston, had fallen to $17,200.27. An increase in the income from investments compensated somewhat and the total was $43,720.43. By now, however, the expenses of the branch organizations had risen to $24,103.47, and the total expenditure for the year was $81,886.86, leaving an excess of expenditure amounting to $38,166.39. As the total of unrestricted bequests in the course of the year was only $18,326.16, it was necessary to draw upon the reserve built up in the previous years to the extent of $19,840.23.

Within two years of this time, it became evident that financially, the program of expansion was gaining rather than losing ground. For various reasons, the expenses of the branch organizations had decreased to $22,039.34, while the income from them increased to $14,353.88. In 1916 the expenses of the branches leaped to $30,944.05, an increase of $8,804.71. The income from this source had increased from $7,376.90 to $21,730.78. Nevertheless, if the figures for branch expenses and income in 1916 be compared with those for 1913, it will be seen that the income had made the greater growth, despite the fact that new branches, a heavy drain, were being formed.

It should be remembered, however, that along with its program of state-wide expansion, the Massachusetts S. P. C. C. was developing new and wider fields of child help, so that there was during this period a very rapid increase in the expenditure of the mother society, from $27,230.77 in 1910 to $46,738.61 in 1913, and to $54,824.35 in 1916, so that in this latter year the total for expenditures was $97,-300.48. The deficit was $30,222.20. Before entering upon this program of expansion, both in territory covered and work accomplished, the directors of the Society had counted on assistance from two sources. They believed that were the activities of the Society well advertised, and were the proper appeals made to the pride and altruism of residents of Massachusetts, there would be a steady growth in membership with a corresponding increase in contributions and donations. Even more important would be the assistance which the Society hoped for in the form of bequests. In neither respect were the directors disappointed. The figures so far quoted show a growth in the total of contributions and donations. More significant were the percentages of

annual increase.   The income figures for 1914 represented
a 13.7 per cent increase over those of the preceding year.
Similarly, the increase in 1915 was 20.3 per cent; in 1916,
22.3 per cent.   Despite the demands of war charities during
1917-18, the income of the Society managed to register an
increase in each of those years, 3.7 per cent in 1917, and
5.4 per cent in the following year.   The income from contributions has increased steadily through 1922.

As was to be expected, the income from unrestricted bequests has shown no such regularity as the income from subscriptions and donations.   The annual figures since 1910
have varied widely, from $12,274.11 in that year to $71,-
368.50 in 1920.   In 1922 the total was over $50,000.   As
has been stated, the directors looked forward to balancing
these bequests against the foreseen annual excesses of expenditure.   In some years the excess has proved greater
than the total of bequests.   In other years the reverse has
occurred.   However, for the period from 1907 to 1922,
the two have balanced each other to within a few thousand
dollars.   In 1912 the income from investments was $18,-
882.99; in 1922 it was $18,039.92.   Evidently the Society
has not found it necessary to cut very deeply into its reserve funds.[1]

Although the limits of territorial expansion were now
reached, it was not yet possible for the Society to make any
radical cut in its expenditures or even to prevent them from
mounting.   By 1919 the total had risen to $139,431.93,
and the annual deficit was $54,098.30.   By the next year
the total was $144,178.56 with a deficit of $43,911.27.
The attention of the directors was now turned to consolida-
ting the gains made by the Society, a labor which proved

[1] These figures are quoted from the annual reports of the Mass. S. P.
C. C. and from memoranda recently furnished by Mr. Lathrop, the secretary of the Society.

quite as expensive as the earlier growth. The president of the Society in his 1920 address said: " We now enter upon a new period which will not be exactly like the last period, but which we hope will be equally one of improvement. The past fourteen years have been a period of development, and development for us on entirely new lines. The next period ought probably to be one of consolidation of the position we have won. Without slacking our vigilance and effectiveness in protecting any child that needs protection of this Society, the future of children's protective work must be even more preventive in its nature." He pointed to the mounting figures for expenditure and insisted that the dependence of the Society on the greatly varying stream of bequests to pay large deficits was disquieting. " We ought to build up our invested funds until they contribute enough to pay the expenses of our general office, and the work of all our branches ought to be paid for where the work is done." [1]

The first step in carrying out this policy was to make as many as possible of the branch societies independent and self-supporting. Heretofore, only the New Bedford branch had enjoyed this distinction. By the end of 1921 there were three others. By January 1923 ten district and branch organizations were self-supporting. In each of these cases the mother society followed the same policy it had with the New Bedford branch, guaranteeing to cover a limited deficit. The directors felt that in the carrying out of this program they would have as an ally the community pride of each municipality where a branch was established. Their judgment has been proven correct. Where the choice was of making the branch self-supporting or else giving up the work, in that neighborhood the community has come to the

[1] *Mass. S. P. C. C., 40th Ann. Rpt.* (1920), p. 8.

support of its organization. It is the hope and expectation of the Society that in the very near future, all twenty-seven of hte district and branch S.P.C.C.s will be maintaining themselves.

During the War an exceedingly large number of the Massachusetts municipalities developed community chests or financial federations for the successful flotation of their war charities. As in other states, some proved successful, others were disastrous failures. The Massachusetts S. P. C. C. dictated to its branches no policy concerning the joining of such federations. Each society was allowed to determine its own course. In most cases they joined a federation where such had been formed in their community. With few exceptions they reported satisfaction with the arrangement. On the other hand, the Worcester branch refused to join the community chest in that city, being the only charitable organization to remain outside of it, and did not find itself discomfited by its position. During 1919 and 1920 some of the federations hitherto successful became too ambitious and collapsed. Several branches of the Massachusetts S. P. C. C. suffered. During the last couple of years saner principles of guidance have been followed by the Massachusetts financial federations, and the S.P.C.C.s have not been unfriendly to them.

Though the Society considers its function preventive, it finds itself called upon to do no small share of protective work. During 1922 it investigated the cases of 5,040 families, 1,090 of which warranted court action. Of the 13,008 children involved, only 2,094 were protected by court action. The following figures indicate the activities of the mother society and the district and branch S. P. C. C.s during 1922:

GENERAL STATISTICS OF THE MASSACHUSETTS S. P. C. C. AND
BRANCHES FOR THE YEAR ENDED OCTOBER 31, 1922 [1]

Districts and Branches	Total families dealt with	Total children involved	Families requiring court action	Children protected by court action	Families not requiring court action	Children protected without court action
Athol......................	36	79	6	13	27	62
Berkshire	95	323	23	37	63	266
Boston.....................	1,917	5,055	569	1,151	1,054	3,342
Brockton...................	226	652	33	75	159	486
Cape Cod...................	130	367	14	22	110	334
East Hampshire.............	50	96	9	5	35	81
Fall River	214	467	36	36	148	372
Fitchburg..................	83	179	4	13	66	154
Franklin	119	273	11	11	79	207
Gloucester	36	89	10	28	21	45
Hampshire	282	695	91	172	185	499
Haverhill..................	123	308	31	43	92	265
Holyoke	100	289	15	26	71	235
Ipswich	21	41	..	..	19	37
Lawrence	113	330	25	53	79	260
Leominster	36	92	5	12	22	64
Lynn	162	387	56	77	94	260
New Bedford	303	709	20	41	194	464
Newburyport	35	77	3	6	26	67
North Attleboro	33	77	4	6	25	58
North Berkshire	23	53	..	..	22	53
North Shore	77	186	19	30	52	137
Peabody	38	81	5	14	30	62
Plymouth...................	15	57	..	..	15	57
Salem	71	162	9	8	59	129
South Middlesex............	61	200	19	36	36	150
Springfield	303	795	31	78	241	653
Taunton	98	288	16	21	73	248
Waltham	55	148	10	32	35	96
Worcester.	185	453	16	48	145	317
	5,040	13,008	1,090	2,094	3,277	9,460

NOTE.—In the above totals, 1,454 children, in 673 families, were not protected. In 355 cases the complaint was unwarranted; in 154 cases the families could not be located; while in 184 cases there was failure to accomplish purpose, because the evidence was insufficient or because the law did not reach the conditions disclosed.

[1] *Mass. S. P. C. C., 42nd Ann. Rpt.* (1922), p. 25.

An important example of a humane society organized for both animal and child protective work and devoting itself almost exclusively to the latter is offered by the Ohio Humane Society, located at Cincinnati. It states its purposes:

I. To compel deserting fathers of families or their responsible relatives to contribute to the support of dependent children, and to cooperate with the officials of the Courts in the prosecution of neglectful, abusive or immoral parents.

II. To protect children—regardless of race, color or creed—from all conditions of neglect, abuse, cruelty or immorality, with a view to the future welfare of the child and the community.

III. To investigate the conditions of children about to become public charges, in order to seek homes for them in placing-out departments, or guiding them through proper channels to relatives or friends as an alternative to institutional placement at public expense.

IV. To direct attention to feeble-minded and epileptic children, stressing the question of their care and support, together with commitment to the proper institutions, where they may receive such training as they are capable of undergoing.

V. To help the unmarried mother to obtain support from the father, and to construct a plan best suited to the needs of herself and her child.

VI. To secure adequate medical treatment through public hospitals and clinics for children or their parents suffering from physical defect, or from the general physical deterioration which marks the deserted family.

VII. To make efforts to re-organize so-called "bad homes" to prevent the breaking up of families with consequent disadvantage to the children.

VIII. To compel derelict adult children properly to support their aged parents, and to insure peaceful old age for those reduced to a state of helplessness by reason of infirmity and illness.

IX. To protect animals from mistreatment, cruelty and abuse, and to enforce the laws relating thereto.[1]

The Ohio Humane Society has serveral times sought to release itself from the necessity of carrying on animal protection. Despite the fact that there exists in Cincinnati another animal protective society, the Hamilton County' S. P. C. A., to which it would gladly turn over its animal work, it has been unable to succeed in doing this without running the risk of forfeiting its charter. Moreover, a share of its income depends upon the maintenance of its activities in behalf of animals, under the provisions of the " Ohio Sheep Fund ". This " Sheep Fund " is composed of the registration fees for dogs and dog kennels in each Ohio county. It was originally intended to reimburse sheep owners whose flocks had been attacked by the wild dogs which used to infest the state many years ago. It was provided that whenever there was a surplus of more than $1000 at the end of a year after paying the claims of the sheep owners, it should be transferred to the treasuries of animal protective societies in the country.[2] There are several humane societies in the state of Ohio whose interest is in child welfare rather than in animal protection, but who are forced to engage in a certain minimum of animal protection to receive a part of their income. Of these the Ohio Humane Society is the most important.[3]

As may be seen from its declaration of purposes, the Ohio Humane Society considers the enforcing of anti-cruelty laws only a minor part of its program. Thus in 1922, of the 1619 new cases investigated by the Society and the

[1] *Ohio Humane Society, Ann. Rpt. for 1921; cf. Community Chest Crier* (Cincinnati), April 2, 1923.

[2] *Ohio R. S.*, sec. 2833.

[3] Manuscript letter of May 11, 1923 from the secretary of the Ohio Humane Society.

4767 cases that it found necessary to rehandle, only 951 cases required court action.[1]   In 1921, besides the cases of cruelty to children, the Society handled 158 cases of illegitimacy and 164 cases of non-support of aged parents.

In carrying out its program, the Ohio Humane Society has found it necessary to enter into the closest possible relations with the other child-welfare organizations of Cincinnati.   Through the influence of the Council of Social Agencies, coordination and harmony have been obtained and the overlapping of work is eliminated.   The Ohio Humane Society is represented at the various conferences and local committees, the executive of the Society serving as chairman of the Cincinnati Boarding Home Bureau, and chairman of the Committee on Illegitimacy, both committees being functional members of the Council of Social Agencies. The Society is also represented on the District Conference Committee, the Public Health Federation, and the Negro Civic Welfare Association.[2]   Finally, it belongs to the very successful Community Chest of Cincinnati.

Until 1910 the Pennsylvania S. P. C. C. had followed a program of strictly protective work in the city of Philadelphia.   In the early years of the decade beginning with 1910 it was influenced by the movement started by the Massachusetts S. P. C. C., and broadened its activities.[3]

In 1913 it announced a program which showed the influence of the new forces that were permeating it:

Our work consists (1) of home conservation through the determined and persistent efforts which we put forth and enlist others in putting forth to secure proper home treatment for

[1] *Community Chest Crier* (Cincinnati), April 2, 1923.

[2] Manuscript letter of May 11, 1923.

[3] William Henry Slingerland, *Child Welfare Work in Pennsylvania* (N. Y., 1915), p. 145.

children where home conditions have been found, upon complaint made, to warrant public interference for their protection; (2) of presenting to the Court the cases of families in which preventive and constructive work has failed, recommending to the Court the removal of children from parents who have proven intolerably cruel or neglectful and have refused every effort toward reformation; (3) of caring for children who have been committed to our custody by the Court and endeavoring, even after having, through the instrumentality of the Court, removed the children, to reconstruct the family life, make the parents again worthy of the care of their children, and return the children to them.[1]

One of its first problems was to divest itself of its child boarding functions. In 1912 it had boarded 3542 children; by 1915 it had reduced this number to 1952. Eventually its children's shelter, maintained at first solely by the Society and later jointly with the Children's Aid Society and the Seybert Institution, was turned over entirely to the latter.[2]

Seeking to obtain greater cooperation among the charitable organizations of Philadelphia, it formed the Children's Bureau to act as a clearing house for the child-welfare agencies of the city. This not proving an entirely satisfactory body, the Philadelphia Welfare Federation was organized in the spring of 1921, to act both as a central charitable bureau and a financial federation.[3]

Hitherto, having confined its activities to Philadelphia and the immediately surrounding territory, it now plans to make itself state-wide. In 1921 the president announced: " The Society must put itself as soon as possible in a position to give more satisfactory service to the eastern

[1] *Pennsylvania S. P. C. C., 37th Ann. Rpt.* (1913), p. 7.

[2] *Pa. S. P. C. C., 38th Ann. Rpt.* (1914), p. 10.

Pa. S. P. C. C., 45th Ann. Rpt. (1921), p. 10.

part of the state outtside of Philadelphia. . . . If the Society
is to give service to the State by means of branch offices and
district committees, we shall have to pay the additional cost
untill such time as the communities helped can pay for their
own welfare work." [1]

Financially, the Pennsylvania society was not so well
equipped to begin a campaign of state-wide expansion as
was the Massachusetts S. P. C. C. It lost rather than
gained ground during the past decade. Its income from
subscriptions was $13,739.53 in 1914, and by 1920 had
sunk to $9,817.70. It has had during these years a steady
excess of expenditure over net income, which it has had to
meet either from its invested capital or from its limited
amount of unrestricted bequests. It has, however, the advantage of receiving grants from the State of Pennsylvania
and from the county and the city of Philadelphia, which
in 1921 amounted to $14,310.66. Its total net income, ex-
clusive of bequests in this year was $43,033.25 and its ex-
penses were $65,175.83.

Another society that has recently undergone a transfor-
mation similar to that of the Massachusetts and Pennsylvania societies, is the Delaware S. P. C. C. Formed in 1879,
its history during its first decade was that of growth and
active development. Thereafter, its founders having been
taken from it by death and change of residence, it slowly
disintegrated until by 1918 it was practically inactive. It
had been managed for many years together with the Delaware S. P. C. A. by the non-support officer of the municipal
court of Wilmington. Though sincere, he was untrained
in social case work. The finances of the Society were
limited; the state appropriated $900 a year, membership dues
amounted to about $120, and fines raised the average an-

[1] *Ibid.*

nual income to between $2000 and $2500. Although the non-support officer declared the interest of the Society was mainly in " preventive " work, it was possible to do little more than prosecute the actual cases of cruelty in the city of Wilmington. When in 1918 an investigation was made of all the child welfare organizations of Delaware, it was advised that the S. P. C. C. unite with the Wilmington Juvenile Court and Probation Association and surrender its individual existence.[1]

The suggestion was not a welcome one to the social workers of Wilmington, and during the following year, several of them succeeded in getting on the board of managers of the S. P. C. C. One of the staff of the Massachusetts S. P. C. C. was invited to become the secretary of the Society and reorganize it. The non-support officer was dismissed as agent and the society dropped all connections with the non-support work and with the S. P. C. A. The type of work was completely changed, following as nearly as possible, with the Society's limited facilities, the program of the Massachusetts S. P. C. C. The policy of an annual financial drive and widespread advertising was adopted, which proved remarkably successful, resulting in large donations and a series of bequests. In 1922, whereas there had been no increase in the income received from public sources and little from dues, donations as a result of a special appeal amounted to $2,247, and bequests to $5000, making a total income for the year of $10,577.13.[2]

In imitation of the policy of the Massachusetts society, the Delaware S. P. C. C. has sought to bring about as complete a cooperation among the Wilmington child-welfare organizations as is possible. In January 1922 the director

[1] C. S. Richardson, *The Dependent, Delinquent and Defective Children of Delaware* (N. Y., 1918), p. 27.

[2] Manuscript letter of April 19, 1923.

of the Society became director of the Children's Bureau of
Delaware, dividing her time between the two organizations,
which, however, have separate boards of managers. In
1923 a full-time secretary and a full-time field-worker were
obtained, and for the first time in its history, the Society
was in a position to attend to cases of cruelty outside of the
city of Wilmington. It looks forward during the next few
years to expanding its work until its becomes state-wide.
Because of the limited extent of the territory it will be called
upon to cover, it plans to utilize the services of local agents
in various parts of the state rather than to establish branch
societies after the Massachusetts model.

The California S. P. C. C. is another society the type of
whose work has changed. It is one of the oldest child-protective societies, having been formed in 1876. Up to the
present, it has confined its work to the city of San Francisco.
In the matter of child protection, the state of California is
very poorly served. It is dotted with humane societies,
but these confine themselves with one exception to animal
protection. In a survey of child welfare work made in
1915, only three child-protective organizations were found
to exist, the California S. P. C. C., the Fresno County
Humane Society, and the Pacific Humane Society.[1] Since
then, the latter two societies have ceased to exist. One new
society to help children has been formed, the Los Angeles
Humane Society for Children.

The California S. P. C. C. asserts its purpose to be
" educational in all matters involving the welfare of children ".[2] It prefers to settle the cases that come before it
out of court and to break up families as rarely as possible.
In 1916, against 135 prosecutions of adults, 742 cases were

[1] William Henry Slingerland, *Child Welfare Work in California* (N. Y.,
1915), p. 172.

[2] *California S. P. C. C., Ann. Rpt. for 1917*, p. 29.

settled out of court, and 919 warnings were given, and of the 130 parents convicted of cruelty, 103 were released from custody on probation. Of the 3,373 children that came to the Society's attention during the same year, only 95 were not permitted to stay with their families.

Some few child-protective societies have for one reason or another neglected to a greater or lesser extent the actual protection of children from cruelty and have devoted their resources to some allied field of child welfare. The Humane Society of Kansas City (Missouri) presents such a case. Within the city there is another society, the Missouri Anti-Cruelty Society, whose agents are active in prosecuting cases of cruelty to either children or animals. The Humane Society of Kansas City has made no attempt to compete with its sister organization. Some time ago it received an endowment for educational propaganda among children and to provide a recreational camp for them; since then practically its entire attention has been turned to this field. It justifies itself by pointing to the educational value of its work:

While the Society's agents have police power, its exercise is neither a primary nor a perpetual function of the Society, since it is and probably ever will be the duty of the police, the public prosecutor, and all authorities and courts having jurisdiction in criminal cases, to apprehend, arrest and prosecute offenders in cruelty cases: and one of the chief reasons for the formation of the Humane Society was to secure the enactment of humanitarian laws, and to educate the people and public officials as to their justice and proper enforcement. When this education is fully accomplished, there will be no more need of a society to prevent cruelty than for a society to prevent murder or arson.[1]

[1] *Humane Society of Kansas City, Ann. Rpt. for 1919.*

The Youngstown (Ohio) Humane Society has devoted itself to the establishment of a detention home for the Juvenile Court and to the establishment of boarding homes for children and the obtaining of hospital attention where needed.[1] The Mansfield (Ohio) Humane Society makes charitable relief an important part of its activities. In the first six months of 1921 it assisted 145 families, representing 798 persons.[2]

In cities and towns where S. P. C. C.s have never been formed, the protection of children has been taken over by other organizations not recognized by the American Humane Association and not to be found in its record. The number and kind of such organizations can in no way be determined. The following may serve as examples.

Louisville, Kentucky, has never had an S. P. C. C. This work has been done by the Child Protective Association of that city, organized in 1914 as a "big sister" movement to assist the Juvenile Court in probation work. In 1917 it separated from the Court and a board of managers was elected. It became a member of the Welfare League. Its procedure has been to receive all reports of cases of mistreatment, neglect and other sins against childhood. It investigates these cases and then reports those requiring action to the appropriate agency.[3]

In Chicago a Juvenile Court Committee was organized in 1899 to pay the salaries of the probation officers of the Chicago Juvenile Court as the original act has made no provision for this. The defect was remedied in 1905. From then until 1909 the Committee cooperated in general

[1] National Humane Review, vol. x, p. 86.

[2] Mansfield Humane Society, 1921 Booklet.

[3] William Henry Slingerland, Child Welfare Work in Louisville (Louisville, 1919), p. 101.

with the Court without taking to itself any particular sphere
of work.   In 1909 it was reorganized as a juvenile protective association and turned its attention to community
conditions affecting child life.   It continued to maintain
close relations with the Juvenile Court and whenever cases
of cruelty to children serious enough to warrant court action
came to its attention, it turned them over to the Court.
Where the offense was less serious, it took the settlement
into its own hands.[1]   Of recent years, however, it has turned
its attention from individual case work to the promotion
of " the study of child problems and by systematic agitation,
through the press and otherwise, to create a permanent
public sentiment for the establishment of wholesome social
agencies ".[2]   Nevertheless, during the year ending November 1923, it dealt with 62 cases of offenses against
children.

The Social Service Bureau of Houston, Texas, was
formed in 1916 by the combination of five independent
organizations occupied with various forms of social work
in the city.   In their combined form they deal with (1)
charitable relief; (2) public health nursing; (3) child welfare (including the supervision of neglected children, and
the prevention of cruelty to children); (4) protection of
women and girls : and (5) settlement work.

The Bureau as it exists at present is a private organization supported in part by public funds (in 1921 it received
$25,500.00 out of a total income of $58,422.06 from the
city of Houston).   It is governed by a private board of
directors, and each department has its departmental committee.   The child welfare department of the Bureau de-

---

[1] U. S. Dept. of Labor, Children's Bureau Publication No. 104, Helen
R. Jeter, *The Chicago Juvenile Court* (Wash., 1922), p. 100.

[2] *The Juvenile Protective Association of Chicago, 21st Ann. Rpt.*
(1923), p. 27.

votes more attention at present to homeless and neglected
children than to the prosecution of cruelists, but it is,
nevertheless, the only child-protective organization of the
city.[1]

Several cities have established forces of policewomen, the
larger part of whose duties involves child protection.   In
New York City, the force of policewomen was provided
for in 1920 by legislative statute.[2]   It is today the largest
and most highly developed body of its kind and its com-
position and activities are described as follows by Police
Commissioner Enright of that city :

There are sixteen policewomen and twenty patrolwomen attached to the police force of this department, who are prin-
cipally engaged in activities for the promotion of the welfare
of women and children.   Their particular duties and functions
in this respect are the investigation of crimes and offenses in
which women and children are concerned, in cooperation with
other divisions and bureaus of the police department in procuring information and evidence in all cases affecting the welfare, safety and protection of women and children. . . . In
all welfare work of this character, women officers cooperate
with recognized civic organizations devoted to welfare work
and court officers having jurisdiction in cases affecting women
and children.[3]

Cincinnati, on the other hand, has detailed a group of regular police officers for child protection, to cooperate with
the Ohio Humane Society. The uniformed officers are
trained and are capable of executing the same processes as
an experienced social worker. They are acquainted with
the technique of writing correct case histories, and are

[1] *The Social Service Bureau of Houston, Texas, Report for 1921.*
[2] *N. Y. Sess. Laws*, 1920, ch. 509.
[3] Manuscript letter of May 14, 1923.

active in problems of social psychiatry and intensive health programs for the child. They are particularly helpful in acquainting the courts and public departments of the plans and aims of the Humane Society, and they have a contact with public departments which is sometimes denied the regular social workers.[1]

In general, the larger cities of the United States are served more or less thoroughly in child-protective work by S. P. C. C.s or humane societies engaging in child work. It is the rural territory in all states that suffers in this respect. As was pointed out in Chapter II on animal protection,[2] in the West there are entire states without any agency whatsoever to protect either animals or children. Moreover, as has been pointed out, most humane societies confine themselves to animal protection. It is thus evident that the regions void of child protective agencies are far more extensive than those unserved by animal societies. Speaking of this lack, the secretary of the child department of the New York State Charitise Aid Association said: " the most flagrant neglect of children that has ever come to my attention has been among the children of American stock in rural communities." [3]

A few societies have made definite attempts to meet this condition. The Massachusetts S. P. C. C. and its branches have agents located in all the centers of population of the state unserved by the branch societies, who are responsible for the condition of the region. Each branch society likewise is expected to serve the rural district surrounding its

[1] Manuscript letter of May 11, 1923 from the secretary of the Ohio Humane Society.

[2] *Vide supra*, p. 26.

[3] *National Conference of Charities and Corrections*, vol. xl, p. 296. *Cf.* introductory chapter of *Rural Child Welfare* (New York, 1922), published by the National Child Labor Committee.

city. In this way the state is thoroughly covered—or will
be, when the Society has completed its projects—by a net-
work of active societies and agents. So far, Massachusetts
is the only state in which such organization has been
effected.

In New York, the State Humane Association employed a
special field agent during 1916 and a part of 1917 to visit
the different local child-saving societies and help them with
advice and suggestions. He also went into the counties
where there were dead societies or no societies for the prevention of cruelty to children, and endeavored to start active
and efficient organizations. Poverty of resources forced
the Association to drop this plan in 1917.[1]

Interorganization among child protective societies has not
been as complete as among animal societies. The New
York societies are members of equal standing with the
animal societies in the State Humane Association; so also
in Pennsylvania. On the other hand, when the California
State Humane Association was formed in 1908, the San
Francisco S. P. C. C. was excluded.[2]

All the child protective societies except the Massachusetts
S. P. C. C. belong to the American Humane Association.
The Massachusetts S. P. C. C. allowed its membership to
lapse because it felt that the Association's activities were so
largely concerned with animal protection, that child protection was slighted.[3] There has been a tendency during the
last few years for some child protective societies to ally
themselves with the Children's Division of the National

[1] *A. H. A., 41st Ann. Rpt.* (1917), p. 4.

[2] Hubbard, *Prevention of Cruelty to Animals in the States of Ill.,
Colo. and Cal.*, p. 104.

[3] *Cf.* C. C. Carstens, "Development of Social Work for Child Protection," in the *Annals of the American Academy of Political and Social
Science*, November, 1921.

Conference of Social Work.   The Massachusetts S. P. C. C.
is a member, and representatives of the Brooklyn, the Pennsylvania, the Delaware and the Essex County (N. J.)
S. P. C. C.s have participated at recent conferences.   This
must not be taken to mean a defection from the American
Humane Association.   All but the Massachusetts S. P. C. C.
continue members of the Association and the secretary of
that society believes that it will soon resume its membership.

The Children's Bureau of the U. S. Department of
Labor has been of much assistance to the movement for
child protection during the past ten years.   A bill for the
establishment of the Bureau was first introduced into Congress in the winter of 1905-6 through the efforts of the
National Child Labor Committee and many cooperating
agences.   Although endorsed by the President and by members of the Cabinet and warmly advocated by members of
both House and Senate, the bill failed to reach a vote.   Reintroduced into the Sixtieth (1908-9) and Sixty-First
(1909-10) Congresses, it suffered the same fate.   The
White House Child Welfare Conference called by President
Roosevelt in 1909 warmly advocated the establishment of
the Bureau.

The bill was again introduced into the Sixty-Second Congress, was passed by both houses, and approved April 9,
1911.   The Children's Bureau began active operations upon
the passage of the legislative, executive and judicial appropriation bill of August 23, 1912, with Miss Julia C.
Lathrop as its first Chief.

The Bureau was intended to investigate and report upon
all matters pertaining to the welfare of children and child
life among all classes of the people, and to investigate
especially the questions of infant mortality, birth rate, or-
phanage, juvenile courts, desertion, dangerous occupations,
accidents, diseases of children, employment and legislation

affecting children in the several states and territories.[1]
This broad program has been followed, and the Bureau has
become a clearing house for information regarding child
welfare in the United States and relating to actual or pending legislation in the several states affecting children.   Up
to 1923 it had issued a valuable series of over 100 pamph-
~s covering the major phases of child welfare.

Finally it should be noted that at the 1910 International
Conference of the American Humane Association, the suggestion was made by the director of the National S. P. C. C.
of London that an international federation of children's protective societies be formed.   His plan included: (1) a central bureau, the headquarters of the federation, located
in London or New York; (2) a permanent secretary; (3)
a library to contain reports, copies of the laws of different
countries on all subjects relating to child welfare; (4) interchange of ideas; (5) active propaganda; (6) the arranging of visits between members of the federated societies;
and (7) international congresses.[2]   The convention took
no action.

The second international humane conference, held in New
York City in October 1923, was attended by representatives
of the leading child-protective organizations in foreign
countries, and it adopted resolutions making renewed efforts
to bring about more definitely organized international cooperation.

The expansion of child protective activities in the period
since 1910 is very noticeable.   The growth of the Massachusetts S. P. C. C during these years is quite unparalleled
in the history of child protection; and except in the cases of

---

[1] *Cf. 62nd Cong., 1st Sess., S. Rpt., no. 141. Vide* also *The Survey,*
vol. xxix, p. 189.

[2] *A. H. A., 34th Ann. Rpt.* (1910), p. 46.

a few small societies in the central part of the United States, there has been general progress throughout the whole movement. The Delaware and the Pennsylvania S. P. C. C.s, electrified into action by the example of the Massachusetts organization, have entered upon ambitious programs of expansion and development.

Finally, too much emphasis cannot be given to the great assistance afforded to all types of child work through the Children's Bureau. The years covered by this study cover also the period of its earliest beginnings and its full, rich development. It now has reached the period of its maturity and is accomplishing all that was hoped for it.

We shall study in the next chapter the significance of the widening scope of " protection " as that term has come to be interpreted by certain societies. In effect, many child protective organizations are doing vanguard service for child *welfare;* they are more flexible than other types of child help organizations, and it is possible for them to take the first steps in opening up new fields of assistance to child life.

CHAPTER XI

Policies and Activities of Child Protective Societies

In 1910 Professor McCrea pointed out that with very few exceptions, child-protective societies in the United States followed the lead of the New York S. P. C. C. in confining themselves to work of a strictly protective nature, leaving broader welfare activities to child organizations of other types.[1] In 1923 this statement is no longer true. The majority of S. P. C. C.s and no inconsiderable number of humane societies have adopted the welfare program of the Massachusetts S. P. C. C.

In the minds of its founders, the New York society was to be an organization for the enforcement of the law. It did not concern itself with the causes which lead to tragedy in the child's life, except as might be incidental to the individual case presented. The Society was primarily concerned with the rescue of the children suffering from brutal treatment or living in degraded surroundings, and it presented such evidence to the court that those responsible for these conditions might feel the heavy hand of the law. This was its corporate purpose and was many times emphasized in its annual reports and in statements before official commissions.[2]

This conception of the functions of the New York S. P. C. C. was embodied in a decision handed down by the New

[1] McCrea, *op. cit.*, p. 136.

[2] *Vide* evidence in Dalett H. Wilson, *Statement on Behalf of Mr. August Heckscher* (N. Y., 1923), submitted to the N. Y. State Commission to Examine Laws Relating to Child Welfare.

York Court of Appeals on January 9, 1900.[1] The New
York State Board of Charities had sought to extend its
supervision over the work of the New York S. P. C. C.
because it was charged by law with the supervision of
private organizations undertaking charitable work, and particularly charitable organizations receiving public funds.
Since the New York S. P. C. C. received $30,000 in the
year 1898 from the Treasury of the City of New York and
maintained a shelter for children, the State Board of Charities considered that it came within the scope of its inspec-
tional duties. The New York S. P. C. C. brought suit to
prevent the Board from performing such inspection and
supervision, on the ground that the Society was not a
charity, but "a subordinate governmental agency". The
Appellate Division of the Supreme Court held that it was a
charity with respect to its shelter work. The New York
S. P. C. C. appealed the case and the Court of Appeals re-
versed the decision, holding that the city's appropriation
was for "doing work that would otherwise devolve upon
the Police Department".[2]

In the course of his decision, Judge O'Brien of the Court
of Appeals stated that "the corporation (New York S. P.
C. C.) was created for the purpose of enforcing laws enacted to prevent cruelty to children, and that is the only
object or purpose of its existence"; and Judge Gray added
in a concurring opinion, "giving it a distinct place from
those institutions which bring of a charitable, eleemosynary,
correctional, and reformatory nature, are made subject to
the authority of the State Board".[3]

[1] *People ex rel. the State Board of Charities v. the New York S. P.
C. C.*, 161 N. Y. 233.

[2] *Vide* review of the decisions in *State Board of Charities, Quarterly
Record*, vol. i, p. 121.

[3] *Ibid.*

The policy of the New York S. P. C. C. was explained by Mr. Elbridge T. Gerry to the first international humane conference held in 1910:

It is the utilization of the voluntary contribution of time, thought, effort and money by citizens to aid suffering childhood, through the law, by the law, and under the law. It is the hand of the law, the fingers of which trace charges of injury to children and fasten the grasp of the law upon the offender. The arm of the law attached to the hand brings the children and the offenders into the Court, where the helpless child is judicially disposed of for reformation, proper education, change of circumstances, probation, or whatever appropriate reformatory means are desirable in the particular case; and the cruelist is punished. *Child rescue* is not *child reformation*. It is not technically " charitable " work. But it places the subject for the charitable work of reformation in the possession and under the control of the societies, associations, institutions and individuals, who are constantly occupied in *charitable* work only, and it terrifies the cruel by the vigor of its prosecutions.[1]

Three years later, Mr. Peter G. Gerry wrote more briefly of the aims of the New York S. P. C. C., that they could be divided into two classes, " the prevention of cruelty to children and the prosecution of cruelists. Our object is to prevent cruelty; to rescue the child who is being ill-treated, and to deter the brutal from similar acts by bringing to punishment all those who injure children." [2] He asserted that only by this specialization of work could the Society become most effective. As to the children involved, the first duty of the Society was " to take the child away from the people who were injuring it ".[3] As late as 1916, the Society could state its primary purpose as " the relentless

---

[1] *A. H. A., 34th Ann. Rpt.* (1910), p. 12.

[2] *National Humane Review*, vol. i, p. 5.

[3] *A. H. A., 37th Ann. Rpt.* (1913), p. 35.

prosecution of those who have made helpless childhood their victim ".[1]

Since 1919 the Society has somewhat broadened its conception of " child protection ". In that year the general manager said in his report:

The assistance and supervision rendered by the Society in the rehabilitation of homes has continued to be a most gratifying feature of its work. Children are removed from the custody of their parents or guardians only when such action has become imperative, and in every case, effort is made to encourage in the guardians a proper sense of their responsibility and a determination to reconstruct their homes upon a better standard, in order that their children may be returned to them. Every effort is made to save the children to their homes.[2]

As a result of considering itself " an arm of the law ", the New York S. P. C. C. has been forced to look upon its shelter work as " incidental and transitory in the temporary care of such children as, for the time being, while the society is enforcing the law in particular cases, are detained in its custody ".[3] For this reason the Society declined to accept Mr. August Hecksher's gift in 1920 in its original form, as this would have involved it in child-welfare work of a nature foreign to its corporate purpose, and it " could not deviate from those lines under any circumstances ".[4] It is significant, however, that in its appeals for financial support, it lays great stress on the welfare features of its shelter work.[5]

[1] *New York S. P. C. C., 42nd Ann. Rpt.*, p. 35.

[2] *New York S. P. C. C., 45th Ann. Rpt.*; cf. Carl C. Carstens, " Development of Social Work for Child Protection," in *Annals of the American Academy of Political and Social Science*, November, 1921.

[3] Concurring opinion of Judge Gray, *cit. supra.*

Dallet H. Wilson, *op. cit.*, p. 4.

Cf. *New York S. P. C. C., 48th Ann. Rpt.* (1923), p. 6.

The attitude of the American Humane Association and particularly of its president, has been distinctly in favor of a conservative policy for child-protective societies. He objects to any other than specifically *protective* work on their part as a duplication of the activities of charitable societies. He believes that child-protective societies should remain strictly law-enforcing organizations.[1] At the most, he considers that they might profit by *studying* the causes of cruelty and delinquency.[2]

The majority of social workers who consider themselves "progressive" look upon this attitude towards child work as primitive and belonging to an age which has past. The concentration of effort upon the individual rather than the environment and the elasticity which were the chief characteristics of this type of social work, were made possible because in the early stages of the movement cases did not have to be dealt with in large numbers.[3]

The newer tendency is to deal with environment: "Efforts are concentrated upon trying to prevent the failure from recurring. . . . Whereas under the old school of thought, the child seldom became an object of attention until he was ill or in difficulties, the movement today concentrates its attention, and is in fact, based on the principle that most of such troubles arise from preventable causes."[4]

In 1909 the Massachusetts S. P. C. C. considered "the tendency of the anti-cruelty societies to become arms of the police a dangerous one". The necessity for prosecution it regarded as a diminishing phase of anti-cruelty work.

[1] Editorial by Dr. William O. Stillman in *National Humane Review*, vol. ii, p. 195.

[2] Editorial in *National Humane Review*, vol. i, p. 84.

[3] Nora Milne, *Child Welfare from a Social Point of View* (London, 1920), p. 12.

[4] *Ibid.*, pp. 13-15.

The need for preventive and remedial measures, on the other hand, it viewed as a rapidly growing one. In addition to the protection of children from bodily harm and from serious neglect and moral injury by invoking the law, it felt it should take upon itself the work of developing conditions of normal family life.[1]

At this period, the Massachusetts S. P. C. C., under the influence of its secretary, Mr. Carstens, was just entering upon a program of development into new fields of child welfare work allied to its protective activities. In the following year, 1910, the board of managers made public announcement in unmistakeable terms of what was to be the policy of the Society for the future:

Your directors have taken the broadest view of the obligations of the Society to the public, and no preconceived notion of what the functions of an S. P. C. C. are, has been allowed to stand in the way of what it has been found that the Society can do. We lay emphasis on the words " prevention " and " children ", and our ideal is to help prevent any of the preventable evils which come to childhood through the imperfections of our social structure, or through the frailties of human nature. We even consider that it comes within the scope of our work to spread abroad the story of our methods and the results of our investigations. We have therefore encouraged our agents, and our General Agent in particular, to take part in conventions, whether held within or without the state, which discuss matters which touch our work, and to serve on committees or on the boards of other charitable organizations. For instance, our General Agent attended in the course of the year (1910) the National Conference of Charities and Corrections at St. Louis. the International Humane Conference, the International Prison Conference at Washington, the State Conference of Charities

[1] Roswell C. McCrea, " Societies for the Prevention of Cruelty to Children," in Hastings H. Hart, *Preventive Treatment of Neglected Children* (New York, 1910), p. 200.

in Fitchburg, and the Ohio Federation of Humane Societies in Cleveland. Our central office is a laboratory where experiments are being constantly made under careful supervision and our deductions are being tested again and again in their practical operation. One cannot carry on this sort of work without becoming an educational agency of considerable importance. In our laboratory we diagnose the causes of family disaster, and we discover the remedy through years, perhaps, of experimentation.[1]

At the American Humane Association convention of that year, the secretary of the Society explained its program of cooperation:

The practical question before us is, can we best render our service to all the children who need us by holding aloof from cooperative relations with other agencies for home betterment, or by entering into such relations? To state the question is, in my judgment, to answer it. Cooperation is the keynote to a larger service to the community. Not the cooperation which will tend towards the absorption of agencies with diverse functions, but the cooperation which will recognize diversity of function as its basis, and will place each problem before the society that will solve it most effectually. Cooperation is fundamentally a question of toleration. It requires a friendly nature, a recognition of values in others. It means "one for all and all for one". We are constantly thrust up against definite and difficult social problems. We are asked every day how can the Society induce a father to care for his offspring? How can the curse that falls upon children from their parents' intemperance be driven out from the home? How can young girls be protected from the influences everywhere around them which tend to rob them of their virtue? Any children's protective society that thinks it can single-handed cope with these and many other questions has either not yet learned the content of these problems, or is ignorant

[1] *Mass. S. P. C. C., Ann. Rpt. for 1910,* p. 9.

in its own conceit. In helping to bring about needed social changes, all agencies must together present a united front. Only thus shall we achieve success.[1]

It will be remembered that in this year the Hampshire branch of the Massachusetts S. P. C. C. organized its confidential exchange and two years later the mother society organized the Children's Welfare League of Roxbury, and in 1913 a confidential social exchange for the city of Boston.

During the intervening years, the Massachusetts Society has occupied itself with an increasing number of preventive types of activity. If anything, it has enlarged upon its earlier program. In 1921 its secretary, Mr. Carstens, speaking of the services that must be rendered in every community by some agency to ensure " a square deal " for all children, outlines the following program for prevention of cruelty to children :

1. Children must be protected from physical brutalities. Though these are less numerous than before, they are always degrading even when not dangerous.

2. Children must be protected from early exhausting and degrading labor. The public now generally frowns upon the child acrobat, but child labor is still in great demand and seems to be in better standing since the war.

3. Children should receive suitable physical care at the hands of their parents and guardians. This includes proper medical and surgical care, recommended by physicians of standing in the community. While an honest difference of opinions is found on certain medical questions among medical men, children's protective agencies have rarely undertaken to enforce medical care where there was clear disagreement among practitioners of unquestioned standing.

4. Children, and particularly girls, need a vigorous agency

[1] *A. H. A., 34th Ann. Rpt.* (1910), p. 63; cf. *Proceedings of the National Conference of Charities and Correction,* vol. xli, p. 162.

in every community for their protection from early sex irregularities. The prosecuting attorneys of many communities are learning to render this protection, but in most places the prosecutions for sexual abuses to girls below the age of consent are apt to be either futile because their testimony is poorly used or brutal and demoralizing to the girl witness. Courts should be required to modernize their procedure so as to give greater protection to the girl without removing reasonable safeguards for the accused.

5. Children should also be protected from immoral associations even where they are not directly concerned in immoral acts. This depends in large measure upon an active cooperation with the police departments of our communities. Most police officers are not appealed to in vain where the welfare of the child is involved, if they can see what it means to the child and if what is asked is legal and reasonable.

6. There may be a difference of opinion as to whether a man should support his wife under all circumstances, but there is none as to the responsibility of a father to support his children. To leave children dependent in a community is coming to be recognized as a crime whose effects are registered upon mind as well as body. The limitations which state lines bring to the enforcement of laws against abandonment and desertion are very serious. Perhaps a satisfactory solution of this problem will come only when the Federal Constitution makes it possible to enforce domestic relations in Federal Courts.

7. The child born out of wedlock needs an active agency in every community to safeguard his reasonable rights. Our communities are beginning to render this service, notably the state of Minnesota. One of the services is the enforcement of maintenance against the father, either by court action or by voluntary acknowledgment of paternity.

8. Crippled children and others suffering from physical or mental defects must be given all the opportunities and training that the science of medicine and the art of education can provide so that as far as possible they may become self-supporting

citizens. Where this is impossible, they should have the protection of good public or private care. This does not preclude a good children's program from urging all reasonable measures for the elimination of the unfit.

9. Children should be protected from constant contact with habitual gamblers, drug users and criminals.[1]

The old conception of the best way to save children from cruelty in their homes was to remove them immediately from their families. This procedure is seriously questioned by social workers. In 1915 the secretary of the Pennsylvania S. P. C. C., speaking of the old conception of the child society as " a hand affixed to the arm of the law ", insisted that it should be discarded. " The new type of society must deal with the family as a unit of treatment. It is a family rehabilitation society." [2]

The Children's Bureau Conferences held in 1919 advised that " no child should be removed from the home unless it is impossible so to reconstruct family conditions or build and supplement family resources as to make the home safe for the child, or to so supervise the child as to make his continued presence safe for the community." The same conference concluded that the ideal solution of the problem of the child in his home is " the rehabilitation of the natural home ". The church, school, and private welfare agencies should all engage in educational processes calculated ultimately to make the home what it ought to be.[3]

The Massachusetts and the Philadelphia S. P. C. C.s make the preservation of the family an important element of their policy. The Ohio Humane Society has constructed its whole program on that basis. Its secretary writes:

[1] C. C. Carstens, *loc. cit.*

[2] *Proceedings of the National Conference of Charities and Correction,* vol. xli, p. 168.

[3] U. S. Dept. of Labor, Children's Bureau Publication No. 60, *Standards of Child Welfare* (Wash., 1919).

Remedial measures should first be invoked, and the help of
the Court should be sought only after these have failed. . . .
A need for thorough social investigation. . . . So long as the
man has any earning power in body or brain, he should be
required to labor at some productive work. He may not be
entirely responsible for abnormal conduct, and may require a
physical and moral renovation. . . . A need of proper tests
and examinations starting with psychological tests. If a man
measures eight, ten or twelve years and has a retarded intellect,
let us establish him on that basis and find employment for him
suited to his disability. . . . If we send a man to prison, we
should assume some of the responsibility of the effect of our
prosecution on his character. We have therefore availed our-
selves of the parole system. . . . We have made special efforts
to find suitable employment for men under parole, and have
had the assistance of employers in many cases. . . . We know
that the usual charges against the wife of infidelity, thriftless-
ness, bad temper, and poor homemaking are often sustained,
and that these qualities frequently literally drive the husband
to desertion. . . . We have in all cases avoided long term
institutional care for children.[1]

Similarly, the Children's Aid and S. P. C. C. of Essex
County, N. J., makes "reconstruction and restoration" its
aims—"When we find a home that has gone to pieces, we
pick up the pieces carefully, draw them together, and build
the structure anew. Not to take the child from an unfit
home, but to make the home fit for him and *keep him in it,*
is our aim."[2]

The Pennsylvania S. P. C. C. carries its practice still
further. Where it has been necessary to remove the children from the influence of the family, the Society continues
a friendly supervision of the parents after the children have
left, in the endeavor to build up the family life again, so

[1] *Ohio Humane Society, Ann. Rpt. for 1920-21.*
[2] *Ch. Aid and S. P. C. C. of Essex Co., 50th Ann. Rpt.* (19—), p. 8.

that it may be safe once more to trust the children with them.   This supervision takes many forms—encouragement, advice, threats, help towards new jobs or new home environment.   Sometimes the shock of the actual loss of the children brings to their senses even the most abandoned parents, and it is possible to return children to them under close supervision.   Of 2,242 children of which the Pennsylvania Society was guardian in the beginning of 1914, 384 were returned to their parents in the course of the year.[1]

Several of the larger S. P. C. C.s have interested themselves in the problem of the desertion of families by husbands and fathers.   The primary activity of the societies when they occupy themselves with this problem is to assist in initiating prosecution of deserters and to cooperate with the courts in bringing them to justice.   There is a wide variance in the legislation of the various states bearing on abandonment and failure to provide for the family. Usually, wilful failure to provide food, care and shelter is included in the statutes covering abandonment, or else special legislation has supplied the deficiency.   Only three states, Colorado,[2] Missouri [3] and Wisconsin,[4] include the abandonment of illegitimate children by their fathers in their general desertion acts.   In some few cases, such as the Colorado statute already noted, the administration of the law is in the hands of the juvenile courts.

To sentence the deserting father to jail for a longer or shorter period would work as much hardship upon the abandoned mother and children as his absence otherwise. Therefore, within the last two decades most of the desertion statutes include the provision that the sentence of the

[1] *Pa. S. P. C. C., 38th Ann. Rpt.* (1914), p. 7.

[2] *Colo. Mills Supp.*, secs. 3021b, c, d, am. by *Sess. Laws*, 1915, no. 35.

[3] *Mo. Sess. Laws*, 1919, ch. 8.

[4] *Wis., Desertion Act of 1911.*

deserting parent may be suspended under bond to observe the conditions imposed by the Court. Thirty-eight states [1] make this stipulation. Not all of these provide that failure to comply with the conditions set by the Court will lead to execution of the sentence.

During recent years another type of legislation in this field has been developed to the interest of the deserted family. Six states [2] allow the forfeited bail or the fine imposed upon the deserting father to be granted to his family. Ten states [3] allow the earnings of the father while in prison to go to his family. The sum allowed varies from the fifty cents a day provided for by Alabama and which is administered by the probation officer,[4] to the sliding scale established by Oregon whereby one dollar a day is allowed where there is but one child living with the mother, and twenty-five cents for each additional child until a maximum of one dollar and seventy-five cents is reached.[5]

As is to be expected, there is variance among the statutes of the individual states. The age of the child that is considered " abandoned " ranges from a lower limit of twelve years in several states to the simple expression " minor ". Alabama has the provision that parents abandoning their children for more than six months lose all their parental rights.[6] In Arizona it is deemed abandonment to send a child to a saloon or a house of ill-fame.[7] In California it is considered abandonment for parents to falsely obtain ad-

[1] The following do not make this provision : Ala., Ariz., Cal., Mo., Mont., N. M., N. C., R. I., S. D. and Tenn.

[2] Cal., Colo., Mass., Okla., Pa. and Utah.

[3] Ala., Cal., Del., Mich., Ohio, Ore., Pa., Utah, Wash. and Wyo.

[4] *Ala. Sess. Laws*, 1915, no. 498, sec. 1.

[5] *Ore. Sess. Laws*, 1913, chs. 19, 244.

Ala. Sess. Laws, 1919, no. 1.

Ariz. P. C., secs. 240-241.

mission of children under fourteen to an asylum.[1]   In Connecticut, when a father fails to comply with the terms of his bond, the selectmen of the town must furnish support for his family.[2]   Massachusetts provides that the appointment of a custodian for the child shall not be allowed as defense by the parents for non-support.[3]   In Mississippi failure to support a child for three months is considered " presumptive evidence of intention to abandon ".[4]   In New Jersey refusal to give a child proper education is considered as non-support and punished as such.[5]   Oregon does not admit as defense for the father in a non-support trial that he has remarried and has other children.[6]

In addition to initiating prosecution in cases of abandonment and non-support, most of the larger societies make it a part of their routine activities to collect from deserting fathers the income allowed by the courts to their families. During 1921 $118,210.16 of such moneys passed through the hands of the Ohio Humane Society.

The Mothers' Pension statutes that have been passed since a beginning was made in Missouri and Illinois in 1911, are intended, like some phases of the recent non-support legislation, to prevent the breaking-up of homes with the corresponding hardships to the children, when the support of the father is removed.   By the end of the 1919 legislative sessions, thirty-nine states had adopted such laws.   The provisions embodied in these statutes vary widely, as to persons to whom aid may be given, the conditions of such aid, and administration, but there is a strong movement to equal-

[1] *Cal. Sess. Laws*, 1905, ch. 568, am. in 1909.
[2] *Conn. Sess. Laws*, 1919, ch. 36.
[3] *Mass. Sess. Laws*, 1909, ch. 148.
[4] *Miss. Sess. Laws*, 1920, ch. 213.
[5] *N. J. Sess. Laws*, 1918, ch. 85.
[6] *Ore. Sess. Laws*, 1921, ch. 125.

ize the operation of the laws in all states, and to make the machinery for supervision and investigation more adequate.[1]

The problem of the unmarried mother and the illegitimate child has occupied the attention of several important child protective societies, particularly the Boston, Cleveland and Cincinnati organizations. In this field American legislation has been very backward. We have three kinds of statutes. Some states make bastardy a criminal offense; others, like Illinois, term it a quasi-criminal proceeding, civil in its nature, but criminal in its procedure; and some few states have provided civil remedies in action brought by the State. In few cases has thought been given to the interests of the child; it is a bastard in law, under moral and legal opprobium. Only recently have North Dakota and Minnesota taken steps to remedy this by providing that the natural child shall have legal right to the father's name and all the other rights of a legitimate child.[2]

The American Humane Association paid special attention to this problem in its 1918 and 1919 conferences. In 1920 an inter-city conference on illegitimacy was held, and the following procedure in cases of illegitimacy was suggested to be embodied in legislation:

1. Birth registration—in cases of illegitimate birth, the name of the father should be recorded only after adjudication of paternity or the father's written consent. The record should be confidential, open to inspection only on Court order, and school and work transcripts should omit the data of parentage.

2. All illegitimate births should be reported to a properly authorized public agency.

[1] U. S. Dept. of Labor, Children's Bureau Publication No. 63. Laura A. Thompson, *Laws Relating to "Mothers' Pensions" in the United States, Canada, Denmark and New Zealand* (Wash., 1919), p. 9.

[2] *Vide Minn. Sess. Laws*, 1917, chs. 210, 211, 220, 231. *Cf.* U. S. Dept. of Labor, Children's Bureau Publication No. 66, *Illegitimacy as a Child Welfare Problem* (Wash., 1920), pt. i.

3. The mother or the public agency should institute paternity proceedings.

4. The father should make provision for the child's maintenance and welfare according to his economic situation, the child remaining under Court jurisdiction during minority.

5. The child should have rights of inheritance. The assumption of the father's name after adjudication of paternity should be permissive.

6. The mother should keep the child during the nursing period (compulsory legislation not recommended).

7. The State should assume further responsibility for the child.[1]

The Ohio Humane Society gives more attention than is usual among child-protective societies to the problem of illegitimate children. The Cincinnati General Hospital Social Service notifies the Society immediately upon the registration of an unmarried mother. A worker is sent to the hospital to interview the case and to provide a plan to cover the care of the mother and child upon dismissal—this without pressing the mother for any definite decision at this time in regard to her permanent plans for herself or her child. After thoroughly examining the previous moral record of the mother, prosecution of the father is initiated by the Society without expense to the client when it is thought advisable. Where a record of promiscuity is discovered, the Society declines to initiate prosecution, though ready to extend aid to the mother by other means.[2]

The St. Louis County Humane Society of Duluth, Minnesota, maintains a home for unmarried mothers where they may remain for six months after the child is born. They are given work outside of the home so arranged that they may nurse the child properly.[3]

[1] *National Humane Review*, vol. viii, p. 67.
[2] *Hospital Social Service*, vol. vii, p. 247.
[3] *A. H. A., 43rd Ann. Rpt.* (1919), p. 29.

In 1910 sixteen states had contributory delinquency statutes.   Without exception, these related only to action by the parents or guardian of the child and in most of them it was provided that the sentence might be suspended under bond. By 1922 thirty-three states punished parents for inciting their children to misdemeanor and the original sixteen states had nearly all amended their statutes so as to make them more inclusive.   These laws are not identical.   They vary for example as to the age of the child concerned; in some cases the age is stated, in others " minor " is the term used, while Rhode Island, Nevada, Kansas and Colorado include " all children under the jurisdiction of the Juvenile Court ".   The phraseology of the offense also varies.   In Louisiana, delinquency of the child " through careless control " is punishable.[1]   Maryland punishes " failure to exercise proper guardianship or connivance at improper guardianship ".[2]   An Oklahoma act of 1913 is directed against " abetting delinquency ".[3]   In Washington, " to subject a child under seventeen to vicious or immoral influences " is punishable.[4]

Not so many states punish contributory delinquency on the part of persons other than the parents.   Only eight states [5] cover the abetting of juvenile delinquency by others than the parents of the child.   Five states [6] guard against one possible incentive to such delinquency by forbidding junk dealers and pawn-shop keepers from dealing with minors.   Eight states [7] punish any adult who encourages a minor to gamble or to smoke in public.

[1] *La. Sess. Laws,* 1916, no. 139.
[2] *Md. Sess. Laws,* 1916, ch. 674.
[3] *Okla. Sess. Laws,* 1913, pp. 868-75.
[4] *Wash. Sess. Laws,* 1913, ch. 160.
[5] Ia., Ky., Mo., N. M., Ohio, Pa., S. D. and Va.
[6] Ill., Ind., N. J., N. Y. and Pa.
[7] Ala., Conn., Ga., Ind., Ky., Nev., Ohio and S. D.

In all states the carnal abuse of girls under a certain age is severely punished. The usual age is eighteen. Mississippi and Tennessee fix the age of consent at twelve years. The New Hampshire statute is phrased "enticing female child".[1]   Seven states[2] provide, however, that the girl shall have been of previous chaste character.   Seven states[3] punish the sexual abuse of boys under a given age, usually sixteen, by special statute; elsewhere the general sodomy laws cover this offence. Several states punish the taking of lewd liberties with children, though without the intent to rape, less severely than more extreme carnal abuse. Delaware punishes the harboring of a girl under fifteen for prostitution by a separate statute.[4]   In Indiana, where the age of consent is set at sixteen, intercourse with a girl under twelve is punished by life imprisonment.[5]   New Mexico punishes especially severely the seduction of a girl under sixteen of unsound mind or under the influence of an intoxicant.[6]

The development of the Juvenile Court during the last fifteen years has resulted in a great lessening of several needless hardships to those children who, for one reason or another, are brought into contact with judicial procedure. It has, moreover, greatly simplified such procedure. Formerly in Detroit, for example, if a man were arrested for non-support, he was taken to the Police Court; if for desertion, to the Recorder's Court; if for the neglect of his children, to the Juvenile Court as originally organized; and in cases of the separation of the parents, the Circuit Court

---

[1] *N. H. P. S.*, ch. 272, p. 8.

[2] Fla., Neb., N. C., Okla., Pa., Tenn. and Wis.

[3] Ia., La., Me., Mich., Mont., Utah and Wash.

[4] *Del. R. C.*, vol. xviii, ch. 686.

[5] *Ind. Sess. Laws*, 1913, ch. 95.

[6] *N. M. Sess. Laws*, 1915, ch. 51.

had jurisdiction. The tendency has been to draw all cases involving children under the jurisdiction of the juvenile courts.

The pioneer stage in the development and scope of juvenile courts lasted up to 1904, and was largely a period of experimentation and of missionary work by individuals such as Judge Lindsay of Denver, Judge Stubbs of Indianapolis and Miss Julia C. Lathrop of Chicago.[1] Following this came the period of volunteer probation resulting in the Big Brother and Big Sister Movements and other volunteer activities. This was after all, only a transition stage, and before long, volunteer workers were replaced by paid staffs. It is still too early to say that in theory or practice, the juvenile courts have reached their complete development.

The juvenile court legislation of today deals with a complicated group of problems; those of the offending adult, of the accused child, of the neglectful and degraded parent, of the incompetent or unfaithful guardian, of the family that is simply poor. This legislation contains provisions concerning methods of complaint, of apprehension, and of detention; the structure and organization of the juvenile courts and their relation to the other tribunals; records, procedure, organization of the probation staff and methods of the disposition of the various kinds of cases; and the relation of the courts to the agencies upon which they must depend—charitable, educational, correctional.[2]

In a few cases, a special juvenile court is created for larger cities or counties. This is the case in Alabama, Colorado, Delaware, Georgia, Indiana, Louisiana, Massachusetts, New York, Tennessee and Virginia. A special

[1] Thomas Dawes Eliot, *The Juvenile Court and the Community* (N. Y., 1914), ch. i.

[2] U. S. Dept. of Labor, Children's Bureau Publication no. 70, Sophonisba P. Breckinridge and Helen R. Jeter, *A Summary of Juvenile Court Legislation in the United States* (Wash., 1920), p. 11.

court is established in the District of Columbia, and in Utah one is provided for each judicial district. In the other districts of these states and in all other states, jurisdiction is vested in courts already existing, with the provision that such courts may be called juvenile courts when acting under the juvenile court law.[1]

Jurisdiction of the juvenile courts with some qualifications in fourteen states[2] extends to children under sixteen years of age, in thirteen states[3] and the District of Columbia to children under seventeen, and in seventeen states[4] to children under eighteen years. In Maryland the age is eighteen for girls and twenty for boys; in California it is twenty-one for boys and girls. A number of states provide that jurisdiction once obtained over any minor may continue beyond these age limits, usually until the child reaches twenty-one.

S. P. C. C.s and humane societies have found it necessary to devote an increasing share of their activities to co-operation with juvenile courts. Formerly many of them were sadly neglectful of such cooperation. A questionaire sent to a large number of juvenile courts in 1910 brought the response that in only six did the officers of the humane societies attend with any regularity, and in thirteen others, they attended only occasionally and then to prosecute.[5]

[1] Exclusive jurisdiction over juvenile cases is given to special courts thus created and to designated courts in Ariz., Ark., Cal., Idaho, Kans., Ky., Md., Mich., Minn., Mont., Nev., N. J., N. M., N. D., Okla., Ore., R. I., S. C., S. D., Wash., and parts of Ala., Colo., Del., Ga., Ill., Ind., La., Mass., Nebr., N. Y., Ohio, Pa., Tenn., Va. and W. Va.

[2] Ala., Colo., Ga., Ind., Iowa, Kans., N. J., N. M., N. Y., Okla., Pa., R. I., Tenn. and Vt.

[3] Ark., Del., Fla., Ill., Ky., La., Mass., Mich., Mo., Mont., N. H., Tex. and Wis.

[4] Ariz., Conn., Idaho, Minn., Miss., Neb., Nev., N. C., N. D., Ohio, Ore., S. C., S. D., Utah, Va., Wash. and W. Va.

[5] *A. H. A., 34th Ann. Rpt.*, p. 17.

This failure on the part of humane societies to understand the significance of the juvenile courts is happily becoming a thing of the past, and today more than one child
protective society finds it of advantage to be housed under
the same roof as the local juvenile court.

With the increasing cooperation between child-protective
societies and juvenile courts, the question of detention homes
maintained by the societies has become of increasing importance.   In 1910 in most of the large cities where juvenile
courts existed, detention homes were provided for the temporary care of children awaiting court action either by the
city, or as in Chicago by volunteer groups of social workers
affiliated with the courts.[1] Usually these were not specially
planned to meet their needs.   In Massachusetts and to a
limited extent in Pennsylvania, Maryland and New Jersey,
children awaiting the action of the courts or found in the
streets or whose parents were in temporary distress, or who
were awaiting placement in family homes, were boarded
in private homes at the expense of the State.[2]

During the past decade, the impossibility of the continuance of such a chaotic condition has been recognized and
among other organizations, the S. P. C. C.s and humane
societies have taken steps to remedy it.   The first children's
shelter was established by the New York S. P. C. C. in
1880, but few other societies copied its example.[3]   In recent years the necessity for children's shelters has been increased by the needs of the juvenile courts, but the municipal and state governments have been lax in establishing
such.   As a result, most child-protective organizations have
either begun to operate children's shelters of their own, or,
in the case of young S. P. C. C.s in rural districts having

---

[1] Hart, *Preventive Treatment of Neglected Children*, p. 60.

[2] *Ibid.*, p. 57.

[3] *National Humane Review*, vol. i, p. 245.

only a few cases to deal with, they have made arrangements
with local charitable institutions to care for any children
coming under their supervision.   The director of one large
S. P. C. C. has asserted that "a society for the prevention
of cruelty to children, which is located in a large city, and
is without a children's shelter, is literally like a pot without
a handle ".[1]

The larger S. P. C. C.s have been confronted with the difficult problem of the segregation of the children coming to
their shelters.   The New York S. P. C. C., for example, receives juvenile delinquents of every degree of depravity on
remand from the Children's Court for short periods.   To
allow these to remain in close contact with temporarily lost
children or those just saved from cruel homes, would be a
great blunder.   The problem is difficult, and its only solution is architectural—the construction of the shelter must be
planned with a view to segregation.   Even the present
shelter of the New York S. P. C. C., empodying the latest
and best views along these lines, has been severely criti-
cised on these grounds.

Of recent years there has been a growing movement for
the coordination and revision of child-welfare legislation in
the several states, based on a comprehensive study of the
conditions surrounding children.   " An organized and cooperative effort to secure legislation based upon the study
of conditions in a State and remedies that have been successful in other States has been substituted for the spas-
modic and often little-considered proposals of legislative
measures by individuals or organizations interested in special
phases of child welfare ".[2]

[1] *A. H. A., 39th Ann. Rpt.* (1915), p. 29.

[2] U. S. Dept. of Labor, Children's Bureau Publication No. 116, Emma
O. Lundberg, *State Commissions for the Study and Revision of Child
Welfare Laws* (Wash., 1924), p. 1.

The first of such code commissions was appointed in Ohio in 1911, and the so-called *Children's Code* of Ohio passed in 1913, resulted from the recommendations of the two commissioners.[1]   Up to the present, twenty-eight states have provided for such commissions, nineteen by acts of their legislatures, and nine by appointment by their governors.

[1] Hastings H. Hart, in *The Survey*, July 19, 1913.

CHAPTER XII

STATE ACTIVITIES IN CHILD PROTECTION

THERE are many persons to-day engaged in child protective work who feel that such work can be done better by the State than by private societies. In 1914 the Secretary of the Pennsylvania S. P. C. C. said at the conference of the American Humane Association held in that year: "This thing that we are doing is, after all, the job of the public authorities. The public ought to protect all citizens, including the children, from cruelty and improper care. As speedily as conditions admit, we should turn over to the public the things we are at present doing."[1] The present secretary of the Massachusetts S. P. C. C. has expressed his opinion that the State should take over the agents, the offices, and the organizations of the child societies and carry out their work. He expects that this will eventually develop in some states. The S. P. C. C.s will then turn to educational work in parenthood, sex hygiene, and recreation, and engage in other activities to raise the standard of family life. In addition, there will always be some specialized case work for them to take charge of.

Mr. C. C. Carstens has pointed out that private societies were necessary in the early development of child protection when the work was experimental, the cases occurring were individual in their application, and elasticity and adaptivity were required of the organization involved. Insofar as any work becomes based on well-established principles, re-

---

[1] *A. H. A., 38th Ann. Rpt.* (1914), p. 25.

quires more permanent care, and involves an element of compulsion or control, it becomes possible for public departments to administer it.[1]

The advantages of state administration have been stated: (1) The prestige and power given to the humane officers by state authority, and the cooperation of all legal authorities; (2) the completeness and effectiveness of the work, covering every remote section of the state; (3) the keeping of a permanent record belonging to the state of every child taken by the state; (4) the supplying of sufficient funds by the state to carry on the work without appealing to charity; (5) the avoidance of all conflict between local, city, and county authorities, or societies, in carrying on humane work; (6) the great improvements in methods of humane work resulting from a uniform system, and from the mobilization and organization of all the forces engaged in humane work.[2]

The state bureaus in Colorado, Minnesota, Montana, Washington and Wyoming, and the Wisconsin State Agent, combine child protection with that of animals. In most cases the emphasis is laid on animal protection. During the biennial period from 1920 to 1922, the Colorado Bureau, which has stated as its policy not to expand either branch of work to the detriment of the other, handled cases involving 1,118 children and 5,183 animals.

In West Virginia, the State Board of Children's Guardians was created in 1919 to take the place of the former Humane Society of the state and to look after the general welfare of the dependent, neglected and homeless normal children of the state. Unlike similar Boards in other states, it is an active prosecuting agency in cases involving cruelty to children and during 1921 and 1922, dealt with 209 such

[1] *Proceedings of the Nat. Con. of Char. & Cor.* (1915), **p. 95.**
[2] *A. H. A., 41st Ann. Rpt.* (1917), p. 61.

cases. In its protective activities, it operates similar to the
state bureaus already mentioned.[1]

Recently in several states, organization for child protection has been developed along county lines. Emphasis has
been placed upon the prevention of child dependency and
cruelty rather than upon the prosecution of cruelists, with
the avowed purpose of preserving the child's own home
wherever possible.[2]

The scope of such work is largely a matter of local expediency. The denser the population, the more opportunity
of separating child welfare and adult work. Local resources are also a matter to be considered, and as always,
much depends upon the attitude of the executive officer and
the adequacy of his assistants. County organization of
child welfare has been most highly developed in Minnesota.
Here the State Board of Control is the official central agency.
It consists of five members, two of whom must be women,
with office terms of six years. In 1917 it was authorized
to create a children's bureau. This bureau had charge of
all fields of child welfare, among others the enforcement of
the child-protective laws of the state, and was intended to
take the initiative to conserve the interests of children wherever adequate provision had not been already made.

Under its supervision, county boards of child welfare were
appointed. By the end of 1921 sixty-nine of the eighty-six
counties of the state were so covered. Each county board
is composed of from five to seven members, of whom at
least two must be women. It is closely affiliated with the

[1] *West Virginia State Board of Children's Guardians, 2nd Biennial
Rpt.* (1922), p. 15.

[2] Emma O. Lundberg, " Unifying County Work for Child Care and
Protection," in U. S. Dept. of Labor, Children's Bureau Publication No.
107, *County Organization for Child Care and Protection* (Wash., 1922),
p. 2.

school system of the county—the county school superintendent is always an ex-officio member. It is expected to cooperate with all the private and semi-public agencies for the benefit of children within its jurisdiction.[1] In addition, the Minnesota Society for the Prevention of Cruelty, a state association supported by state funds, operates throughout the state.

North Carolina is beginning a similar system of county boards. In 1917 the State Board of Charities and Public Welfare was created.[2] The statute provided for county organization for child welfare similar to that in Minnesota, permissive but not obligatory. No counties adopted the plan. In 1919 it was made compulsory,[3] and provision was made for cooperation with a state-wide system of juvenile courts.

The Illinois Childrens Commission in 1921, approving of the Minnesota plan for child welfare, recommended:

In order to crystallize the potentialities of the counties and local communities, both urban and rural, the Department of Public Welfare should promote the formation, by the officials and citizens, of local committees which might be known as county welfare boards. Experience has shown that such boards do much to prevent duplication of effort and to arouse interest, and lead to a common understanding of community resources and responsibilities, and a fine spirit of cooperation in service for the common good.[4]

Child protection would be one of the duties of such county welfare boards.

[1] William W. Hodson, " Organization and Development of County Child-Welfare Boards in Minnesota," in Children's Bureau Pub. No. 107, *cit. supra.*

[2] *N. C. Sess. Laws,* 1917, ch. 170.

[3] *N. C. Sess. Laws,* 1919, ch. 46.

[4] *Illinois Childrens Commission, Report for 1921,* p. 7.

In Alabama the Board of County Welfare movement has developed along different lines. During the past few years, the advisory committees of the county juvenile courts have exercised the functions of county welfare boards. To a limited extent, the work of these advisory committees had been coordinated and given unity by the State Department of Child Welfare organized in 1920, which among other duties, enforced the child labor and child protection laws.[1] Recent legislation has superseded this rudimentary type of county child-welfare organization by providing for a fully developed system of county boards. Each county board is to be appointed by the judge of the county juvenile court upon resolutions to the effect by the board of county commissioners and the county board of education. It is provided that each board shall have the power to appoint an agent or county superintendent of child welfare.[2]

Pennsylvania has likewise laid the foundation for a system of county welfare boards. The state departments of Health, Labor and Industry, Public Instruction, and Public Welfare have entered into cooperation to further this work. The Commonwealth Committee of six members was organized to serve as a clearing house for public welfare plans. Upon invitation from any responsible group of citizens within a county it undertakes the organization of a county welfare board, whose chairman will be appointed by the Committee.[3]

Finally, there should be noted the rudimentary county organization which has been sponsored in New York by the department of county agencies of the New York State Charities Aid Association. In 1908 the Dutchess County committee of the Association was organized. A trained

[1] *Alabama Childhood*, vol. i, no. 4, pp. 34, 62.
[2] *Ala. Sess. Laws*, 1923, no. 369.
[3] Lundberg, *loc. cit.*

agent was obtained to undertake welfare work. She found that the protection of the children of the county was an important part of her work. "Unbelievably bad conditions were found in the county, and the most revolting crimes against childhood were discovered." The agent frequently secured evidence and became prosecuting witness in proceedings both to rescue children and to punish adult offenders. In 1917 the Dutchess County committee was constituted by statute the Dutchess County Board of Child Welfare and its activities expanded.[1]

This movement for the protection of children through county agencies is still too young for us to judge of its results. The few states that have interested themselves in this field are still experimenting with administrative agencies. Analysis and valid criticism must wait yet a few more years before passing authoritative judgment.

[1] H. Ida Curry, " County Organization for Child-Welfare Work in New York State by the New York State Charities Aid Association," in Children's Bureau Pub. no. 107, *cit. supra.*

APPENDICES

EXPLANATORY NOTE TO APPENDICES I AND II

THE following synopsis of laws has been condensed to the utmost according to the principles expressed on pages 21 and 22. It is hoped that the form of organization adopted will facilitate rather than confuse reference.

In Appendix I, legislation affecting the welfare of animals has been broadly classified under the heads, (1) OFFENSES FORB'DDEN UNDER PENALTY, (2) POWERS AND DUTIES OF POLICE OFFICERS, (3) SOCIETIES FOR ANIMAL PROTECTION, and (4) HUMANE EDUCATION. Legislation upon OFFENSES FORBIDDEN UNDER PENALTY has been further classified under provisions for (1) GENERAL NEGLECT, (2) TRANSPORTATION OF ANIMALS, (3) DISABLED, DISEASED, DECREPIT AND DYING ANIMALS, (4) MISCELLANEOUS, and (5) VIVISECTION.

In Appendix II, legislation relating to the protection of children has been classified under the heads, (1) OFFENSES AGAINST CHILDREN FORBIDDEN UNDER PENALTY, (2) REGULATION OF INSTITUTIONS CARING FOR CHILDREN, (3) S. P. C. C.s AND HUMANE SOCIETIES, and (4) CHILDREN'S CODE COMMISSIONS. Legislation upon OFFENSES AGAINST CHILDREN FORBIDDEN UNDER PENALTY is further classified under provisions for (1) GENERAL CRUELTY, (2) ABANDONMENT, DESERTION, NON-SUPPORT BY PARENT OR GUARDIAN, (3) EXHIBITIONS AND EMPLOYMENTS, (4) OBSCENE LITERATURE, (5) ADMITTANCE TO RESORTS, (6) SALES TO MINORS, (7) CARNAL ABUSE, and (8) MISCELLANEOUS.

The main characteristics of each type of legislation are set forth in the summary at the head of each column, with identifying boxed letters and figures. Where these letters and figures appear against the name of a state, it is understood that such legislation is to be found upon the statute books of the state, and reference is given to the specific acts or statutes embodying it. Conditioning clauses are noted where significant. To emphasize the chronological sequence of the acts, reference is made for statutes subsequent to 1910 to the collections of session laws of the various years rather than to compilations or codifications that have been made since that date.

In legal citations, where the year is given, the reference is to the public or session laws of that year. The usual abbreviations for the states are used.

am. Amending
ch. Chapter

no. Number
p. Page

ALA. *Code: Code of 1907.*

ARK. *S. & H.: Sandels and Hill, Digest of Arkansas Statutes, 1894.*

ARIZ. *P. C.: Penal Code, 1901.*

CAL. *P. C.: Penal Code. C. C.: Civil Code.*

COLO. *Mills Supp.: Mills' Annotated Statutes, Supplement of 1905.*
Mills: Mills Annotated Statutes.

CONN. *G. L.: General Laws of 1902.*

DEL. *R. C.: Revised Code of 1893.*

D. C. References are to Federal Laws.

FLA. *R. S.: Revised Statutes of 1906.*

GA. *Code: Code of 1895.*

IDAHO *P. C.: Penal Code of 1901.*

ILL. *S. & C.: Starr and Curtiss, Annotated Statutes of 1896.*
J. & A.: Jones and Addington, Supplement to Starr and Curtiss, 1903.

IND. *Burns: Burns' Annotated Statutes, 1908.*

IOWA *Code: of 1897.*

KANS. *G. S.: General Statutes of 1905.*

KY. *Stat.: Statutes of Kentucky, 1909.*

LA. *R. L.: Revised Laws of 1904.*

ME. *R. S.: Revised Statutes.*

MD. *P. G. L.: Public General Laws of 1904.*

MASS. *R. L.: Revised Laws of 1902.*

MICH. *C. L.: Compiled Laws of 1905.*

MISS. *Code: Code of 1906.*

MO. *A. S.: Annotated Statutes of 1906.*

MONT. *P. C.: Penal Code of 1907.*

NEB. *C. S.: Cobbey's Annotated Statutes of 1903.*

NEV. *C. L.: Compiled Laws of 1900.*

N. H. *P. L.: Public Laws of 1901.*

N. J. *G. S.: General Statutes of 1895.*

N. M. *C. L.: Compiled Laws of 1907.*

N. Y. *P. C.: Penal Code.*
C. & G.: Cummings and Gilbert, General Laws.

N. C. *R.: Revisal of 1905.*

N. D. *P. C.: Penal Code of 1899.*

OHIO *R. S.: Revised Statutes of 1906.*

OKLA. *G. S.: General Statutes of 1908.*

ORE. *B. & C.: Ballinger and Cotton, Codes and Statutes, 1901.*

PA.

R. I. *G. L.: General Laws of 1896.*

S. C. *Crim. Code: Criminal Code of 1902.*

S. D. *Code: Code of 1903.*

TENN. *Code: Code of 1896.*

TEX. *P. C.: White's Annotated Penal Code of 1901.*

UTAH. *C. L.: Compiled Laws of 1907.*

VT. *P. S.: Public Statutes of 1906.*

VA. *Code: Code of 1904.*

WASH. *Ball. Supp.: Supplement of 1903 to Ballinger's Code of 1897.*
Ball. Code: Ballinger's Code of 1897.

W. VA. *Code: Code of 1906.*

WIS. *S. & B.: Sanborn and Berryman's Revised Statutes of 1898.*
S. & S.: Sanborn and Sanborn's Revised Statutes (1899-1906).

WYO. *R. S.: Revised Statutes, 1899.*

APPENDIX I

SUMMARY OF STATE LAWS FOR ANIMAL PROTECTION

(*Through the Legislative Sessions of 1922*)

I

DEFINITIONS

(a) " Animal ": any living creature other than man.

(b) " Torture ", " Torment ", " Cruelty ": every act, omission or neglect causing or permitting unnecessary or unjustifiable pain, suffering or death.

(c) " Owner ", " Person ": corporations included; acts of agents or employees of corporations include the corporation in legal liability incurred.

ALA.
ARK.   (a) (b) (c) *S. & H.*, sec. 1531.
ARIZ.
CAL.   (a) (b) (c) *P. C.*, sec. 599b.
COLO.   (a) (b) (c) *Mills*, sec. 117.
CONN.   (a) *G. L.*, sec. 2815.
DEL.   (a) Reads: " pigeons and all brute creatures ": *R. C.*, vol. 14, ch. 414, sec. 6, p. 403.
D. C.   (a) (c) *1892*, Act of June 25, sec. 31.
FLA.   (a) (b) (c) *R. S.*, sec. 3156.
GA.   (b) *Code*, sec. 705.
IDAHO   (a) (b) *1909*, p. 175.
IOWA
KANS.
KY.
LA.
ME.
MD.   (a) (b) *P. G. L.*, art. 27, sec. 68.
MASS.   (a) (b) (c) *1914*, ch. 669.
MICH.   (a) (c) *C. L.*, sec. 11748.
MINN.   (a) (b) *R. L.*, sec. 5151.
MISS.

MO.
MONT.
NEB.
NEV.
N. H.
N. J.
N. M.
N. Y.   (a) (b) *P. C.*, sec. 669.
N. C.
N. D.
OHIO   (a) (b) (c) *R. S.*, sec. 3721.
OKLA.
ORE.
PA.
R. I.   (a) (c) *G. L.*, ch. 114, sec. 7.
S. C.   (a) (c) *Civil Code*, sec. 2126; see also *Crim. Code*, sec. 630.
S. D.   (a) (b) (c) *1903*, ch. 9, sec. 13.
TENN.   (a) (b) (c) *Code*, sec. 2870.
TEX.   (a) (b) *1913*, ch. 88, sec. 12.
UTAH   (a) (c) *C. L.*, sec. 4459.
VT.   (a) (c) *P. S.*, sec. 5808.
VIR.
WASH.   (a) (b) (c) *Ball. Supp.*, sec. 7411.
W. VA.   (a) (b) (c) *1919*, ch. 118.
WIS.
WYO.   (a) (b) (c) *R. S.*, sec. 2287.

II

Offenses Forbidden Under Penalty
General Neglect

(a) Overloading, overdriving, unnecessary or unjustifiable beating, killing, mutilating or maiming.

(b) Failure to provide necessary and proper food, drink and shelter.

(1) Outsider may provide food, etc., after reasonable time.

(2) Expense chargeable to owner, and a lien on animals cared for.

(3) Immunity from prosecution for entry.

ALA.   (a) *Code*, sec. 6233.
            (b) *ibid.*

ARK.   (a) *S. & H.*, secs. 1516, 1521.
     (b) *ibid.* To impounded animal: *S. & H.*, sec. 1518.
       (1) 12 hrs., (2), (3) *S. & H.*, sec. 1519.

ARIZ. (a) *P. C.*, pt. i, title xiv, ch. 13, par. 537, am. by *1907*, ch. 4.
     (b) *ibid.*

CAL.   (a) *P. C.*, sec. 597. " Cruelly " struck out, so that any use,
       when unfit, is punished: *1909.*
     (b) *P. C.*, sec. 597.
       (1), (2), (3) *P. C.*, sec. 597e.

COLO. (a) *Mills*, sec. 104.
     (b) *ibid.* To impounded animal: *Mills*, sec. 105. Certain
       wild animals: *1909*, ch. 167.
       (1) 12 hrs., (2), (3) *Mills*, sec. 106.
       State Bd. of Stock Inspectors may relieve range stock;
       animals may be sold after 30 days: *1909*, ch. 210;
       1913, ch. 152.
       Person entitled to lien on animal may sell same after
       giving due notice to owner and proper publicity to
       sale: *Mills*, sec. 114, am. by *1907*, ch. 116.

CONN. (a) *G. L.*, sec. 1331.
     (b) *ibid.*
       (1) *G. L.*, sec. 1375. Agents of Conn. Hum. Soc.:
       G. L., secs. 2808-2810.
       (2) *G. L.*, sec. 1375.

DEL.   (a) *R. C.*, vol. 14, ch. 414, sec. 1, p. 403.
     (b) *ibid.*

D. C. (a) *1871*, Act of Aug. 23.
     (b) *ibid.*

FLA.   (a) *R. S.*, secs. 3595, 3596.
     (b) *ibid.*

GA.   (a) Cruelty forbidden in very general terms: *Code*, sec. 703.

IDAHO (a) Reads: " Cruelly whips, beats or ill-treats ": *P. C.*, sec.
       5083.
     (b) In enclosure 48 hrs. without food, 24 hrs. without water:
       P. C., sec. 5062; *1909*, p. 175.
       (1) 12 hrs.: *1909*, p. 175.

ILL.   (a) *S. & C.*, p. 1261.
     (b) *ibid.*

IND.   (a) Docking of lambs, dehorning of cattle, and clipping of
       horses specifically excepted: *Burns*, sec. 2499.
     (b) *ibid.*

IOWA   (a) *1907*, ch. 174.
        (b) *ibid.* To impounded animal: *Code*, secs. 2338, 4972.
           (1) 12 hrs., (2) *Code*, secs. 2338, 4972.

KANS.   (a) Reads: " Maim, beat or torture any horse, ox or other cattle ": *G. S.*, sec. 2348; see also secs. 3180, 2418.
        (b) See *G. S.*, sec. 2418.

KY.   (a) *Stat.*, sec. 3167.

LA.   (a) Reads: " Beat, maim, disable, starve ": *R. L.*, sec. 816.

ME.   (a) *R. S.*, ch. 125, secs. 34, 51; ch. 128, sec. 1, am. by *1907*, ch. 23. " Dog " added: *1909*, ch. 208.
        (b) *R. S.*, ch. 125, sec. 53, am. by *1905*, ch. 113. " Keeping or leaving sheep on barren islands of coast " during Dec., Jan., Feb., Mar., *prima facie* evidence of abandonment: *R. S.*, ch. 125, secs. 34, 51.
           (1), (2), (3) *R. S.*, ch. 125, secs. 34, 51.

MD.   (a) Cruelty in any form: *P. G. L.*, art. 27, sec. 67.

MASS.   (a) *R. L.*, ch. 212, secs. 70, 71.
        (b) *ibid.*
           (1), (2) Owner must be notified; period of care not to exceed 60 days, this applies in any case where animals are taken: *R. L.*, ch. 212, sec. 74.

MICH.   (a) *C. L.*, sec. 11739.
        (b) *ibid.*
           (1), (2) Officer or humane agent: *1913*, no. 321.

MINN.   (a) *R. L.,* sec. 5152.
        (b) *ibid.*
           (1) " Or animal exposed in cold ", officer may relieve, (2) *R. L.*, sec. 5160, am. by *1907*, sec. 398.

MISS.   (a) *Code*, secs. 1091, 1092, 1094.
        (b) *ibid.*

MO.   (a) *A. S.*, sec. 2298; see also sec. 1988.
        (b) *A. S.*, sec. 2298. To impounded animal; sec. 2299.

MONT.   (a) *P. C.*, sec. 8774.
        (b) *P. C.*, sec. 8776. To impounded animal: *P. C.*, sec. 8774. Sheep: *1909*, ch. 116.

NEB.   (a) *C. S.*, sec. 2129, am. by *1905*, ch. 185. " Maltreat " added: *1911*, p. 174. To pluck feathers from live fowl, or expose animal tied on street for more than 4 hrs. at time: *C. S.*, sec. 2128.
        (b) *C. S.*, sec. 2130. To impounded animal: *C. S.*, sec. 2132.
           (1) 24 hrs., (2), (3) *C. S.*, sec. 2132.

NEV.   (a) Or pluck feathers from live bird or fowl: *C. L.*, sec. 4873; see also secs. 4874, 4875.

N. H.   (a) *P. L.*, ch. 267, sec. 1; see also ch. 266, sec. 13.

N. J.   (a) *G. S.*, p. 34, sec. 17; p. 36, sec. 29; p. 1068, sec. 102; p. 1098, sec. 258.
   (b) *ibid.*   To impounded animal: *G. S.*, p. 35, sec. 20.
      (1) 12 hrs., (2) 20% additional, (3) *G. S.*, p. 35, sec. 26.

N. M.   (a) *C. L.*, sec. 1134.
   (b) *ibid.*

N. Y.   (a) *P. C.*, sec. 655. Unjustifiably running a horse attached to a vehicle; a resident leaving the State to elude this is punishable as if the act were done in the state: *P. C.*, secs. 666, 667.
   (b) To impounded animal: *P. C.*, sec. 657.
      (1), (3) *C. & G.*, *1867*, ch. 375, sec. 4.

N. C.   (a) *R.*, sec. 3300.
   (b) To impounded animal: *R.*, sec. 3311.

N. D.   (a) *P. C.*, sec. 7560.
   (b) Or hitch uncovered in cold storm, or in night time; all incorporated municipalities with water supply must furnish water in troughs, May 1, to Nov. 1; diseased animals must not be watered at such: *P. C.*, sec. 7560.
      (1), (2) Officer may provide: *P. C.*, sec. 7560, am. by *1911*, ch. 2.

OHIO   (a) *R. S.*, sec. 6951. "Overworks" added: *1910*, p. 118.
   (b) *R. S.*, sec. 6951.
      (1), (2), (3) *R. S.*, sec. 3725.

OKLA.   (a) *G. S.*, sec. 1466.
   (b) *ibid.*   To impounded animal: *G. S.*, sec. 1468.

ORE.   (a) *B. & C.*, sec. 1943.

PA.   (a) *1860*, Act of March 31; *1869*, Act of March 29; *1903*, Act of April 24. Dehorning of cattle legalized: *1895*, Act of June 25.
   (b) *1911*, p. 654.
      (1), (2) Officer may relieve and has lien: *1911*, p. 654.

R. I.   (a) *G. L.*, ch. 114, sec. 1, am. by *1898*, ch. 548.
   (b) *ibid.*
      (1) Officer or agent of R. I. S. P. C. A., (2) *G. L.*, ch. 114, sec. 4.

S. C.   (a) *Crim. Code*, secs. 623-625.
   (b) *ibid.*

S. D. (a) Also tight check-rein, and riding or working 6 consecutive hours without food: *1903*, ch. 9, sec. 5; see also *Civil Code,* secs. 1397, 2319.

(b) *1903*, ch. 9, sec. 5. To impounded animal: *1903*, ch. 9, sec. 8.

(1) 12 hrs., (2), (3) *1903*, ch. 9, sec. 8.

TENN. (a) *Code*, sec. 2875. "Any act of furtherance of cruelty": *Code*, sec. 2863.

(b) *Code*, sec. 2875; see also secs. 2859, 2860.

(1), (2), (3) *Code*, secs. 2859, 2860.

TEX. (a) "Wilful killing or wounding or poisoning or abuse of any animal": *P. C.*, art. 787, am. by *1901*, ch. 121; *1913*, ch. 88, sec. 1.

(b) To impounded animal: *1913*, ch. 88, sec. 2.

(1) Officer or agent of hum. soc.; any person may relieve impounded animal after 12 hrs.; (2), (3) *1913*, ch. 88, secs. 3, 6, 7.

UTAH (a) *C. L.*, sec. 4453; see also sec. 4428.

(b) Animals on the range excepted: *C. L.*, sec. 4453.

In any case of cruelty peace officer may take and deliver animals to pound master; owner is chargeable for expense: *C. L.*, sec. 4456.

VT. (a) *P. S.*, sec. 5809.

(b) *ibid.*

Anti-cruelty laws applied to unorganized towns and gores: *1908*, no. 164.

VIR. (a) *Code*, sec. 3796a, cl. 1. Reckless driving of a hired horse: *Code*, sec. 3797.

(b) *Code*, sec. 3796a, cl. 1.

(1) agents of hum. soc., (2) notice must be given before sale: *Code*, sec. 3796a, cls. 6, 7, 8.

WASH. (a) Also driving with too tight check-rein or with chafing harness, or at night after 6 consecutive hours without food: *Ball. Supp.*, sec. 7411.

(b) Also when impounded: *Ball. Supp.*, sec. 7411.

(1) 24 hrs., (2), (3) *Ball. Supp.*, sec. 7411.

Cutting off more than half of ear or ears of a domestic animal: *Ball. Code*, sec. 7410. Cruel plucking or killing of fowl: *Ball. Code*, sec. 7407.

W. VA. (a) *Code*, sec. 4365.

(b) Also when impounded: *ibid.*

(2) Animal and attached vehicle: *Code*, secs. 501, 502.

WIS.   (a) *S. & S.*, sec. 4445, am. by *1913*, ch. 473.
            (b) *S. & S.*, sec. 4445.
WYO.   (a) *R. S.*, sec. 2274; see also sec. 5118. Dehorning cattle not
            cruelty: *R. S.*, sec. 2288.
            (b) *R. S.*, sec. 2274. To impounded animal: *R. S.*, sec. 2275.
                (1) 12 hrs., (2), (3) *R. S.*, sec. 2276.

III

OFFENSES FORBIDDEN UNDER PENALTY
TRANSPORTATION OF ANIMALS

(a) In vehicle or otherwise with legs tied or crowded in
other ways.
    (1) Peace officer may take charge and provide for care
    of such animals. Expense chargeable to owner and
    a lien on the animals.
(b) Livestock in transit on boats and railroads must be
unloaded, rested, fed and watered every A hours for a period
of B hours. When railroad so provides, expense is chargeable to owner and is a lien on animals.
    (1) Exception made in case of accident or unavoidable
    circumstances. (2) Exception made where space,
    opportunity for rest, etc., is provided on cars. (3)
    Sheep need not be unloaded at night if within 36 hr.
    period.
    (4) Average speed of C miles per hr. must be maintained.
    (5) Animals to be unloaded within D hours of arrival.

ALA.
ARK.   (a) *S. & H.*, sec. 1520.
                (1) *ibid.*
ARIZ.
CAL.   (a) *P. C.*, sec. 597a; see also *1905*, ch. 472.
                (1) *ibid.*
            (b) A = 36 hrs., B = 10 hrs.: *P. C.*, sec. 369b.
COLO.   (a) *Mills*, sec. 104.
                (1) Officer of Col. Hum. Soc.: *Mills*, sec. 110.
            (b)
                (4) C = 10 mi. per hr., accidents excepted: *1910*, ch. 5,
                sec. 21, am. by *1921*, ch. 68.
                (5) D = 2 hrs.: *ibid.*

CONN.   (a) *G. L.*, sec., 1331.
           (b) A = 28 hrs., B = 5 hrs.: *G. L.*, sec. 1336.
                (2) *ibid.*

DEL.   (a) *R. C.*, vol. xiv, ch. 414, secs. 2, 3.
                (1) *ibid.*

D. C.   (a) *1871*, Act of Aug. 23.

FLA.   (a) *R. S.*, secs. 3595, 3596.
           (b) *R. S.*, secs. 3397, 3398.
                (1) Vessels detained by storm excepted: *ibid.*

GA.

IDAHO   (a) *1895*, p. 40; *1909*, p. 175.

ILL.   (a) *S. & C.*, p. 1261.
           (b) A = 36 hrs., B = 5 hrs.: *S. & C.*, p. 1261, am. by *1907*,
                p. 264.
                (1) *ibid.*

IND.   (a) *Burns*, sec. 2502.
           (b) A = 28 hrs., but extended to 36 hrs. on shipper's request;
                B = 5 hrs.: *Burns*, sec. 2503, am. by *1913*, ch. 248.
                (1), (3) *ibid.*

IOWA   (a) *1907*, ch. 174.
           (b) A = 28 hrs., B = 5 hrs.: *Code*, sec. 4970.
                (1), (2) *ibid.*
                (4) Must be carried at "highest practicable speed";
                    Bd. of Ry. Com'rs. to judge: *1907*, ch. 115, am. by
                    1913, ch. 180.

KANS.   (a) *G. S.*, sec. 2419.
           (b) Following provision only—must be carried at a rate not
                less than 15 mi. per hr., not including stops for feeding:
                1907, ch. 276, am. by *1909*, ch. 191.

KY.

LA.

ME.   (a) *R. S.*, ch. 125, sec. 34.
           (b) A = 28 hrs; time limit for unloading; animals may be
                seized for violation of law; cars must be boarded in in
                winter: *R. S.*, ch. 125, secs. 41-47, am. by *1909*, ch. 135.
                (1), (3) *ibid.*
                (4) Animal freight in transit must have preference
                    over other freight: *ibid.*

MD.

MASS.   (b) A = 28 hrs: *R. L.*, ch. 212, sec. 73.
                (2) *ibid.*

240 APPENDIX I [240

MICH.   (a) *C. L.*, sec. 11741; *1913*, no. 321.
          (1) *1913*, no. 321.
        (b) A = 28 hrs., B = 5 hrs.: *C. L.*, sec. 11742.
          (1), (2) *ibid.*
          (4) Animal freight in transit must have preference over other freight: *1913*, no. 389.

MINN.   (a) *R. L.*, sec. 5153.
        (b) A = 24 hrs.: *R. L.*, sec. 5153; see also sec. 2025.
          (5) D = 5 hrs.: *1919*, ch. 322.
        Stockyards at terminal market points must have sanitary watering and feeding troughs: *1919*, ch. 231.

MISS.   (a) *Code,* sec. 1096.

MO.   (a) *A. S.*, sec. 2298.

MONT.   (a) P. C., sec. 8777.

NEB.   (b) A = 28 hrs.: *C. S.*, sec. 2133.
          (1), (2), (3) *ibid.*
          (4) C = 18 mi. per hr. except on short branch lines where C = 12 mi. per hr.: *1905*, ch. 107.
          (5) D = 90 min.: *1905*, ch. 5, am. by *1911*, ch. 2.
        Rys. must maintain sheds for large shipments of hogs; *1911*, ch. 90.

NEV.   (a) *C. L.*, sec. 6873.
          (1) *ibid.*
        (b) A = 36 hrs., B = 5 hrs.: *1903*, ch. 94.
          (1) *ibid.*

N. H.   (a) *P. L.*, ch. 267, sec. 3.
          (1) *ibid.*
        (b) *P. L.*, ch. 267, secs. 4, 5, 6.

N. J.   (a) *G. S.*, p. 35, secs. 19, 24.
          (1) If sold, due notice of sale must be given: *ibid.*

N. M.

N. Y.   (a) *P. C.*, sec. 659.
        (b) A = 28 hrs., B = 5 hrs.: *P. C.*, sec. 663, am. by *1916*, ch. 173.
          (1) *ibid.*

N. C.   (a) *R.*, sec. 3302.
          (1) *ibid.*

N. D.   (b)
          (4) C = 20 mi. per hr.: *1903*, ch. 144.
        Person bedding or feeding stock on cars must not be interfered with: *1901*, ch. 22.

OHIO   (b) A = 24 hrs.; *R. S.*, sec. 6951.

OKLA. (a) *G. S.*, sec. 1469.

ORE. (a) *B. & C.*, sec. 1943.
 (b) A = 28 hrs., but extended to 36 hrs. on shipper's request; B = 5 hrs.: *B. & C.*, secs. 4306-4308.
  (1), (2), (3) *ibid.*
  (4) C = 12 mi. per hr. on long distances, 8 mi. per hr.
  on short, for large lots: *1911*, ch. 136.

PA. (a) *1869*, Act of March 29.
  (1) *ibid.*

R. I. (a) *G. L.*, ch. 114, secs. 3, 4.
  (1) Officer or agent of R. I. S. P. C. A.: *ibid.*
 (b) A = 28 hrs., but extended to 36 hrs. on shipper's request;
 B = 5 hrs.: *G. L.*, ch. 114, sec. 4.
  (1), (2) *ibid.*
  (5) D = 2 hrs., with exceptions: *1916*, no. 475.
 Animals must not be loaded more than 2 hrs. before departure: *ibid.*

S. C. (a) *Crim. Code*, sec. 626.
 (b) A = 28 hrs., B = 5 hrs.: *Crim. Code*, sec. 627; see also
 Civil Code, sec. 2125.
  (1), (2) *ibid.*

S. D. (a) *1903*, ch. 9, sec. 7.

TENN. (a) *Code*, secs. 2852, 2861.
  (1) *ibid.*

TEX. (a) Birds or poultry: *1913*, ch. 88, secs. 4, 5.
  (1) *ibid.*

UTAH (a) *C. L.*, sec. 4455.

VT. (a) *P. S.*, secs. 5809, 5810.
 (b) A = 28 hrs., B = 5 hrs.: *P. S.*, secs. 5812, 5813.
  (1), (2) *ibid.*
 Rys. must supply covered yards for live stock and running
 water between May and Nov.: *P. S.* secs. 4472-4475.

VIR. (a) *Code*, sec. 3796a, cl. 1.
 (b) Rys. must supply water to cattle in pens: *1920*, ch. 489.

WASH. (a) *Ball. Supp.*, sec. 7411.
  (1) *ibid.*
 (b) A = 48 hrs., B = 2 hrs.: *Ball. Code*, sec. 7403. (This
 is either repealed or supplemented by *Ball. Supp.*, sec.
 7411.)
  (1), (2) *ibid.*

W. VA.   (a) *Code,* sec. 4365.
                    (1) Officer of the W. Va. Hum. Soc.: *Code,* sec. 497.
           (b) Rys. must supply water during transit; fine for neglect:
           1919, ch. 29.

WIS.   (a) *S. & S.,* sec. 4445.
           (b) Following provision only: livestock in transit in mixed
           lots must be properly separated; rys. must feed and
           water unloaded stock detained more than six hours:
           S. & B., sec. 1799a.

WYO.   (a) R. S., sec. 2274.
                    (1) In any case of cruelty: *R. S.,* sec. 2280.

IV

Offenses Forbidden Under Penalty

Disabled, Diseased, Decrepit and Dying Animals

(a) Abandonment forbidden.
    (1) Peace officer may kill abandoned animal on affirma-
        tive judgment of two citizens, (2) One of whom
        must be a veterinarian, (3) One of whom may be
        chosen by owner.
    (4) Attached vehicle to be put in safe custody by officer.
    (5) Expense is chargeable to owner and is a lien on
        vehicle and contents.
(b) Selling or offering for sale.
(c) Use or exposure, or working when unfit for labor.
(d) Refusal to kill such on demand of proper authorities.

ALA.   (a) *Code,* sec. 2833.
                    (1) *ibid.*
           (c) Driving when unfit for labor: *Code,* sec. 6233.

ARK.   (a) *S. & H.,* secs. 1526, 1527.
                    (1) *ibid.*
                    (4) And in any case where an arrest for cruelty is
                    made: *ibid.*
           (b) *S. & H.,* sec. 1522.
           (c) *S. & H.,* sec. 1522.
           (d) *S. & H.,* sec. 1523.

ARIZ.   (c) *1907*, ch. 4.

CAL.   (a) *P. C.*, sec. 597f.
               (1) For which owner cannot be found on officer's initiative : *ibid.*
               (5) Any animal cruelly treated or unfit for labor may be cared for until fit to return to owner : *ibid.*
            (b) Another's : *P. C.*, sec. 596.
            (d) Within 12 hrs; does not apply to animal on owner's premises under proper care : *P. C.*, sec. 599e.

COLO.   (a) *Mills*, sec. 104.
               (1) *Mills*, sec. 113.
               (5) Officer of Col. Hum. Soc. may take charge of abandoned animals and charge expense to owner; this is lien on animals : *Mills*, secs. 111, 112, am. by *1907*, ch. 116.

CONN.   (a) *G. L.*, sec. 2811.
               (1) Agent of Conn. Hum. Soc.: *ibid.*

DEL.   (a) *R. C.*, vol. 14, ch. 414, sec. 2, p. 404. Justice of Peace may order killing and removal; fines and forfeitures go to S. P. C. A. involved : *R. C.*, vol. 16, ch. 382, p. 405.
            (c) *R. C.*, vol. 14, ch. 414, sec. 1, p. 403.

D. C.   (a) *1892*, Act of June 25, sec. 4.
               (1) *ibid.*
               (4) *ibid.*
               (5) When animal is allowed to lie more than 3 hrs. after notice : *ibid.*
            (c) *1871*, Act of Aug. 23.

FLA.   (a) *R. S.*, secs. 3595, 3596. Such may be destroyed on due notice after proper legal process : *R. S.*, sec. 3159.

GA.   (a) Any person may apply to local justice and kill on his order; such person is still liable to owner for damages : *Code,* sec. 1755.

IDAHO   (a) *1909*, p. 175.
               (1) Or on veterinary surgeon's judgment, or with owner's consent : *ibid.* (Statute adjudged unconstitutional for lack of notice, etc., to owner : 155 *Ill. Appeal Rep.*, 310.)
            (b) Of famished animals, *i. e.*. 48 hrs. without proper food, 20 hrs. without water : *P. C.*, sec. 4749.
            (c) *1909*, p. 175.

ILL.   (a) *S. & C.*, p. 1261.
            (c) *S. & C.*, p. 1261.

IND.   (a) *Burns*, sec. 2505; see also sec. 2502.
               (1) " 3 reputable ", (2), (3) *ibid.*

IOWA   (a) Peace officer may provide for an abandoned animal:
        Code, sec. 2337.   May be destroyed on due notice after
        proper legal process: *Code*, sec. 2339.
        (c) *1907*, ch. 174.

KANS.   (a) *G. S.*, sec. 2420; see also sec. 2419.
            (1) *i. e.*, agent of Hum. Soc. may, provided appraised
            value is not over $5; Soc. must compensate owner
            unless abandonment is wilful, and appraisers must
            be paid by Soc.: *ibid.*
        (c) *G. S.*, sec. 2419.

KY.   (a) *1910*, ch. 23.
            (1) With owner's consent, or on veterinary surgeon's
            judgment: *ibid.*
        (b) "Disabled horse"; humane officer may arrest vender,
        1910, ch. 23.

LA.   (b) At auction; auctioneer's license subject to forfeiture:
        1908, no. 289.

ME.   (a) *R. S.*, ch. 125, sec. 53, am. by 1905, ch. 70; see also *R. S.*,
        ch. 125, sec. 48.   Animal may be destroyed after notice
        and proper legal process: *R. S.*, ch. 125, sec. 49.
        (b) At auction; auctioneer's license subject to forfeiture;
        others fined; sales to hum. soc. for humane killing per-
        mitted: *1917*, ch. 158.

M.D.   (a) *P. G. L.*, art 27, sec. 65.
            (1) *i. e.*, provided appraised value is not over $5;
            hum. soc. must compensate owner unless abandon-
            ment was wilful and cruel: *ibid.*

MASS.   (a) *R. L.*, ch. 96, sec. 13; see also *1907*, ch. 363, am. by
        1915, ch. 125.
            (1) *i. e.*, agent of Mass. S. P. C. A., provided that
            appraised value is not over $5; Soc. must com-
            pensate owner unless abandonment was wilful, and
            must pay appraisers: *ibid.*
        (b) At auction; auctioneer's license subject to forfeiture:
        1906, ch. 185.   Hum. soc. may purchase for human
        killing: *1913*, ch. 281.
        (c) Except to convey for humane purposes: *1906*, ch. 185.
        Worn-out horses of city dpts. to be turned over to Red
        Acre Farm: *1908*, ch. 133.

MICH.   (a) *1913*, no. 321.
        (c) *1913*, no. 321.

MINN.   (a) *R. L.*, sec. 5152.
        Animals with infectious diseases included in anti-cruelty
        law: *R. L.*, sec. 5159.

MISS.   (a) *Code,* sec. 1092.
                (1) " Three respectable citizens "; *ibid.*
                Isolation and killing of glandered animals included in anti-
                cruelty law: *Code,* secs. 1096, 1097.

MO.   (a) " Cruelly abandon to die ": *A. S.,* sec. 2298.
           (b) *A. S.,* secs. 2321, 2322.
           (c) *A. S.,* sec. 2298.

MONT.   (a) *P. C.,* sec. 8775.

NEB.   (a) *C. S.,* sec. 2134.
                (1) Magistrate or chief of police may appoint per-
                son to kill such : *ibid.*

NEV.   (a) *C. L.,* sec. 4873.
                (1) On his own initiative : *ibid.*

N. H.   (a) " Disabled animals ": *P. L.,* ch. 267, sec. 3.
                (1) 3 citizens : *ibid.*
                (5) *ibid.*
           (b) " Sell or exchange ": *1909,* ch. 8.   Or purchase, *1913,*
                ch. 69.

N. J.   (a) *G. S.,* p. 36, sec. 29.

N. M.   (c) *C. L.,* sec. 1138; see also *1899,* ch. 8.

N. Y.   (a) *P. C.,* sec. 656, am. by *1907,* ch. 1921.   Or allow to lie
                in public place more than 3 hrs. after notice : *1922,*
                ch. 260.
                (1) Of with writen consent of owner; Amer. S. P.
                C. A. agent may kill : *P. C.,* sec. 656, am. by *1907,*
                ch. 192; *1922,* ch. 260.
                (4) *P. C.,* sec. 656, am. by *1907,* ch. 192.
                (5) *ibid.*
           (b) *P. C.,* sec. 658.
           (c) *P. C.,* sec. 658.
           (d) *P. C.,* sec. 658.

N. C.

N. D.   (c) *P. C.,* sec. 7560.

OHIO   (a) *R. S.,* sec. 6951.

OKLA.   (a) *G. S.,* sec. 1467.
                (1) *ibid.*
                (4) *ibid.*
                (5) *ibid.*

ORE.   ⌣   (a) *B. & C.,* sec. 1943.
           (c) *B. & C.,* sec. 1943.

PA.   (a) *1913*, no. 308; see also *1869*, Act of March 29.
          (1), (3) *ibid.*
                In any cruelty trial, magistrate may direct killing
                of animal unfit for use: *ibid.*
      (b) *1909*, no. 245.
      (c) *1909*, no. 245.

R. I. (a) *G. L.*, ch. 114, sec. 10.
       (c) *G. L.*, ch. 114, sec. 2.

S. C. (a) *Crim. Code*, sec. 626.
          (1) *Crim. Code*, sec. 663, am. by *1907*, p. 484.
          (4) *ibid.*
          (5) *ibid.*
       (c) *Crim. Code*, sec. 626.

S. D. (a) *1903*, ch. 9, sec. 6.
       (c) *1903*, ch. 9, sec. 6.
       (d) *1903*, ch. 9, sec. 6.

TENN. (a) *Code*, sec. 2866.
          (1) *ibid.*
       Officer may care for any animal of an arrested person and
       deliver same into proper custody: *Code*, sec. 2867.

TEX.   (a) *1913*, ch. 88, sec. 8.
          (1), (3) *ibid.*
       Abandoned animal and personal property may be sold
       after 5 days' public notice if owner be known and 10 days'
       notice if he be unknown: *1913*, ch. 88, secs. 8, 9.

UTAH   (a) *C. L.*, sec. 4455.
          (1) *i.e.*, provided appraised value is not over $5;
              Utah Hum. Soc. must reimburse owner, unless kill-
              ing is necessary because of cruel treatment, and
              must pay appraisers: *C. L.*, sec. 4459x4.
       (c) *C. L.*, sec. 4454.

VT.   (a) *P. S.*, secs. 5809, 5810.

VIR.   (a) Code, sec. 3796a, cl. 5.
          (1) If the two disagree, they must name a third, whose
              judgment is final: *ibid.*

WASH. (a) This covers case of animal in enclosure when owner can-
           not be found: *Ball. Supp.*, sec. 7411.
          (1) Officer must do this on his own initative: *ibid.*
              If animal is allowed to run loose more than three
              hours after owner has been notified, it is considered
              abandoned: *ibid.*
       (c) *Ball. Supp.*, sec. 7411.

W. VA.   (a) Code, sec. 4365.
          (1), (3) Code, secs. 498-500, am. by *1919*, ch. 118.
          (5) Humane officer must take charge of abandoned or
              cruelly treated animal and care for same: *ibid.*
WIS.   (a) *S. & S.*, sec. 4445.
          (b) Hum. soc. may purchase decrepit horse for purpose of
              killing: *1909*, sec. 2636r.
          (c) *S. & S.*, sec. 4445.
WYO.   (a) *R. S.*, secs. 2274, 2281, 2283, 2284.
          (1), (2) *ibid.*
          (4) *ibid.*
          (5) *ibid.*

V

Offenses Forbidden under Penalty
Miscellaneous Offenses

(a) Maliciously killing or maiming another's animal in
any way.

(b) Intentional poisoning or exposure of poison for purposes
of killing.

(c) Animal fighting.

    (1) Property so used subject to seizure, (2) Trainers,
owners, spectators, owners and letters of premises,
punishable.

(d) Trap-shooting at live birds.

(e) Use of dogs as draft animals.

(f) Docking of horses' tails.

    (1) Mutilated condition of tail is *prima facie* evidence of
act, (2) Necessary surgical operations excepted, (3)
Provision for registration of docked horses.

ALA.   (a) Except in case of trespass beyond a lawful fence: *Code,*
              secs. 6230, 6231. Dogs: *Code,* sec. 6234.
          (c) Keeping a cockpit, or fighting cocks in a public place:
              Code, secs. 6467, 6468.
ARK.   (c) *S. & H.*, sec. 1517; see also sec. 1893.
          (2) Spectators by implication only: *ibid.*
ARIZ.   (a) *P. C.*, par. 536. To kill or attempt to kill a licensed
              dog: *1905*, ch. 39.
          (b) Another's, except dogs: *P. C.*, par. 534; see also par. 560.
          (d) *1921*, ch. 167.

CAL.   (a) Wilfully or neglectfully while hunting: *P. C.*, sec. 384a, am. by *1907*, ch. 295.

     (c) Or worrying in any way: *P. C.*, secs. 597b, c, am. by *1907*, ch. 456.

        (2) *ibid.*

     Officer may enter and arrest without warrant: *P. C.*, sec. 597d.

     (f) *P. C.*, secs. 597a, b. c, d, am. by *1907*, ch. 220.

        (1), (2), (3) *ibid.*

     Use of the bristle bur, etc., on horses: *1903*, ch. 129.

COLO.   (b) *Mills*, sec. 1424.

     (c) Also to release any animal to be shot at or pursued by dogs; fines go to Col. Hum. Soc.: *Mills*, sec. 107, 108; *1905*, ch. 99.

        (2) *ibid.*

     (d) *1905*, ch. 99.

     (f) Use of unregistered docked horse *prima facie* evidence; this does not apply to pure-bred stallions or mares brought into State for exhibition: *Mills*, Supp., secs. 119a, b, c, d, and *1905*, ch. 98.

        (1), (3) *ibid.*

CONN.   (a) *G. L.*, sec. 1218.

     (b) *G. L.*, sec. 1218.

     (c) *G. L.*, secs. 1396-1398.

     (f) *G. L.*, secs. 1332, 1333.

        (1) *ibid.*

DEL.   (b) "Another's": *1909*, ch. 244.

     (c) *R. C.*, vol. 14, ch. 414, sec. 1, p. 403.

        (2) *ibid.*

     Betting on cockfight forbidden: *R. C.*, vol. 12, ch. 102, sec. 3, p. 394.

D. C.   (c) *1892*, Act of June 25, sec. 6.

        (2) *ibid.*

     (f) *1892*, Act of June 5, sec. 5.

FLA.   (a) Even when driving from one's premises where proper fence is lacking: *R. S.*, secs. 3390-3392, 3398.

     (b) *R. S.*, secs. 3390-3392, 3398. Phosphate plants must guard against injury to animals by proper fences: *R. S.*, sec. 3394.

     (c) Between man and animal: *R. S.*, sec. 3253.

     A person cruel to another's animal is liable to usual penalties and added damages: *R. S.*, secs. 3157, 3402.

GA.   (c) Promoting cockfighting in any way or betting on same: *Code*, sec. 412.

IDAHO   (a) Or cruelly beat or injure one's own: *P. C.,* secs. 5081,
         5082; *1909,* p. 175.
         (b) *P. C.,* secs. 5081, 5082; *1919,* ch. 145.
         (c) Dog or cock: *P. C.,* sec. 4777.
             (2) *ibid.* Spectators included; sheriff may enter:
             1909, p. 175
         (f) *1909,* p. 175.

ILL.   (a) *S. & C.,* p. 1326.
         (b) Does not cover exposure of poison for sheep-killing
         dogs: *S. & C.,* p. 1326.
         (c) *S. & C.,* p. 1262.
             (2) *ibid.*
         (d) *1905,* p. 77.
         (f) *S. & C.,* p. 413.
             (2) *ibid.*

IND.   (a) *1913,* ch. 61.
         (b) "Administering": *Burns,* sec. 2322.
         (c) *Burns,* secs. 2501, 2504.
             (1) *Burns,* sec. 2504; (2) *Burns,* sec. 2501.
         (d) Or animals: *Burns,* sec. 2501.

IOWA   (c) Or exhibiting pictures of fight: *Code,* secs. 4971, 4973-
         4975.
             (2) Spectators by implication: *ibid.*
         (d) *1904,* ch. 96.
         (f) *1904,* ch. 135. "Except horses and colts used for breed-
         ing and show purposes": *1917,* ch. 341.

KANS.   (a) *G. S.,* secs. 2179, 2180. Owner may recover for mali-
         cious killing of dog: *1913,* ch. 331.
         (b) *G. S.,* secs. 2179, 2180.

KY.   (a) *Stat.,* secs. 3164, 3165. "Tame deer": *Stat.,* sec. 3169.
         (b) *Stat.,* secs. 3164, 3165. "Dogs": *Stat.,* sec. 358.
         (c) *Stat.,* sec. 3667.
             (2) Spectators included only as "bettors": *ibid.*

LA.   (a) *R. L.,* sec. 815; see also *R. L.,* p. 369.

ME.   (a) *R. S.,* ch. 128, sec. 1, am. by *1907,* ch. 83, am. by *1909,* ch.
         134.
         (b) *R. S.,* ch. 128, sec. 1., am. by *1907,* ch. 83. "Dog" in-
         serted; "of domestic animals", raised to felony; others
         remain misdemeanor: *1909,* ch. 208.
         (c) Officers may enter to arrest: R. S., ch. 125, secs. 37, 38, 39.
             (1), (2) *ibid.*
         (f) Proceeds from fines go to Maine State S. P. C. A.: *R. S.,*
         ch. 125, sec. 52.

Traps set for animals must be visited once in 24 hrs. and trapped animals removed: *1907*, ch. 160.

Exhibition of bears except in menagerie: *R. S.*, ch. 125, sec. 40.

Preparation of or participation in movie film involving cruelty to animals: *1921*, ch. 53.

MD.   (a) Cattle: *P. G. L.*, art. 27, sec. 73.

MASS.   (a) *R. L.*, ch. 208, sec. 98.

(b) *R. L.*, ch. 208, sec. 98. " Or entice away or attempt to poison a dog ": *1913*, ch. 551.

(c) Officers have right of entry and search: *R. L.*, ch. 212, secs. 79, 82-86. Warrants on complaint to search houses where birds or dogs are kept or trained for fighting: *1918*, ch. 99.

   (1), (2) *R. L.*, ch. 212, secs. 79, 82-86.

(d) *R. L.*, ch. 212, sec. 78.

(f) *R. L.*, ch. 212, sec. 72.

To set steel traps with teeth jaws, or with more than 6 in. spread, or to fail to visit traps once in 24 hrs.: *1913*, ch. 626.

MICH.   (b) Except for rats: *C. L.*, 11598.

(c) *C. L.*, secs. 11740, 11743, 11744; *1899*, no. 234.

   (1), (2) *ibid.*

(d) Permitted if birds are killed at once: *C. L.*, secs. 11740, 11743, 11744; *1899*, no. 234.

(f) *1901*, no. 45, sec. 1; *1905*, no. 322.

   (1), (2), (3) *ibid.*

MINN.   (b) *R. L.*, sec. 5157; see also *1905*, ch. 53.

(c) *R. L.*, secs. 5154, 5158.

   (1), (2) Owner of premises included: *ibid.*

Between Nov. 1 and May 7, clipped horses must be blanketed when standing in unsheltered place: *R. L.*, sec. 5155.

MISS.   (a) Or one's own: *Code*, sec. 1099.

(c) Duty of officer to enter and arrest: *Code*, sec. 1093.

   (2) *ibid.*

(d) *Code*, sec. 1098.

MO.   (a) *A. S.*, secs. 1986, 1987.

(b) *A. S.*, secs. 1986, 1987.

(c) *A. S.*, sec. 2300.

   (1), (2) *ibid.*

MONT.   (a) *P. C.*, sec. 8781.

(b) Another's: *P. C.*, sec. 8778.

(c) *P. C.*, sec. 8780.

   (2) *ibid.*

NEB.   (a) *C. S.*, secs. 2124-2127.
         (b) *C. S.*, secs. 2124-2127.
         (c) Bull or bear-baiting: *C. S.*, sec. 2136. Cock-fighting: *C. S.*, sec. 2137.
         (d) *C. S.*, sec. 2375j, k.
         (f) *C. S.*, sec. 3295.
         Pitfalls and old wells must be filled to avoid danger to animals: *C. S.*, sec. 3225.
         Leaving team hitched in unclement weather for 2 hrs.: *1911*, ch. 174.

NEV.   (b) Exposing for another's dog: *1903*, ch. 24.
         (c) *C. L.*, secs. 4873-4875.
             (1), (2) *ibid.*

N. H.   (b) *P. L.*, ch. 266, sec. 15.
         (c) *P. L.*, ch. 271, secs. 19, 20.
             (2) *Ibid.*
         (d) *P. L.*, ch. 267, sec. 7.
         (f) *1907*, ch. 39.
             (1), (2) *ibid.*

N. J.   (a) *G. S.*, p. 1068, sec. 101; p. 1074, sec. 138.
         (c) *G. S.*, p. 35, sec. 27; p. 36, sec. 18; p. 1791, sec. 22.
             (1), (2) *ibid.*
         (d) *1904* (special sess.), ch. 1.
         (e) Cart with contents also subject to seizure: *G. S.*, p. 36, secs. 28, 29.
         To drive horse or beast of burden on public highway when intoxicated: *1917*, ch. 201.
         To sell feed for livestock in bags with tags attached by metal fasteners: *1920*, ch. 121.

N. M.   (a) *C. L.*, secs. 1135-1137. Dog, cat, domesticated fowl or bird: *1912*, ch. 38.
         (b) *C. L.*, secs. 1135-1137.

N. Y.   (b) *P. C.*, sec. 660. " Another's ": *1910*, ch. 81.
         (c) Place may be entered and searched by officer: *P. C.*, secs. 664, 665; *C. & G.*, p. 226; *1875*, chs. 97, 246.
             (1), (2) Spectators by implication only: *ibid.*
         (e) Permitted if license is taken out and number is painted on vehicle: *C. & G.*, p. 1064, sec. 65.

N. C.   (a) In any place not surrounded by a lawful fence, or animals in range: *R.*, secs. 3313, 3314; see also sec. 3504.
         (b) Applies to exposure of poisonous shrubs: *R.*, sec. 3318.
         (c) *R.*, sec. 3301.
             (2) *ibid.*
         Traps for wild animals must be enclosed so as to safeguard domestic animals: *1909*, ch. 436.

N. D.   (a) Or torture or beat one's own: *P. C.,* sec 7559
(b) Another's: *P. C.,* sec. 7558.
(c) *P. C.,* sec. 7561. Or maliciously instigate a fight between animals; officer must arrest offender if bidden by a citizen: *P. C.,* secs. 7562, 7563.
  (2) Spectators by implication only: *P. C.,* sec. 7561.

OHIO   (a) *R. S.,* secs. 3723, 6850, 6851.
(b) *R. S.,* sec. 6852; see also secs. 4212-1, 4214, 6863, 6856-1; *1919,* p. 1231.
(c) *R. S.,* secs. 6952, 6952-1.
  (1), (2) *ibid.*
(d) *R. S.* sec. 6952-2.
(f) Or pulling of hairs from mane or withers: *R. S.,* sec. 6951-1.
  (2) *ibid.*
Township trustees may maintain watering troughs on highways: *1919,* p. 65.

OKLA.   (a) *G. S.,* sec. 1856.
(b) *G. S.,* sec. 1470.
(c) *G. S.,* secs. 1740, 1741.
  (2) Spectators included by implication: *ibid.*

ORE.   (a) *B. & C.,* secs. 1814, 1815.
(b) *B. & C.,* secs. 1814, 1815. Placing of poisoned grains for birds: *1913,* ch. 232, secs. 24, 29. Poison may be placed in enclosed premises by owner between sunset and sunrise: *1917,* ch. 22.
(d) *1905,* ch. 76; *1913,* ch. 232, sec. 30.
To cut off more than half of ear of domestic animal: *B. & C.,* secs. 2078, 2079.
To allow barbed wire to lie exposed near livestock: *1921,* ch. 308.
Any helpless or crippled wild bird or animal may be captured for humane purposes: *1913,* ch. 232, sec. 24.

PA.   (a) This does not cover case of animal in act of killing another animal: *1903,* Act of April 24.
(b) *1903,* Act of April 24.
(c) *1869,* Act of March 29; *1872,* Act of April 3; *1876,* Act of April 17.
  (1), (2) *ibid.*
Beating cow's udder or not milking: *1911,* p. 178.
Hours of work for animals limited to 15 in 24, and to 90 in week in any city of 1st or 2nd class: *1913,* no. 438.

R. I.　　(a) (b) "Killing, wounding or poisoning" another's animal;
　　　　　　triple damages: *G. L.*, ch. 279, sec. 22, am. by *1913*, ch.
　　　　　　919.
　　　　　(c) Officers have right of entry: *G. L.*, ch. 114, secs. 11-16,
　　　　　　am. by *1900*, ch. 747, sec. 2; see also *G. L.*, ch. 283,
　　　　　　sec. 15.
　　　　　　　(1) Proceeds from sale of birds go to S. P. C. A. in-
　　　　　　　volved: *ibid.*
　　　　　(d) Also use of premises for such purposes: *G. L.*, ch. 114,
　　　　　　sec. 17.

S. C.　　(a) Includes injuries to another's animals in one's own un-
　　　　　　enclosed fields: *Crim. Code,* secs. 170-174, 180.
　　　　　(c) Cockfighting anywhere in state: *1917*, no. 18; see *Crim.
　　　　　　Code,* sec. 298.
　　　　　　　(1), (2) *ibid.*

S. D.　　(c) Officers may enter where a fight or preparations for
　　　　　　one are in progress: *1903*, ch. 9, secs. 9, 10.
　　　　　　　(2) *ibid.*
　　　　　(f) *1903*, ch. 9, sec. 5.

TENN.　(a) *Code,* secs. 6508-6511.
　　　　　(b) *Code,* secs. 6508-6511.
　　　　　(c) *Code,* sec. 2858.
　　　　　　　(2) *ibid.*
　　　　　Traps must be visited within 36 hrs. after being set: *1913*,
　　　　　ch. 21.

TEX.　　(a) *P. C.*, art. 787, am. by *1901*, ch. 121; see also *P. C.*, art.
　　　　　　786.
　　　　　(b) *P. C.*, art. 787, am. by *1901*, ch. 121.
　　　　　(c) *1907*, ch. 76.
　　　　　　　(1), (2) *ibid.*
　　　　　Dogs may not be killed when worrying stock where fence
　　　　　is insufficient: *P. C.*, art. 799.

UTAH　(a) *C. L.*, secs. 4427, 4428.
　　　　　(b) *C. L.*, secs. 4427, 4428.
　　　　　(c) Dog, cock or bull: *1911*, chs. 120, 123, am. by *1913*, chs.
　　　　　　83, 86; see also *C. L.*, secs. 4454, 4457.
　　　　　　　(1), (2) *ibid.*
　　　　　(f) *C. L.*, secs. 4459-4459x2.
　　　　　　　(1) *ibid.*

VT.　　　(a) *P. S.*, sec. 5815.
　　　　　(b) *P. S.*, sec. 5815.
　　　　　(d) *P. S.*, sec. 5811.
　　　　　Traps must be visited once in 48 hrs.: *P. S.* sec. 5330.

VIR. (a) *Code,* sec. 3724.
      (b) Or one's own to prevent possession by another: *Code,* sec. 3724.
      (c) *1910,* p. 330; see also *Code,* sec. 3792. Between man and animal: *Code,* secs. 3693, 3694.
         (1), (2) *1910,* p. 330.
      (d) *1906,* ch. 254; *1910,* p. 687.

WASH. (a) *Ball. Code,* sec. 7159.
      (b) *Ball. Code,* sec. 7159. When poison is exposed for noxious animals, notice must be given to neighbors: *Ball. Code,* sec. 7279.
      (c) *Ball. Supp.,* sec. 7411.
         (2) Without warrant: *ibid.*
      (f) *Ball. Supp.,* sec. 7411.

W. VA. (a) *Code,* sec. 4265.
      (b) Dogs not included: *Code,* sec. 4265.
      (c) *Code,* sec. 4365.
         (2) *ibid.*

WIS. (a) *S. & S.,* sec. 4445.
      (b) *S. & S.,* sec. 4445.
      (c) *S. & S.,* sec. 4445.
         (2) Spectators not included: *S. & B.,* sec. 4445b.
      (f) *S. & B.,* sec. 4445d.
      Wanton failure to milk a cow: *S. & B.,* sec. 4445a.

WYO. (a) *1909,* ch. 40; see also *R. S.,* sec. 5025.
      (c) *R. S.,* sec. 2277.
         (2) Keeper of fighting place specified only: *ibid.*

VI

OFFENSES FORBIDDEN UNDER PENALTY

VIVISECTION

(a) Exhibition of vivisected animals in public schools forbidden.

(b) Properly conducted experiments permitted only under authority of regularly incorporated medical college.

ALA. (a) *1919,* act. 695.
ARK.
ARIZ.
CAL. (b) *P. C.,* sec. 599c.
COLO.

CONN.

DEL.

D. C.

FLA.

GA.

IDAHO   (b) In medical schools and universities: *1909*, p. 175.

ILL.   (a) *1909*, p. 415; *1911*, p. 395.

IND.

IOWA

KANS.

KY.

LA.

ME.

MASS.   (a) *R. L.*, ch. 42, sec. 21.

MICH.   Unlawful to perform various specified operations without anesthesia: *1907*, on. 244, sec. 6, am. by *1909*, so. 143.

MINN.

MISS.

MO.

MONT.

NEB.

NEV.   Anti-cruelty law shall not apply to such experiments on animals: *C. L.*, sec. 4877.

N. H.

N. J.   (b) *G. S.*, p. 33, sec. 17.

N. M.

N. Y.   (b) *C. & G.*, p. 227; *1886*, ch. 593, sec. 10.

N. C.

N. D.

OHIO.

OKLA.   (a) *G. S.*, sec. 6645.

ORE.

PA.   (a) *1905*, no. 41.
    (b) In scientific schools and where biological products are produced for protection against disease: *1911*, p. 654.

R. I.

S. C.

S. D.   (a) *Political Code*, ch. 22, sec. 144.

TENN.

TEX.

UTAH

VT.

VIR.

WASH.   (a) *Ball. Supp.*, sec. 2457.

          (b) " Regularly incorporated college or university of state ":
          Ball. Supp., sec. 7411.

W. VA.

WIS.   (b) For scientific research: *1913*, ch. 473.

WYO.

VII

POWERS AND DUTIES OF POLICE OFFICERS

(a) May enter building or enclosure where (1) animals are kept for unlawful purposes, (2) law dealing with cruelty to animals is being violated.

(b) Offenders may be arrested without warrant.

(c) Must prosecute all violations of anti-cruelty law coming to their notice.

ALA.   (b) By any person; such person entitled to $2 from fine: *Code*, sec. 6233.

          Counties may employ and pay humane officer: *1911*, p. 112, am. by *1919*, no. 244.

ARK.   (a) (1), (2) On issuance of warrant: *S. & H.*, sec. 1530.

          Any officer may interfere to prevent cruelty: *S. & H.*, sec. 1525; see also sec. 1529.

ARIZ.

CAL.   (a) (1), (2) On issuance of warrant: *P. C.*, sec. 599a.

COLO.   (c) Members of Colo. Hum. Soc. may require any peace officer to arrest offenders or to take charge of abused animals: *Mills*, sec. 116.

CONN.   (a) (1), (2) On issuance of warrant: *G. L.*, sec. 1495.

DEL.   (a) (1) On issuance of warrant; proceeds from sale of captured animals go to Del. S. P. C. A.: *R. C.*, vol. 14, ch. 414, sec. 3, p. 404.

          (b) *R. C.*, vol. 14, ch. 414, sec. 5, p. 403.

D. C.   Commissioners authorized to detail one or more police officers to aid Wash. Hum. Soc.: *1892*, Act of June 25, sec. 2.

FLA. (a) On issuance of warrant: *R. S.*, sec. 4084.
   (b) *R. S.*, secs. 3401, 3158.

GA. Duty of Sheriff to furnish list of offenders to prosecuting officer: *1922*, no. 517.

IDAHO (a) (2) *1909*, p. 175.

ILL. Governor authorized to appoint officer for 2 yr. term at Lake, E. St. Louis and Peoria to enforce humane laws, particularly around stockyards: *S. & C.*, p. 402.

IOWA

IND. (a) (1), (2) *Burns*, sec. 2504; see also sec. 1923.
   (c) *Burns*, sec. 2505.

KANS.

KY. (c) Agent of S. P. C. A. may, police officers must, arrest offenders: *Stat.*, sec. 3257.

LA.

ME. (c) *R. S.*, ch. 125, sec. 53.
   Humane officer appointed by governor on application of county commissioners: *1917*, ch. 36.

MD. (a) (1), (2) On issuance of warrant: *P. G. L.*, art. 27, sec. 66.

MASS. (a) (2) *i.e.* where suspected: *R. L.*, ch. 212, sec. 75.
   (b) *R. L.*, ch. 212, secs. 74, 80.
   (c) *R. L.*, ch. 212, sec. 76.
   Humane agents may inspect places where animals are held for transport or slaughter: *1910*, ch.fl 590.

MICH. (a) (1), (2) On issuance of warrant: *C. L.*, sec. 11744.
   (b) And animals or other property delivered to pound master: *C. L.*, sec. 11743.
   (c) See *C. L.*, secs. 11746, 11747.

MINN.

MISS. (a) (1) *Code*, sec. 1093.

MO.

MONT.

NEB. (b) *C. S.*, sec. 2131.

NEV. (c) *C. L.*, secs. 4868, 4872.

N. H. (b) *P. L.*, ch. 267, sec. 8.
   (c) *P. L.*, ch. 267, sec. 10.

N. J. (a) (1), (2) On issuance of warrant: *G. S.*, p. 35, sec. 25.
   (b) *G. S.*, p. 14, sec. 46.

N. M.

N. Y...

N. C.

N. D.   Governor authorized to appoint human agent; no salary, but his expenses paid: *Pol. Code, secs.* 1586, 1587.

OHIO   Officer or agent or member of humane society may interfere to prevent cruelty: *R. S.,* sec. 3720. May require peace officer to arrest offenders, and take and deliver animals to hum. soc.: *R. S.,* sec. 3722.

OKLA.

ORE.   (a) (2) On issuance of warrant: *B. & C.,* secs. 1705 *et seq.*

PA.   (a) (2) *1911,* p. 654.
                (b) And may remove a sick or disabled animal from any street car: *1891,* Act of June 20.

R. I.   (a) No search may be made after sunset unless authorized by magistrate on satisfactory cause: *G. L.,* ch. 114, sec. 6.
                (b) *G. L.,* ch. 114, sec. 5, am. by *1898,* ch. 548, am. by *1900,* ch. 747, sec. I.
                (c) *G. L.,* ch. 114, sec. 8.

S. C.   (a) (2) On issuance of warrant: *Crim. Code,* sec. 629.
                (b) Animals must be cared for; expense chargeable to owner and lien on animals: *Crim. Code,* sec. 628.
                (c) *Crim Code,* sec. 631.

S. D.

TENN.   (a) On issuance of warrant: *Code,* sec. 2869.

TEX.

UTAH.   (a) (1), (2) On issuance of warrant: *C. L.,* sec. 4457.

VT.   (a) *P. S.,* sec. 5817.
                (b) Owner must be notified and animals cared for at owner's expense: *P. S.,* sec. 5816.
                (c) *P. S.,* sec. 5818.

VIR.   (a) (1), (2) On issuance of warrant; *Code,* sec. 3796a, cl. 4.

WASH.   (a) (1), (2) Warrant necessary except where animals are being fought: *Ball. Supp.,* sec. 7411.
                (b) Only where animals are being fought: *Ball. Supp.,* sec. 7411.
                Members, agents and officers of humane society may prosecute: *Ball. Supp.,* sec. 7411.

W. VA.   (c) Misdemeanor to interfere with humane officer: *1919,* ch. 118.
                Humane officer making arrest and detaining vehicle, has lien on same; may make public sale of animal, after due notice: *1919,* ch. 118.

WIS.   See *1919,* ch. 359.

WYO.   Any officer or agent of Wyo. Hum. Soc. may interfere to prevent cruelty: *R. S.,* sec. 2279; see *1919,* ch. 32.

VIII

Societies for Animal Protection

(a) May be incorporated as agencies for the enforcement of anti-cruelty laws and for other humane purposes.

(b) Officers and agents have powers as peace officers within the scope of the societies' activities.

(c) Officers and agents must have certificates of appointment and wear badges.

(d) Fines imposed for violation of anti-cruelty laws go to S. P. C. A. involved.

ALA.   (b) In counties over 200,000: *1915*, no. 165.

ARK.   (d) *S. & H.*, sec. 1528.

ARIZ.

CAL.   (a) Not new ones that duplicate the style or name of previously existing ones: *1905*, ch. 434, am. by *1913*, ch. 325, 279; see also *1903*, ch. 63 and *1905*, ch. 389.
   (b) Members also when duly authorized: *1905*, ch. 434, am. by *1913*, ch. 279; see also *1903*, ch. 63, and *1905*, ch. 389.
   (c) *1913*, ch. 279.
   (d) *1905*, ch. 434; see also *1903*, ch. 63, and *1905*, ch. 389. These are repealed by *1913*, ch. 325 which provides that an S. P. C. A. may receive not more than $500 per month from county funds in lieu of fines (*vid. supra, p.*——).
   Affecting power of humane officers to carry weapons: *1913*, ch. 279.

COLO.   (b) Members of Colo. Hum. Soc. may interfere to prevent an act of cruelty: *Mills*, sec. 109.
   (c) *Mills* sec. 115.
   (d) Officers to be paid usual fees for services, chargeable as costs to offenders and reimbursed to Soc.: *Mills*, sec. 116.
   Colo. Hum. Soc. constituted a State Bureau of C. & A. Protection: *Mills Supp.*, secs. 416a, b, c, d, e, f, g.

CONN.   For powers and duties of Conn. Hum. Soc., see *G. L.*, sec. 2807.
   (b) Governor to appoint agents of Conn. Hum. Soc. special officers: *1919*, ch. 255, am. by *1921*, ch. 128.
   (d) Conn. Hum Soc. shall receive not more than $2000 annually from State: *G. L.*, sec. 2816.

DEL.

D. C.   Officers and members of Hum. Soc. not to receive witness fees: *1892*, Act of June 25, sec. 1.

FLA.   (a) *R. S.*, secs. 3401, 3158
   (b) *ibid*

GA.   (d) One-half: *Code*, sec. 704.

IDAHO

ILL.   (d) *S. & C.*, pp. 1413, 1414.

        Governor to appoint humane officers. *1877*, Act of March 25, am. by *1885*, Act of June 30, am. by *1905*, p. 76.

IND.   One member of police force in every city is a humane officer — three in cities of 1st Class; this humane officer must attend meetings of humane society where one is or-organized: *Burns,* sec. 8795; *1909,* ch. 120.

IOWA

KY.   (a) *Stat.,* secs. 3258.

KY.   (a) *Stat.,* sec. 3258.

        (b) *ibid.*

        (d) One-half fines: *1912,* ch. 253.

LA.   (a) *R. L.,* p. 222.

        (b) *R. L.,* p. 222; *1914,* no. 28.

        (d) One half: *R. L.,* p. 751. Proceeds of sale of dog tags in New Orleans go to La. S. P. C. A.; *1906,* no. 179, am. by *1908,* no. 201.

        La. S. P. C. A. must catch and impound stray dogs: *1906,* no. 179, am. by *1908,* no. 201.

ME.   (d) Fines are paid into county treasury; allowance is made for expenses of travel and investigation by officers and agents: *R. S.,* ch. 125, sec. 53, am. by *1905,* ch. 107.

MD.   (a) *P. G. L.,* art. 27, secs. 59-61.

        (b) *ibid.*

        (d) One-half: *ibid.*

MASS.   (a) *R. L.,* ch. 125, secs. 1-12; see also *R. L.* ch. 208, sec. 123, and *1906,* ch. 227.

        (b) Governor may appoint Mass. S. P. C. A. agents special police: *1912,* ch. 384.

        (d) After deducting expenses of prosecution, except in case of docking when one-half only is paid to Mass. S. P. C.A.: *R. L.,* ch. 212, secs. 76, 77.

        Agents may inspect places where animals are kept for transport and slaughter: *1912,* ch. 384.

MICH.   (a) *1899,* no. 206; *C. L.,* secs. 8914-8925, 11745; see also sec. 8423, am. by *1907,* no. 132, and *1901,* no. 101.

        (b) Governor may appoint agents at state humane marshals: *1899,* no. 206; *C. L.,* secs. 8914-8925.

MINN.   (a) *R. L.,* sec. 3125. The Minn. S. P. C. constituted a State Bur. of C. & A. Protection: *1905,* ch. 274.

        (b) Minn. S. P.C. may appoint representatives in counties, and an agent at large: *R. L.,* secs. 3125, 3126.

(d) Fees allowed from costs: *R. L.*, sec. 3128. Counties and municipalities may subsidize not more than $2400 a year; this not for salaries: *R. L.*, sec. 3127, am. by *1913*, ch. 31; see also *R. L.* sec. 5154.

MISS.   (d) In cities of 2nd Cl.: *1915*.
2nd Cl. cities have power to prevent cruelty: *ibid*.

MO.   (d) In cities of 2nd Cl.: *1913*, p. 434.

MONT.   St. Bur. of C. & A. Protection: *1903*, ch. 115; see *1909*, ch. 36; *1911*, ch. 127.

NEB.

NEV.   (a) *C. L.*, secs. 4868-4872.
(b) *ibid*.
(c) *ibid*.
(d) *C. L.*, sec. 8766.

N. H.   (a) *1895*, ch. 1, sec. 1; *P. L.*, ch. 267, sec. 9.
(b) *P. L.*, ch. 267, sec. 9.
(d) *P. L.*, ch. 267, sec. 12; *1905*, ch. 24.

N. J.   (a) N. J. S. P. C. A. with district and county societies: *1908*, chs. 118, 119, 120, 148.
(c) Penalty for improper wearing of badge: *G. S.*, pp. 32, 33; see also p. 37, secs. 31, 35.
(d) One-half to N. J. S. P. C. A.: *G. S.*, pp. 32, 33; see also p. 37, secs. 31, 35. Whole fine to county S. P. C. A.s: *1908*, ch. 118. Proceeds of dog-license fees go to district S. P. C. A.s for sheltering dogs found at large unlicensed: *1902*, ch. 22.

N. M.

N. Y.   (a) Amer. S. P. C. A.: *1866*, ch. 469. Other societies, but work must not be duplicated in any county: *C. & G.*, pp. 2290 *et seq*, secs. 70-72; *1905*, ch. 271; *1906*, ch. 489. Additional societies in Yonkers: *1911*, ch. 621.
(b) *P. C.*, sec. 668. After authorization by sheriff: *C. & G.*, p. 2290.
(d) *P. C.*, sec. 668. Humane societies to receive dog-license taxes: *1917*, ch. 161 (superseding *C. & G.*, p. 222 et *seq*; *1894*, ch. 115; *1895*, ch. 412; *1902*, ch. 495; *1911*, ch. 718). Counties authorized to appropriate funds, to require reports and prescribe rules: *1911*, ch. 663.

N. C.

N. D.

OHIO   (a) Ohio Hum. Soc. with local and county branches: *R. S.*, sec. 3714. Local societies: *R. S.*, secs. 3717, 3718.
(b) *ibid*.
(d) *R. S.*, secs. 6908, 6951.

OKLA. State accepts gift of $1000 to be banked for 250 years at 4 per cent; final sum to be used for P. C. A.: *1913*, ch. 69.

ORE.

PA. (d) *1891*, Act of June 9. For sale of infirm horses: *1909*, p. 443. County Com. may appropriate money for local S. P. C. A.: *1921*, ch. 80.

R. I. (a) *1907*, ch. 1446; *1909*, ch. 534.
(b) *1907*, ch. 1446.
(d) *G. L.*, ch. 114, sec. 8.
No recognizance for costs required of any agent of the R. I. S. P. C. A.: *G. L.*, ch. 229, sec. 14, am. by *1896*, ch. 421.

S. C. (d) One-half to S. P. C. A.; fines, costs, etc., are lien on animals involved: *Crim. Code*, secs. 631, 632.

S. D. (a) *1903*, ch. 9, secs. 1, 2, 3, 4.
(b) *ibid.*
(c) *ibid.*

TENN. (a) *Code*, sec. 2864.
(b) *ibid.*
(d) *Code*, sec. 2868. Fines collected in cities and towns of over 36,000 may be turned over to any S. P. C. A.: *1907*, ch. 310.
Counties of 70,000 to 90,000 may pay $50 per month to any officer of S. P. C. A. for his services: *1907*, ch. 57.
City Humane Board established in Nashville: *1909*, ch. 64.

TEX. (a) St. Bur. of C. & A. Prot.: *1913*, ch. 56.
(c) *1913*, ch. 88, sec. 10.
Member of Tex. Hum. Soc. may require officer or agent to make arrests and take possession of cruelly treated animals: *1913*, ch. 88, sec. 11.

UTAH (d) Less expenses of prosecution to Utah Hum. Soc.: *C. L.*, sec. 4459x3.
Hum. Soc. may designate county agents to be appointed by sheriff as dep. sheriffs without compensation: *C. L.*, sec. 4458.

VT. (b) A misdemeanor to interfere with such: *1917*, ch. 237.

VIR. (a) *Code*, sec 3796a, cl. 2.
(b) *ibid.*
(c) *ibid.*
(d) One-half; but name of officer involved must be endorsed to warrant: *Code*, sec. 3796a, cls. 10, 13.

WASH. Only one entitled to privileges of act in each county: *Ball. Supp.*, sec. 7411. A State Hum. Bur.: *1913*, ch. 107.
(b) *Ball. Supp.*, sec. 7411.
(c) *ibid.*
(d) County humane societies: *ibid.* Humane societies receive dog-license tax in cities of 1st, 2nd, 3rd cl.: *1919*, ch. 6.

W. VA.   (b) W. V. Hum. Soc: *Code,* secs. 495, 496.
        W. V. Hum. Soc. is a State Bd. of C. & A. Prot.: *Code,* sec. 15J, am. by *1907*, ch. 40.

WIS.   (b) *S. & B.,* sec. 1636k. Badger Soc. agents given police powers: *1911*, ch. 258.
        (d) Counties may appropriate for anti-cruelty soc. and pay expenses of agent: *1909*, ch. 65; *1913*, ch. 106.
        State Humane Agent: *1919*, ch. 359.

WYO.   (a) Wyo. Hum. Soc. constituted a St. Bur. of C. & A. Prot.: *1907*, ch. 82; *1913*, ch. 99. Superseded by Commissioner of C. & A. Prot.: *1919*, ch. 32.
        (d) *R. S.,* ses. 2278.
        Members of Wyo. Hum. Soc. may require officers to make arrests, take possession of animals, and deliver to proper officers; officers and agents are allowed usual fees: *R. S.,* sec. 2285, 2286.

IX

HUMANE EDUCATION

(a) Instruction in common schools.

(b) Included on programs of normal schools.

ALA.   (a) Time optional with teachers: *1919*, Act. 695.
        (b) *ibid.*

ARK.

ARIZ.

CAL.   (a) *Political Code,* par. 1665. am. in *1921.*

COLO.   (a) 2 lessons not less than 10 min. each per wk.: *Mills Supp.,* sec. 4043.

CONN.   (a) *1921*, ch. 45.

DEL.

D. C.

FLA.   (a) Not less than 30 min. per wk.

GA.

IDAHO

ILL.   (a) Not less than 30 min. per wk.: *1909*, p. 415; *1911*, p. 395.
        (b) *ibid.*

IND.

IOWA

KANS.

KY.   (a) 30 min. per wk. compulsory: *1920*, ch. 74.

LA.

ME.   (a) Not less than 30 min. per wk.: *1917*, ch. 228; see also R. S., ch. 15, sec. 86.

MD.

MASS.

MICH.   (a) A portion of time in all public schools: *1913*, no. 227.

MINN.

MISS.

MO.

MONT.   (a) *Political Code*, sec. 912.

NEB.

NEV.

N. H.   (a) " Prescribed reading course ": *1909*, ch. 49; *1921*, ch. 85.

N. J.

N. M.

N. Y.   (a) Amendment to education law; time to be prescribed by Bd. of Regents: *1917*, ch. 102.
          (b) *1917*, ch. 210.

N. C.

N. D.   (a) 2 lessons of 10 min. each per wk.: *1905*, ch. 108.

OHIO

OKLA.   (a) Not less than 30 min. per wk.: *G. S.*, secs. 6663, 6664.

ORE.   (a) Not less than 30 min. per wk.: *1921*, ch. 410.

PA.   (a) Not more than 30 min. per wk., up to and including 4th grade.: *1905*, no. 41; see also *Laws,* sec 1607.

R. I.

S. C.

S. D.   (a) Not less than 10 min. per wk.: *Code,* ch. 22, sec. 144.

TENN.

TEX.   (a) " Once each week "; *1907*, ch. 169.

UTAH

VT.

VIR.

WASH.   (a) 10 min. per wk.: *1909*, ch. 97, title iii, sec. 2.

W. VA.

WIS.   (a) Not less than 30 min. per month: *1913*, ch. 506; *1917*, ch. 102.

WYO.   (a) 2 lessons not less than 10 min. each per wk.: *1901*, ch. 8.

APPENDIX II

SUMMARY OF STATE LAWS FOR CHILD PROTECTION

(Through the Legislative Sessions of 1922)

I

OFFENSES AGAINST CHILDREN FORBIDDEN UNDER PENALTY
GENERAL

(a) To wilfully cause or permit life or health of any child to be endangered.

(b) To unnecessarily expose to weather.

(c) To cruelly torture or punish.

(d) To neglect or deprive of necessary food, clothing and shelter.

(e) To endanger its morals.

ALA.	
ARK.	(e) Gaming with a minor: *S. & H.,* secs. 1808, 1809.
ARIZ.	(a) *1907,* ch. 12.
CAL.	(a) (c) *P. C.,* sec. 273a.
COLO.	(a) (b) (c) *Mills Supp.,* sec. 411.
CONN.	(a) Child under 16; *1921,* ch. 81.
	(b) (c) (d) *G. S.,* sec. 1160.
	(e) *1921,* ch. 81.
DEL.	(a) (c) *R. S.,* vol. 16, ch. 150, sec. 1.
D. C.	(c) Child under 18: *Code of 1905,* sec. 814.
FLA.	(c) (d) *R. S.,* sec. 3236.
GA.	(a) (b) (c) (d) *1922,* p. 49.
IDAHO	
ILL.	(a) (b) (e) *S. & C.,* pp. 1262-1264.
IND.	Cruel treatment or overworking: *Burns,* sec. 2622.
IOWA	

KANS.   (a) (b) (c) (d) Boy under 14 or girl under 16; search warrant may be issued and child removed: *G. S.*, secs. 4397, 4398. Under 18: sec. 4434.

KY.   (a) (b) Under 16: *Stat.*, sec. 3254.
(c) (d) By parent or guardian: *1916*, no. 139.
(e) *1910*.

LA.

ME.

MD.

MASS.

MICH.   (a) (b) (c) Officer may search on issuance of warrant: *C. L.*, sec. 11507.

MINN.   (a) *R. L.*, sec. 4935.
(c) Under 16, or compel to labor more than 10 hrs. per day: *R. L.*, sec. 4940.
(e) *R. L.*, sec. 4935.

MISS.

MO.   (c) Parent or adopted parent of legitimate or illegitimate child who unlawfully assaults or beats: *1921*, H. B. 334.

MONT.   (c) (d) *P. C.*, sec. 8348.

NEB.   (a) *C. S.*, secs. 1744-1746.
(c) (d) By parent or custodian of child under 16: *1921*, ch. 52; see also *C. S.*, secs. 1744-1746.
(e) *C. S.*, secs. 1744-1746.

NEV.

N. H.   "Habitual cruelty": *P. S.*, ch. 265, sec. 1.

N. J.   (a) (c) *1903*, ch. 59.

N. M.

N. Y.   (a) (e) Under 16 (New York City excepted) : *P. C.*, sec. 289.

N. C.

N. D.

OHIO   (a) (c) (d) *R. S.*, secs. 6984, 6985. Under 18: *1913*, pp. 873-874.
(e) *1913*, pp. 868-873.

OKLA.   (b) (c) (d) *C. S.*, sec. 692.

ORE.

PA.   (a) (c) (d) *1860*, Act of March 31; *1879*, Act of June 11.
(e) *1907*, Act of June 7.

R. I.

S. C.	(c) (d) Enforceable as are laws for P. C. A.: *Crim. Code,* secs. 135, 136.
S. D.	
TENN.	(a) (b) To expose to weather with intent to injure: *1919,* ch. 150.
TEX.	
UTAH	(a) (b) (c) (d) Boys under 14, girls under 16: *C. L.,* secs. 720x29, 720x30.
VT.	(a) (c) (d) Of child under 10 by person over 16 having care of same: *P. S.,* sec. 5723.
VIR.	(a) *1908,* ch. 282.
	(c) *ibid.; 1914,* ch. 228; *1920,* ch. 186.
	(e) *1914,* ch. 228; *1920,* ch. 186.
WASH.	(a) *1919,* ch. 17.
	(c) (d) Or compel to labor for unreasonable time: *Ball. Code,* sec. 7071.
	(e) *1919,* ch. 17.
W. VA.	(a) (c) (d) (e) *Code,* sec. 4218.
WIS.	(c) Under 16: *1909.*
WYO.	(a) (b) (c) (d) *R. S.,* secs. 2291, 2293, 2298.

II

OFFENSES AGAINST CHILDREN FORBIDDEN UNDER PENALTY
ABANDONMENT, DESERTION, NON-SUPPORT BY PARENT OR
GUARDIAN

(a) Abandonment.

(b) Wilful failure to provide food, care, shelter, etc.

(c) Dependent or neglected condition of children.

(d) Sentence for above or contributory delinquency by parent or guardian may be suspended under bond to observe conditions imposed by court.

(e) Failure to comply with such conditions leads to execution of sentence.

(f) Forfeited bail or fines of father go to wife or guardian of children.

(g) Earnings of father while imprisoned go to family.

ALA.   (a) Of child under 16: *1915*, no. 498, sec. 1.   Parents abandoning children for more than 6 months lose all rights: *1919*, no. 181.

(g) County in which father is sentenced to hard labor shall pay probation officer $.50 per day to be expended for family: *1915*, no. 498, sec. 1.

ARK.   (a) (b) Of wife or legitimate children under 12 by father or custodian: *1909*.

(c) *1911*.

(d) *1911*.

ARIZ.   (a) (b) Child under 16; it is deemed abandonment to send a child to saloon or house of ill-fame: *P. C.*, secs. 240, 241.

CAL.   (a) Of child under 14, or falsely obtains admission for such to an asylum: *1905*, ch. 568; *1909*.

(b) *1905*, ch. 568.   Or medical attendance: *1915*, ch. 374.

(c) *1909*, ch. 133.

(f) *1911*.

(g) Not to exceed $1 per day of work: *1911*.

COLO.   (a) Uniform Desertion Act: *1911*.

(b) For wife and legitimate or illegitimate child (under 16, *1911*) under 18: *Mills Supp.*, secs. 3021b, c, d, am. by *1915*, no. 35.

(c) *1905*, chs. 81, 125.   Juvenile courts given jurisdiction: *1909*; *1915*, no. 296.

(d) (e) *Mills Supp.*, secs. 3021b, c, d, am. by *1915*, no. 35.

(f) *1915*, no. 35.

CONN.   (a) Of child under 6: *G. S.*, sec. 1158.

(b) *G. S.*, sec. 1343.

(c) *1907*, ch. 69.

(d) *G. S.*, sec. 1343; *1907*, ch. 69.   On failure to comply with terms of bond, selectmen of town shall furnish support provided for: *1919*, ch. 36.

Court may order payment by person liable for support of minor: *1911*.

DEL.   (a) *R. S.*, vol. 18, ch. 229, sec. 1.

(b) *ibid*.   Under 16: *1913*, ch. 262.

(d) (g) *1913*, ch. 262.

D. C.   To expose child under 14 with view to abandonment: *Code of 1905*, sec. 814.

FLA.   (a) (b) *R. S.*, secs. 3228, 3236, 3569.

(d) *R. S.*, sec. 3569, am. by *1913*, ch. 6483.

GA.   (a) *Code,* sec. 114.
              (d) *1915,* no. 10.

IDAHO   (a) Of child under 6: *P. C.,* sec. 4693; *1915,* ch. 83.
              (b) *P. C.,* sec. 4692; *1915,* ch. 83.
              (c) *1905,* p. 110, am. by *1907,* pp. 231-232.
              (d) *1915,* ch. 83; see also *1905,* p. 110, and *1907,* pp. 231-232.

ILL.   (a) (b) Of child under 12: *S. & C.,* p. 1226.
              (c) *1899,* Act of April 21, am. by *1905,* p. 86.
              (d) (e) *S. & C.,* p. 1226.
              See also *J. & A.,* p. 160.

IND.   (a) *Burns,* sec. 2622; see also sec. 2635.
              (b) Of child under 14: *1913,* ch. 358, am. by *1915,* ch. 179; *1915,* ch. 73.
              (c) *Burns,* secs. 1645-1649.
              (d) (e) *1913,* ch. 358, am. by *1915,* ch. 179.

IOWA   (a) (b) *Code,* sec. 220; *1907,* ch. 170.
              (c) *1909.*
              (d) (e) *Code,* sec. 2220; *1907,* ch. 170.

KANS.   (c) (d) *1907,* ch. 177, am. by *1911.*

KY.   (a) Of child under 6: *Stat.,* secs. 3255, 3256, am. by *1916,* ch. 6. Includes pregnant wife: *1922,* ch. 19.
              (b) Of child under 14: *Stat.,* secs. 3255, 3256, am. by *1916,* ch. 6.
              (c) *1907,* ch. 177.
              (d) *1907,* ch. 177. Sentence suspended under good behavior: *1916,* ch. 6.

LA.   (b) (d) (e) *R. L.,* p. 335.

ME.   (b) (d) (e) *1907,* ch. 42.
              (g) *1911.*

MD.   (a) Of child under 3 by custodian: *1910.*
              (b) *P. G. L.,* art. 27, secs. 69, 70, am. by *1908,* ch. 694.
              (c) *1914,* ch. 171.
              (d) *1908,* ch. 694; *1916,* ch. 674.
              (e) *P. G. L.,* art. 27, am. by *1908,* ch. 694.

MASS.   (a) (b) Of child under 10: R. L., ch. 83, sec. 10, am. by *1905,* ch. 269. By mother: *1909.* Appointment of custodian shall not be defense for non-support: *1919,* ch. 148.
              (c) Bonded to appear in 1 year: *1911,* ch. 456; *1914,* ch. 520; see also *1916,* ch. 243.
              (f) *1914,* ch. 520.

MICH.   (a) Of child under 16: *C. L.* sec. 7789, am by *1921,* no. 114.
              (c) *C. L.,* sec. 11507.
              (d) (e) *1907,* no. 44, am. by *1921,* no. 114.
              (g) *1907,* no. 44.

MINN.   (a) Of wife and family when children are under 16 or unable to support themselves: *1911*; *1916*, ch. 213. Power of parents to assign children to institutions regulated: *1916*, ch. 221.
(b) Under 15: *R. L.*, sec. 4934.
(c) Under 17: *1907*, ch. 92.
(d) (e) *R. L.*, sec. 4934.

MISS.   (a) Of child under 16 by either parent, or pregnant wife by husband; failure to support for three months "presumptive evidence of intention to abandon": *1920*, ch. 212.
(b) By either parent: *ibid*.
(d) For two years with regular reports to court: *ibid*.
(e) *ibid*.

MO.   (a) (b) Of child under 15: *1911*. "Without regard to whether the child was born in lawful wedlock": *1919*, ch. 8. Parents of legitimate, legitimized or adopted child under 16 criminally liable for abuse or neglect to provide: *1909*.

MONT.   (a) Of child under 15: *1917*, ch. 78.
(b) *P. C.*, secs. 8345, 8346.

NEB.   (a) (b) *C. S.*, sec. 2375a, am. by *1909*.
(c) *1921*, ch. 52.
(d) (e) *1905*, ch. 196.

NEV.   (a) (b) *1913*, ch. 272.
(c) Prosecution vested in Juvenile Court: *1911*.
(d) (e) *1913*, ch. 272.

N. H.   (a) Of children under 14: *P. S.*, ch. 265, sec. 1.
(b) Under 4: 1905, ch. 108; see also *1907*, chs. 1, 71.
(d) *ibid*.

N. J.   (a) (b) By either parent or person who has control over minor, or who refuses to give him proper education: *1916*, no. 45; *1917*, ch. 61; *1918*, ch. 85.
(c) *1905*, ch. 203.
(d) With supervision by probation officer; humane society must go on bond: *1905*, ch. 203; see also *1918*, ch. 85.
(e) *1917*, ch. 61; *1918*, ch. 85.
Parents or guardians desiring to offer care, control or adoption of child or ward to another through medium of press must secure consent of Commissioner of Char. & Cor. or be guilty of "cruelty to children"; does not apply to state institution or child-placing society: *1920*, ch. 180.

N. M.   (a) *C. L.*, sec. 1335.
           (c) *1917*, ch. 85.
N. Y.   (a) Of child under 14: *P. C.*, sec. 287.
           (b) *P. C.*, sec. 287a; see also sec. 288.
           (c) Under 16: *1910*.
           (d) *1910*.
           If all parties consent, court may, in the interest of all
           parties, discontinue proceedings: *1911*.
N. C.   (a) (b) *R.*, secs. 3335, 3336; see also secs. 180, 181.
           Court may make order on property or labor of convicted
           deserter for support of wife or children: *1917*, ch. 259.
N. D.   (a) (b) Of child under 15: *1905*, ch. 1; see also *P. C.*, secs.
           7172-7174.
           (d) (e) *ibid.*
OHIO   (a) *R. S.*, sec. 6984a; see also *R. S.*, sec. 3110.
           (b) Under 16; *R. S.*, secs. 3140-3142.
           (c) *R. S.*, ch. 6b.
           (d) (e) *R. S.*, secs. 3140-3142.
           (g) 50 cents per day to children under 16: *1913*, p. 907.
OKLA.   (a) (b) Of child under 12: *1915*, ch. 149.
           (d) (f) *ibid.*
ORE.   (a) (b) Female children under 18, males under 16: *1917*,
           ch. 136. No defense against non-support that the father
           has remarried and has children by this or other marriage:
           1921, ch. 125.
           (d) (e) *1907*, ch. 78.
           (g) $1 per day for wife and one child, $.25 per additional
           child; limit $1.75 per day: *1913*, chs. 19, 244.
PA.   (a) (b) *1907*, Act of May 29. Includes illegitimate child-
           ren: *1917*, ch. 290. Abandoned wife may sue husband
           civilly: *1913*, no. 97. Courts may assue writs of attach-
           ment against property of deserter: *1913*, no. 50.
           (d) (e) When separated from family: *1903*, Act of March 13.
           (f) (g) Under supervision of probation officer: *1913*, no. 330.
R. I.   (a) (b) *1907*, ch. 1447, sec. 2.
           (c) Under 17: *1910*.
S. C.   (a) (b) (d) *1910*.
S. D.   (a) (b) *Code*, secs. 340, 341.
           (c) *1909*, ch. 275.
TENN.   (a) Of child under 16 a felony: *1907*, ch. 56; *1915*. Each
           day to constitute a separate offense: *1909*.
           (b) A misdemeanor: *1915*.

TEX.   (a) Person who abandons wife or children to be fined as vagrant: *1909*.
    (b) Under 12: *1907*, ch. 62.
    (c) *1907*, ch. 109.
    (d) (e) *1907*, ch. 62.

UTAH   (a) Of child under 6: *C. S.*, secs. 4224, 4225. Sale or other disposition of children for money or other thing of value a felony: *1919*, ch. 28.
    (b) Under 16: *C. S.*, secs. 4224, 4225; *1921*, ch. 148.
    (c) *C. L.*, secs. 720x37-41.
    (d) *C. S.*, secs. 4224, 4225; *1921*, ch. 148.
    (f) (g) $1 for each day's work done by prisoner: *1911*; *1921*, ch. 148.

VT.   (a) (b) (d) *1915*, no. 107; see also *P. S.*, secs. 5722, 5726, and *1919*, ch. 91.

VIR.   (a) (b) Under 14: *1915*, ch. 114.
    (c) *Code*, sec. 3795a, ch. 7.
    (d) Under a probation officer: *1912*, ch. 170.

WASH.   (b) (c) (d) Under 18: *1907*, ch. 103.
    (g) *1913*, ch. 28.

W. VA.   (a) *Code*, secs. 4216, 4218. Legitimate or illegitimate child under 16: *1917*, ch. 51.
    (b) (d) (g) *Code*, secs. 4216, 4218; *1917*, ch. 51.

WIS.   (a) (b) Legitimate or illegitimate child under 16: *1911*.
    (d) On condition of weekly payment for support: *ibid*.

WYO.   (a) (b) Under 15: *1913*, ch. 81; *1915*, ch. 72.
    (c) With or without bond: *ibid*.
    (d) (g) *ibid*.

III

Offenses against Children Forbidden under Penalty Contributory Delinquency

(a) General statute.

(b) By parent or guardian.

(c) Purchasing junk or receiving articles for pawn from minor.

(d) Encouraging minor to gamble or to smoke in public.

ALA.   (b) *Code*, sec. 6460, am. by *1915*, no. 506, sec. 10.
    (d) Or allowing him to be at one's gaming table: *Code*, sec. 6989.

ARK.   (b) *1911*.
ARIZ.
CAL.   (b) *1911*.
           To send or direct minor under 18 to saloon, gambling or immoral house: *1907*, ch. 294; see also *1905*, ch. 568.
COLO.   (b) *1907*, ch. 155 Juvenile Court given jurisdiction: *1909*; *1915*, no. 317.
CONN.   (b) *1907*, ch. 69.
           (d) Inducing minor to procure liquor: *1909*.
DEL.
D. C.
FLA.   (b) *1915*, ch. 6909, no. 100.
GA.   (b) *1915*, no. 210.
           (d) For adult to game with minor; father has right to proceed against such person: *Code,* secs. 402, 3872.
IDAHO   (b) Under 18: *1905*, p. 110, am. by *1907*, pp. 231, 232; *1909*.
ILL.   (b) *1899*, Act of April 21, am. by *1905*, p. 86.
           (c) *1911*.
IND.   (b) *Burns,* secs. 1645-1649.
           (c) *1911*.
           (d) *Burns,* sec. 2468.
IOWA   (a) Or send to improper place: *1921*, ch. 238.
KANS.   (b) *1907*, ch. 177, am. by *1911*.
KY.   (a) *1910*.
           (d) Or to counsel minor under 18 to smoke: *Stat.,* sec. 3589.
LA.   (b) Through careless control: *1916*, no. 139.
ME.
MD.   (b) *1914*, ch. 171. Failing to exercise proper guardianship or conniving at improper guardianship: *1916*, ch. 674.
MASS.   (b) By mother: *1909*. By parent, guardian or custodian: *1916*, ch. 243.
MICH.   (b) *1907*, no. 314.
MINN.   (b) Under 17: *1907*, ch. 92.
           To assist, procure or induce minor to enter saloon: *1911*.
MISS.
MO.   (a) Knowingly to contribute to delinquency of child: *1921*, S. B., 247: H. B. 155.
           (b) *1907*, p. 231.
MONT.   (b) *P. C.,* secs. 9435-9439.

NEB.
N.EV.   (b) *1909*.
            (d) To gamble with a minor: *C. L.,* secs. 4946, 4949.
N. H.
N. J.   (b) *1905,* ch. 160.
            (c) *1903,* ch. 255.
N. M.   (a) *1917,* ch. 85.
N. Y.   (b) *1910*.
            (c) Under 16; *P. C.,* sec. 290.
N. C.   (b) *1915,* ch. 222.
N. D.
OHIO   (a) *1913,* pp. 868-873.
            (b) *R. S.,* ch. 6b.
            (d) To entice to gamble: *1913,* p. 906.
OKLA.   (b) " Abetting delinquency ": *1913*.
ORE.   To induce minor to visit house of prostitution: *B. & C.,*
            secs. 1924-1927.
PA.   (a) *1909*.
            (c) *1899,* Act of April 11.
R. I.   (b) Under 17: *1910*.
S. C.
S. D.   (a) *1909,* ch. 275.
            (d) *ibid.*
TENN.   To entice to enter where intoxicants are sold: *1903,* ch. 63.
TEX.   (b) *1907,* ch. 109.
UTAH   (b) *C. L.,* secs. 720x37-41.
VT.
VIR.   (a) Under 18: *1920,* ch. 186.
            (b) Under 17: *1910; 1914,* ch. 228.
WASH.   (b) " To subject child to vicious or immoral influences ":
            1907, ch. 11, am. by *1911,* and *1913,* ch. 160.
W. VA.   (b) *1915,* ch. 70.
WIS.   (b) *S. & S.,* sec. 4581i, am. by *1915,* ch. 177.
WYO.

IV

OFFENSES AGAINST CHILDREN FORBIDDEN UNDER PENALTY
EXHIBITIONS AND EMPLOYMENTS

(*Not child-labor*)

To apprentice, exhibit, or use any minor.

(a) Where intoxicants are sold.

(b) On stage.

(c) For immoral purposes.

(d) For begging.

(e) In dangerous business or exhibition.

(f) For peddling.

(g) At rag-picking, etc.

(h) Church, school, musical or other entertainments for educational or scientific purposes excepted.

ALA.

ARK.   (a) (b) Under 16, (c) (e) *1909*.
            (h) *1915*, no. 169, sec. 6.

ARIZ.   (a) Or allow to loiter: *1907*, ch. 13.
            (d) Or exhibitions in public street by child under 16: *P. C.*,
            sec. 242.

CAL.   (b) (c) (d) (e) (h) *P. C.*, secs. 272, 273.

COLO.   Under 14.
            (a) (b) (c) (e) (h) *Mills Supp.*, secs. 409, 410.

CONN.   (a) On pain of revocation of license: *G. S.*, sec. 2682.
            (c) (d) (e) (h) *G. S.*, sec. 1163.

DEL.   (b) (c) (d) (e) *R. C.*, vol. 16, ch. 150, secs. 2, 3.

D. C.   Under 18.
            (b) (d) (e) *Code of 1905*, sec. 814.

FLA.   (a) *1915*, ch. 6918, no. 112.
            (b) (c) (d) (e) (f) (h) *R. S.*, sec. 3237.

GA.   (b) (c) *Code,* secs. 706, 707.

IDAHO

ILL.   (a) Under 14: *J. & A.*, p. 223, sec. 1.
            (b) (c) (d) (e) (f) (h) Under 14: *S. & C.*, pp. 1262-1264.
            (g) *1911*.

IND.   Under 15.
            (a) (b) (c) (d) Suspected place maybe searched: *Burns,*
            secs. 2623-2627; see also *1921*, ch. 132, secs. 22, 23, 24.

IOWA

KANS.   Under 14.
(b) (d) (e) *R. S.*, sec. 4434.
Under 18 in any hypnotic or mesmeric exhibition : *G. S.*, sec. 4433.

KY.   Under 16.
(c) (d) (e) (f) *Stat.*, sec. 3252.

LA.   (a) (b) (c) (e) *R. L.*, p. 991; *1908*, no. 301, sec. 1.
Does not apply where permitted by Juv. Ct.: *1913*, no. 184.

ME.   (a) (b) (c) (d) (e) *1905*, ch. 123, sec. 9.

MD.   (a) Under 16: *P. G. L.*, art. 27, secs. 320, 321.
Under 14.
(b) (d) (e) *P. G. L.*, art. 27, secs. 318, 423.
No street vendor nor performer may have a child under 8: *P. G. L.*, art 27, sec. 322.

MASS.   (d) *R. L.*, ch. 212, sec. 52; see also sec. 24.
Under 15 in any public exhibition, (h) *R. L.*, ch. 106, secs. 45, 46.

MICH.   Under 16.
(b) (c) (d) (e) *C. L.*, sec. 5553.

MINN.   Under 18.
(b) (c) (d) (e) *R. L.*, sec. 4939.
Or outside of home between 6 P. M. and 7 A. M., or as messenger to house of prostitution: *ibid.*

MISS.

MO.   Under 14.
(a) (b) (c) (d) (e) (g) (h) *A. S.*, secs. 2186-2190; *1907*, p. 86; see also *A. S.*, sec. 2353.

MONT.   (a) Under 16, (h); or street exhibitions: *P. C.*, sec. 8347.

NEB.   (c) (e) *1907*, ch. 67, sec. 13.

NEV.   (a) *1903*, ch. 103.

N. H.   (b) Under 14, (h) *P. S.*, ch. 265, sec. 3.

N. J.   Under 18.
(b) (c) (d) (e) *G. S.*, pp. 1117, 1118 secs. 27-31.

N. M.

N. Y.   Under 16.
(b) (c) (d) (e) (g) (h) *P. C.*, secs. 291, 292.
Messenger boys must not be allowed to have any connection with saloons or disorderly houses: *P. C.*, sec. 292a.
In the making of moving-pictures: *1916*, ch. 278.

N. C.

N. D.

OHIO   (b) (c) (d) (e) (f) (h) *R. S.,* secs. 6984, 6985.
            (h) Excepts child that takes part without remuneration:
            1911; *1913*, p. 906.

OKLA.

ORE.   Under 16, in any exhibition where fee is charged, without permission of judge of Juv. Ct.: *1909*, ch. 129.

PA.   Under 15.
          (a) (b) (c) (e) *1879*, Act of June 11.
          Under 18, in any exhibition without consent of parents:
          1901, Act of May 16.

R. I.   (c) (d) (e) (f) (g) (h) *1897*, ch. 475, secs. 1, 2.
          Under 16 as acrobat, gymnast, etc., permitted with written consent of mayor of city or pres. of town council: *ibid.*

S. C.

S. D.   (a) (b) (c) (d) *1915*, ch. 306.

TENN.

TEX.

UTAH

VT.

VIR.   Under 14.
          (b) (c) (d) (e) (f) *Code,* sec. 3795a, cls. 2, 3.

WASH.

W. VA.   (a) Or in brewery or bottling establishment: *1911*.
          (b) (c) (d) (e) *Code,* secs. 4219, 4220.

WIS.   Under 14.
          (c) (e) *S. & B.,* sec. 4587a.
          As paid musician, except with parent, and (f) *1907*, ch. 418.

WYO.   Under 14.
          (a) (b) (c) (d) (e) (f) (g) (h) *R. S.,* secs. 2289, 2298, 2304; see also sec. 2290.

V

OFFENSES AGAINST CHILDREN FORBIDDEN UNDER PENALTY
OBSCENE LITERATURE

(a) To show, publish, give or sell to minor such literature, prints, etc.

(b) To permit a minor to distribute such.

ALA.   (a) *Code*, secs. 7427-7429.

ARK.   (a) *S. & H.*, secs. 1819-1821, 1824.

ARIZ.   (a) *P. C.*, secs. 283-286.
        To use indecent language before a minor: *P. C.*, sec. 274.

CAL.   (a) *P. C.*, secs. 311-314.
        To use indecent language before a child: *P. C.*, sec. 415;
        see also sec. 568.
        To indulge in lewd practice before a child: *1907*, ch. 413.

COLO.   (a) *Mills*, secs. 1324, 1327, 1328.

CONN.   (a) *G. S.*, sec. 1325; see also secs. 1476, 1477.

DEL.   (a) *R. C.*, vol. 18, ch. 229, sec. 6.

D. C.

FLA.   (a) Of marking of school places in obscene way by others
        than pupils: *R. S.*, secs. 3540, 3541, 4083.

GA.   (a) *Code*, secs. 394, 395.

IDAHO

ILL.   (a) (b) *S. & C.*, pp. 1312, 1313; see also p. 1335.

IND.   (a) Or expose for sale: *1909*, ch. 33.
        Criminal news or stories; *Burns*, sec. 2359-2361.

IOWA   (a) Or introduce into home, or give to minor, or use phono-
        graph for indecent songs: *Code*, secs. 4951-4958.

KANS.   (a) *R. S.*, secs. 2345-2350. Immoral postcards: *1913*, ch. 181.
        Minors must be excluded from trials where vulgar evi-
        dence is produced: *R. G.*, sec. 4384.

KY.   (a) Or giving account of crime: *Stat.*, secs. 3669-3744.

LA.   (a) *R. L.*, p. 400.

ME.   (a) (b) *R. S.*, ch. 125, sec. 15.

MD.   (a) And reports of criminal deeds: *P. G. L.*, art. 27, secs.
        338-340.

MASS.   (a) Or figures, images, etc.: *1913*, ch. 259.

MICH.   (a) Sell or furnish to minor: *C. L.*, secs. 5557, 5558; see also
        secs. 11724, 11987(2).
        To use obscene language before a child: *C. L.*, secs. 11737,
        11738.

MINN.   (a) (b) Or show in public to minor: *R. L.*, secs. 4954-4957.
        Printed matter devoted largely to criminal news: *1917*,
        ch. 242.

MISS.   (a) *Code*, sec. 1292.

MO.   (a) Or criminal news: *A. S.*, secs. 2177, 2180, 2181, 2188.

MONT.   (a) Or criminal news to minor under 16, (b) *P. C.*, secs. 8391-8393.

NEB.   (a) Or criminal news: *C. S.*, secs. 2369, 2370.
         (b) *C. S.*, sec. 2372; see also secs. 2373, 2374.

NEV.

N. H.   (a) (b) Under 16: *P. S.*, ch. 265, secs. 6-8, am. by *1913*, ch. 31.

N. J.   (a) *G. S.*, pp. 1057, 1058, secs. 44, 45; p. 1096, sec. 253.

N. M.

N. Y.   (a) (b) *P. C.*, sec. 317.

N. C.   (a) *R.*, sec. 3731.

N. D.   (a) (b) Under 18: *P. C.*, secs. 7213-7216; see also secs. 7206-7209, 7864.

OHIO   (a) *R. S.*, secs. 7027; 7027-1, 2, 3, 4, 5; 7028; 7120.

OKLA.   (a) *G. S.*, secs. 1667-1669; see also sec. 2023.

ORE.   (a) Or criminal literature: *1903*, p. 67.

PA.   (a) Or give or show: *1887*, Act of May 6; see also *1860*, Act of March 31; *1897*, Act of May 12.

R. I.   (a) *1900*, ch. 752.
         Indecent shows forbidden: *1900*, ch. 745.

S. C.   (a) *Crim. Code*, secs. 296, 297.

S. D.   (a) *Code*, secs. 371-374; see also *Code of Crim. Proc.*, sec. 238. Moving pictures or indecent slides: *1913*, ch. 241.

TENN.   (a) *Code*, sec. 6770.

TEX.   (a) *P. C.*, art. 365.

UTAH   (a) *C. L.*, secs. 4247-4250.

VT.   (a) *P. S.*, secs. 5894, 5895.

VIR.   (a) *Code*, secs. 3791, 3952.

WASH.   (a) (b) *Ball. Code*, secs. 7246, 6860.

W. VA.   (a) Under 16: *1917*, ch. 51.

WIS.   (a) Or criminal literature: *S. & S.*, sec. 4590; see also *S. & B.*, secs. 4842, 4632.

WYO.

VI

Offenses against Children Forbidden under Penalty
Admittance to Resorts

To allow minors to enter, (1) unaccompanied by or without consent of parent or guardian.

(a) Where intoxicants are sold.

(b) Where obscene plays are performed.

(c) Where game of chance or playing for wager is in progress.

(d) Theatre, movie-house, dance-hall or show-place.

(e) House of prostitution.

(f) Billiard, pool or bowling hall.

ALA.   (c) (f) *Code*, sec. 7992.

ARK.   (a) *S. & H.*, secs. 1810, 1811.
        (c) *S. & H.*, secs. 1808, 1809, am. by *1911*.
        (f) Or permit minor under 18 to play pool: *1911*.

ARIZ.   (a) (1) Under 16: *P. C.*, sec. 269.

CAL.   (a) Or permit minor under 18 to visit: *1905*, ch. 514.
        (d) *1909*.
        To furnish minor under 18 with ticket to cockfight: *1909*.

COLO.   (a) (1), (b) (1), (c) (1), Or any place dangerous to morals: *Mills*, sec. 1352.

CONN.   (a) (1) *G. S.*, secs. 1360, 1395. No person excused from testifying, but no such testimony shall be used against him: *1911*.
        (c) (d) *G. S.*, secs. 1360, 1395.

DEL.   (a) (1) Under 18: *R. C.*, vol. 18, ch. 229, sec. 3.
        (b) *ibid.*
        (c) (1) *R. C.*, vol. 18, ch. 237.
        (d) *R. C.*, vol. 18, ch. 229, sec. 3.

D. C.

FLA.   (c) Or permit minor to play: *R. S.*, sec. 3575.
        (f) Play or loiter: *1913*, ch. 6489.

GA.   (c) To allow minor to play in such: *Code*, secs. 402, 3872.
        (f) (1) *Code*, sec. 413.

IDAHO   (a) *P. C.*, sec. 4694, am. by *1909*.
        (e) *P. C.*, sec. 4691.
        (f) Under 20: *1913*, ch. 123.

ILL.   (a) (1), (d) (1) *1907*, p. 305.

IND.   (a) Male under 16, female under 17: *Burns,* sec. 2488.
            Loitering in saloon not to be permitted: *Burns,* secs.
            8328, 8329.
            (c) (f) *Burns,* sec. 2475-2477.

IOWA   (a) *Code,* sec. 2448.
            (f) *Code,* sec. 5002.

KANS.

KY.   (f) (1), *Stat.,* sec. 3577.

LA.   (f) Under 17: *1912,* no. 25.

ME.   (a) (b) (c) Under 16: *1905,* ch. 123, sec. 7.

MD.   (c) (f) In certain counties: *1916,* chs. 140, 205, 479.

MASS.   (b) Under 14, to any resort after sunset: *R. L.,* ch. 102,
            sec. 184.
            (e) Under 17: *1907,* no. 55, am. by *1910.*

MICH.   (a) (b) (c) (d) (f) Under 17: *1907,* no. 55.
            Where tobacco is sold: *1909.*

MINN.   (a) *1909.*
            (d) Under 18 to dance hall: *1913,* ch. 570, sec. 7.
            (e) Under 18, or invite to enter: *1907,* ch. 320.
            (f) *R. L.,* sec. 4937; *1913,* ch. 572.

MISS.   Betting or gambling with minor or permitting at one's
            tables: *Code,* secs. 1211, 1212.

MO.   (c) Parents may sue for money lost by minor when gamb-
            ling: *1919,* H. B. 156.
            (e) To permit female under 18 to enter or remain in bawdy
            house: *A. S.,* sec. 2202.
            (f) (1) *A. S.,* sec. 439; see also sec. 3428.

MONT.   (c) (1), (f) (1), Under 18: *1917,* ch. 29.

NEB.   (f) *C. S.,* sec. 2311.

NEV.   (a) Or loiter in *C. L.,* sec. 5074; *1911.*
            (c) *C. L.,* secs. 4946, 4949.

N. H.   (a) (1), (b) (1), (c) (1), Under 18: *P. S.,* ch. 265, sec. 2.

N. J.   (a) *G. S.,* p. 1110, sec. 325.
            (c) (1) Under 16: *1903,* ch. 255.
            (d) (1) Manager liable who admits child under 18 unaccom-
            panied in public dance hall or concert saloon, or under 16
            unaccompanied in theatre or moving-picture show: *1911.*
            (f) Fines go to poor fund: *1903,* ch. 122.

N. M.   (c) Under 18, or pupil, to play in any saloon, drug or to-
            bacco store: *1901,* pp. 18, 19, secs. 2, 3; *1903,* ch. 119,
            sec. 6.

N. Y.   (a) (1) *P. C.*, sec. 290, am. by *1910*.
        (c) Under 16 to reputed house of ill fame or opium den:
        P. C., sec. 290.
        (d) (1) Except in school, church or educational institution
        not operated for profit: *P. C.*, sec. 290, am. by *1910*.
        (f) *ibid.*

N. C.   (a) (1), (f) (1), Under 18: *R.*, sec. 3729; *1907*, ch. 953.

N. D.   (f) Under 18, must not be permitted to play or be employed
        in pool, billiard, bowling or card room: *1907*, ch. 128;
        see also *1905*, ch. 137.

OHIO   (a) (1) *R. S.*, secs. 6943—6943-3; see also sec. 4364-21.
        (c) *R. S.*, sec. 6998.
        (e) *R. S.*, sec. 7025.
        (f) *R. S.*, sec. 6998.

OKLA.

ORE.   (a) *B. & C.*, secs. 1977, 1924-1927; see also *1909*, ch. 79.
        (c) Or allow to loiter in or ʽ˜ play: *ibid.*
        (f) *ibid.*

PA.   (a) (1) Under 18, or in any place dangerous to health or
        morals: *1885*, Act of May 28.
        (e) Under 16, or opium den: *1907*, Act of May 29.
        (f) Under 18: *1905*, Act of April 18.

R. I.   (d) (1) Boys under 14, girls under 16: *1907*, ch. 1467.

S. C.   (d) Does not apply to Y. M. C. A. or private homes, where
        playing is social, without fee: *1910*.

S. D.   (a) (1) *Pol. Code*, sec. 2846.

TENN.   (f) (1) *Code*, secs. 6825-6830.

TEX.   (a) *1909*.
        (f) (1) *1905*, ch. 75.

UTAH

VT.   (a) *P. S.*, sec. 5150.

VIR.   (a) (c) (e) (f) *1910*; *1914*, ch. 228.

WASH.   To allow minor to play cards in one's home without con-
        sent of parent or guardian: Ball. Code, sec. 7314.

W. VA. (a) Under 18, or any place dangerous for health or morals:
        Code, secs. 4221, 4222.

WIS.   (a) (1) *S. & S.*, sec. 1657a, am. by *1909*.
        (d) Girl under 17 to dance hall: *S. & S.*, sec. 1057a.
        (f) *S. & B.*, sec. 4575.

WYO.   (b) Or harbor or employ in a brothel: *S. S.*, secs. 2290, 2293,
        am. by *1915*, ch. 6.
        (f) (1) *1915*, ch. 118.

VII

OFFENSES AGAINST CHILDREN FORBIDDEN UNDER PENALTY
SALES TO MINORS

To sell to minor, (1) unaccompanied by or without consent of parent or guardian.

(a) Intoxicant.
(b) Cigarettes, (bb) Tobacco in any form.
(c) Candy containing liquor.
(d) Hand-explosive contrivances.
(e) Toy pistols.
(f) Air rifles.
(g) Firearms or dangerous weapons.

ALA.   (a) (1) Or furnish, except on prescription of physician:
          Code, sec. 7354. Parent has right of action: *Code*, sec.
          2467.
          (b) Or furnish, or materials for such: *Code*, sec. 6466.
          (g) *Code*, sec. 6896.

ARK.   (bb) Or give: *S. & H.*, secs. 1812, 1813; *1899*, no. 75, am.
          by *1921*, ch. 490.

ARIZ.   (a) (1) Under 16, or give: *P. C.*, sec. 270.
          (bb) Under 21, or furnish: 1905, ch. 36, am. by *1917*, ch. 9.

CAL.   (a) Under 18: *1905*, ch. 514.
          (bb) Under 18: *1911*.

COLO   (a) (1) *Mills*, sec. 1353.
          (bb) Or give to minor under 16: *Mills Supp.*, secs. 411a, b.
          (d) *1905*, ch. 102.

CONN.   (a) *G. S.*, secs. 2696, 2711.
          (b) *G. S.*, sec. 1361.
          Gift devices involving chance: *G. S.*, sec. 1404.

DEL.   (a) Or procure for: *1907*, ch. 145.
          (b) Or furnish, or materials for such, to minor under 17:
          R. C., vol. 19, ch. 783.
          (g) *1911*.

D. C.   (g) *Code of 1905*, sec. 857.

FLA.   (a) *R. S.*, sec. 3552.
          (b) Or furnish, or procure, or materials for such, to minor
          under 18: *R. S.*, sec. 3608; *1907*, ch. 5716.
          (g) (1) *R. S.*, sec. 3627.

GA. (a) (1) Father has right of action against person who fur-
nishes such without his permission: *Code,* secs. 3871, 444.
(b) Or furnish, or materials for such: *Code,* sec. 497.
(g) *Code,* sec. 344.

IDAHO (a) Or give: *P. C.,* sec. 4716.
(bb) Or give: *P. C.,* secs. 4767, 4768, am. by *1913,* ch. 150.
(g) Or explosives: *1913,* ch. 177.
To sell poison to minor under 16, except on written order
of adult: *1905,* p. 324, sec. 13.

ILL. (a) Or give, or buy or procure for, without order of parent
or physician: *S. & C.,* pp. 1590, 1592.
(bb) (1) Or furnish to minor between 7 and 18, or permit
to smoke on one's premises: *S. & C.,* p. 1349; *1907,* p. 265.
(e) Toy pistol shooting blank cartridges: *1913,* p. 257.

IND. (a) *Burns,* secs. 2486, 2487.
(bb) Under 16, or furnish, or advise to use: *Burns,* secs.
2478, 2479. More carefully reenacted in 1909.
(d) (e) (g) *Burns,* secs. 2346, 2347.

IOWA (a) Or give to, or procure for, except on order of parent
or physician: *1907,* ch. 22.
(bb) Under 16: *Code,* secs. 5005, 5006.
(e) (g) *Code,* sec. 5004.

KANS. (a) Treating or giving by any but parent, guardian or physician: *G. S.,* sec. 3763.
(bb) Sale or giving away to minor under 21; *1917,* ch. 166.
(e) (g) *G. S.,* secs. 4431, 4432.
Drugs to minor under 15: *G. S.,* sec. 2346.

KY. (a) (1) *Stat.,* sec. 3663.
(b) Under 18, or furnish such or materials for such: *Stat.,*
sec. 3589.
Poison to child under 15 without consent of parent or
prescription of physician: *Stat.,* sec. 3588.

LA. (a) Or furnish or obtain for, or allow to loiter in saloon:
1906, no. 93.
(b) Or materials for such: *R. L.,* p. 394.
(g) Concealable: *R. L.,* p. 915.

ME. (a) Under 16: *1905,* ch. 123, sec. 8, am. by *1909.*
(b) Under 16, or give: *R. S.,* ch. 129, sec. 25.
(f) Under 14: *1917,* ch. 302.
(g) Under 16, except by parents or teachers of marks-
manship: *1909.*

MD. (a) *P. G. L.*, art. 27, sec. 324, am. by *1916*, ch. 31.

(bb) (1) Under 15, except as agent of employer; other person may not purchase for: *P. G. L.*, art. 27, secs. 325-327; *1919*, ch. 835.

(e) (g) Except rifles and fowling pieces: *P. G. L.*, art. 27, secs. 328, 398.

MASS. (e) (f) *1909*, ch. 102, sec. 92.

MICH. (a) Or give: *1909*.

(bb) Or furnish to minor under 17, except on order of parent or guardian: *C. L.*, secs. 11534, 11535.

(d) (e) Under 13: *C. L.*, secs. 11530-11532.

MINN. (a) Or give: *1911*.

(bb) Under 18, or furnish: *R. L.*, sec. 4939; *1907*, ch. 386, am. by *1919*, ch. 348.

(g) (1) Under 18, without written consent of police officer or magistrate: *1917*, ch. 244.

MISS. (a) *Code*, secs. 1758, 1775. Or for transportation co. to deliver to minor: *1914*, ch. 127.

(bb) (1) Under 18: *Code*, sec. 1082.

(g) *Code*, sec. 1107. Or for father to allow son under 16 to carry: *Code*, sec. 1108.

Poison: *Code*, sec. 1328.

MO. (a) (1) *A. S.*, sec. 2179; see also sec. 2995.

(b) Under 18, to give or sell to by self or agent: *1919*, H. B. 290.

MONT. (a) Or give, or send a minor to purchase: *P. C.*, sec. 8380; *1915*, ch. 41.

(bb) Or give: *P. C.*, sec. 8381.

NEB. (a) Or give: *C. S.*, secs. 7157, 7158.

(bb) Under 18: *C. S.*, secs. 2361, 2362.

Poison: *C. S.*, sec. 2098.

NEV. (a) *1903*, ch. 103.

(bb) Under 18, except on order of parent or guardian: *C. L.*, secs. 1250, 4822-4824.

N. H. (a) *1903*, ch. 95, sec. 15.

(bb) *P. S.*, ch. 265, sec. 5; *1895*, ch. 7., sec. 1.

(d) Fire crackers over 6 in. x 1 in. or potash dextrine explosives: *1907*, ch. 87.

(e) *P. S.*, ch. 265, sec. 4.

N. J. (a) *1906*, ch. 114, sec. 10. Or give to minor under 18: *1908*, ch. 185, sec. 3.

(e) (1) *1903*, ch. 169.

(g) (1) *ibid.*

N. M.   (a) (bb) (1) Under 18 or any student of public school, or give: *1901*, pp. 18, 19.

N. Y.   (a) (bb) Under 18: *1917*, ch. 564.
(g) Under 16: *P. C.*, sec. 409.

N. C.   (a) To unmarried minor, to purchase for, or to give except as sacrament: *R.*, secs. 3523-3525.
(b) Under 17, or aid in getting, or materials for such: *R.*, secs. 3804, 3805.
(g) *R.*, sec. 3832.

N. D.   (a) Or give or treat, except by order of parent or physician: *P. C.*, sec. 7617.
(bb) *P. C.*, sec 7338; *1913*, ch. 69.

OHIO   (a) (1) Or furnish: *R. S.*, secs. 6943—6943-3.
(b) Under 16, or furnish: *R. S.*, sec. 4364-38.
(d) (e) Under 16: *1913*, p. 906.
(g) *R. S.*, secs. 6986a, b.

OKLA.   (a) Or give: *1909*.
(b) Or give: *C. S.*, secs. 1454, 1455; see also sec. 1865.

ORE.   (a) Or deliver to; penalty, loss of license: *1907*, ch. 21.
(bb) (1) Under 18, or give: *B. & C.*, secs. 1980, 1981; *1917*, ch. 244.
(d) Other than firecrackers: *1903*, p. 309.
(g) *ibid.*

PA.   (a) *1854*, Act of May 8; *1881*, Act of May 10.
(bb) *1901*, Act of July 10: *1903*, Act of April 4, am. by *1905*, Act of March 16.

R. I.   (a) *G. L.*, ch. 102, secs. 13, 48.
(d) Nor blank cartridges: *1905*, ch. 1244. Firecrackers of other than gunpowder to be neither sold nor used: *1896*, ch. 342.

S. C.   (a) Or furnish: *1907*, pp. 470, 480, secs. 15, 47, 49.
(b) Or furnish, or materials for such; half fine goes to informer: *Crim. Code*, sec. 320.
(e) Or caps or cartridges for same: *Crim. Code*, sec. 610, am. by *1903*, p. 123.

S. D.   (a) *1909*, ch. 247; *1913*, ch. 256.
(bb) (1) Under 21: *1917*, ch. 153.

TENN.   (a) Or furnish: *1903*, ch. 63; see also *Code*, secs. 6785, 6786.
(bb) (1) Under 17: *1905*, ch. 2; see also *Code*, sec. 6793; *1897*, ch. 30; *1903*, ch. 208.
(g) *Code,* sec. 6792.
Poison, without order of parent or guardian, to child under 10: *Code*, sec. 6749.

TEX.   (b) (1) Or give, or deliver; disposition of liquor made to minor by agent shall be deemed act of principal: *1907*, ch. 116, am. by *1909*.

UTAH   (a) Or furnish, or procure for: *C. L.*, sec. 1249.
           (bb) Under 18, or opium or narcotic: *C. L.*, sec. 4469.
           (e) (g) Under 14, or give: *C. L.*, sec. 4281.

VT.   (a) *P. S.*, 5150.
           (bb) (1) Or furnish: *P. S.*, secs. 5903, 5904, am. by *1912*, no. 235.
           (c) *1906*, no. 50.

VIR.   (a) School pupil, or procure for: Code, sec. 3828.
           (bb) (d) (e) (g) Under 12, or furnish: Code, sec. 3828a.

WASH.   (a) (1) Under 21: *Ball. Code*, secs. 7313, 7315, am. by*1919*, ch. 17.
           (bb) *Ball. Code*, sec. 7317; *1907*, ch. 148.
           (d) (e) Under 16: *Ball. Code*, sec. 7324.

W. VA.   (a) Unless by prescription: *Code*, sec. 933.
           (bb) Under 16, or opium, or to furnish: *Code*, sec. 4402; *1913*, ch. 16. To sell tobacco, cigarettes or weapons to inmates of reform school: *Code*, sec. 1787.
           (g) *Code*, sec. 4338.

WIS.   (a) "Whether upon the written order of parents or in any manner whatsoever": *1909*.
           (bb) *S. & B.*, sec. 4608e.
           (c) Or drug: *1907*, ch. 168.
           (d) (e) *S. & B.*, sec. 4397a.

WYO.   (a) (bb) Under 16: *R. S.*, secs. 2292, 2293.
           (g) *Stat.*, sec. 5900.

VIII

Offenses against Children Forbidden under Penalty
Carnal Abuse

Of female under A yrs. by male over B yrs., a felonious offence of high degree, punishable under extreme provisions for rape.

ALA.   A = 12, B = 16: *Code*, sec. 7699.
           A = between 12 and 16; boy under 16 excepted: *1915*, no. 97.

ARK.   A = 16: *1899*, no. 12; see also *S. & H.*, sec. 1456.

ARIZ.   A = 17, B = 14: *P. C.*, secs. 230, 231; see also secs. 236. 238.

CAL. A = 18: *P. C.*, sec. 261, am. by *1913*, ch. 122; see also *P. C.*, secs. 262, 266, 277.

COLO. A = 18, B = 18; if male is under 20, sentence may be commuted to commitment to state reform or industrial school: *1907*, ch. 165; see also *Mills*, secs. 1325, 1326, 1330, and *1905*, ch. 94.

CONN. See *G. S.*, secs. 1149, 1310, and *1907*, ch. 175.

DEL. A = 18: *1895*, ch. 127. A = 7: *R. C.*, ch. 127, sec. 10.

Lascivious playing when A = 16: *1895*, ch. 126; see also *1905*, ch. 203.

To harbor a girl under 15 for prostitution: *R. C.*, vol. 18, ch. 686.

D. C. A = 16: *Code of 1895*, sec. 808; see also secs. 812, 813.

FLA. A = 18 of previous chaste character: *R. S.*, sec. 3521, am. by *1915*, ch. 6974; see also *R. S.*, secs. 3221, 3222.

GA. See *Code*, secs. 93, 94, 98.

IDAHO A = 18, B = 14: *P. C.*, secs. 4911-4914; see also secs. 4689, 4690.

ILL. A = 15, B = 17: *1907*, p. 266; see also *1905*, pp. 162, 164, and *J. & A.*, p. 420.

IND. A = 16: *Burns*, sec. 2250; see also secs. 2354-2356.

B = 17 with inmate of industrial school for girls; life sentence when girl is under 12: *1913*, ch. 95.

IOWA A = 18: *Code*, sec. 4760.

Lewd act of person over 18 with child under 13: *1907*, ch. 173.

KANS. A = 18: *G. S.*, sec. 2107; see also secs. 2108-2112, 2307, 4435.

KY. Male or female under 18: *1922*, ch. 17.

LA. A = btw. 12 and 18, B = 17: *1908*, no. 84; *1912*, no. 192.

Taking indecent liberties with child under 16: *1912*, no. 202.

ME. Person over 21 taking indecent liberties with any child under 16: *1913*, ch. 62.

MD. A = 14; also A = btw. 14 and 16, B = 18: *P. G. L.*, art. 27, secs. 369, 370.

MASS. A = 16: *R. L.*, ch. 207, sec. 23.

MICH. A = 16: *C. L.*, secs. 11489, 11493.

A = 14, B = 14; also to debauch child under 15, or to take girl under 17 to house of prostitution: *C. L.*, secs. 11719, 11725.

Marriage of girl under 16 prohibited and made void: *1919*, no. 352.

MINN.	A = 18: *R. L.*, sec. 4927, am. by *1909*; see *R. L.*, secs. 4926, 4927, 4932.
MISS.	A = 12: *1908*, ch. 171; see also *Code*, secs. 1025-1081.
MO.	Age of consent 18; rape under 15: *1913*, p. 218.
MONT.	A = 18: *1913*, ch. 16. Lewd act by person over 18 with child under 16: *1913*, ch. 59.
NEB.	Chaste girl under 18, by male over 18: *C. S.*, sec. 2061; see also secs. 2260, 2290.
NEV.	A = 14, B = 15: *C. L.*, sec. 4698.
N. H.	Enticing female child: *P. S.*, ch. 272, sec. 8.
N. J.	A = 16: *1905*, chs. 157, 159; see also *1906*, ch. 65.
N. M.	A =14, B = 14: *C. L.*, sec. 1090; see also secs. 1094, 1095, 1349. With girl under 16 of unsound mind, or under influence of intoxicant: *1915*, ch. 51.
N. Y.	A = 18: *P. C.*, sec. 278; see also secs. 282, 303.
N. C.	"Virtuous" female between 10 and 14: *R.*, sec. 3348.
N. D.	A = 18, B = 14: *1903*, ch. 149; see also *P. C.*, secs. 7157, 7158, 7161, 7162, 7165, 7167.
OHIO	A = 12: *R. S.*, sec. 6817. A = 16: *R. S.*, sec. 1816; see also sec. 7022. A = 18: *R. S.*, sec. 6824. A = 16, B = 18: *1915*.
OKLA.	A = 14, B = 14: also female between 14 and 16 of previous chaste character: *G. S.*, secs. 1818, 1819, 1821, 1822, 1825, 1826.
ORE.	A = 16, B = 16: *B. & C.*, sec. 1760; see also sec. 1928, and *1907*, ch. 91.
PA.	A = 16, of good repute: *1885*, Act of May 28; *1887*, Act of May 19; see also *1860*, Act of March 31.
R. I.	A = 16: *G. L.*, ch. 281. Age in case of child abduction, 18: *1909*.
S. C.	A = 14; and under 16, by male over 14, after abduction: *Crim. Code*, secs. 287, 288.
S. D.	A = 18; *1907*, ch. 11. B = 14: *Code*, secs. 326-334; see also *1909*, ch. 255. Age of abduction 18: *1909*.
TENN.	A = 12; from 12 to 21 a felony; evidence as to female's lack of chastity admissible if over 14; no conviction when female over 12 is lewd or kept: *1911*.

TEX. A =15, B = 14: *P. C.*, arts. 633-640; see also arts. 630, 967, 969, am. by *1903*, ch. 136.

UTAH A = btw. 13 and 18: *C. L.*, sec. 4221; see also sec. 4223.
Indecent assault on male or female under 14, distinguished from rape or attempt to commit rape, a felony: *1909*.

VT. A = 16: *1915*, no. 103.

VIR. A = 14: *Code*, sec. 3680; see also sec. 3678.

WASH. A = 18: *Ball. Code*, sec. 7062; see also *1907*, ch. 35.

W. VA. A = 16: *1920*, ch. 90.

WIS. A = 18, previously chaste: *S. & S.*, sec. 4580.
Or to take lewd liberties with such: *1915*, ch. 611.

WYO.

IX

Offenses against Children Forbidden under Penalty

Miscellaneous

GA. Indigent orphan may be separated from guardian if cruelly treated: *Code*, sec. 2543.
Corporal punishment of minor by employer forbidden; minor may claim damages: *Code*, sec. 2620.

IND. To encourage immoral practice with ward of Industrial Girls' School: *1913*, ch. 237.

IOWA Abducting child under 16: *1911*.

KANS. Superintendent of Public Instruction must censor moving picture films: *1913*, ch. 294.

MASS. Bound-out girls from industrial school are discharged from all obligation for service if misused or cruelly treated: *R. L.*, ch. 86, sec. 42.

MINN. Important illegitimacy statutes: *1917*, chs. 210, 211, 220, 231.

MO. Masters punishable for neglect of apprentices: A. S., sec. 1857.

NEV. Children not to be allowed to play nickel-in-slot machines: *1907*, ch. 212.

N. H. Cities and towns may have curfew law for minors under 16; parents responsible for infractions: *1913*, ch. 172.

N. Y. Greater N. Y. charter amended to permit appointment of 30 police women " for moral protection of women and minors ": *1920*, ch. 509.

S. D.   Only licensed physician, without consent of parent, may hypnotize a minor: *1911*.

VIR.   Minor convicted of misdemeanor may be punished by stripes in lieu of fine or imprisonment: *Code*, sec. 3902a.

WYO.   To mesmerize minor for show, or for other purpose, except with consent of parent for medical purposes: *1913*, ch. 87.

X

DISPOSITION OF DEPENDENT AND NEGLECTED CHILDREN

Such children may be separated from those in control and be committed by court to

(a) State home, (b) County home, (c) Proper private family home;

(d) If necessary they may be committed to hospital for care and treatment;

(e) They may be placed in family home by children's agency, (f) Or by such in proper private institution.

(g) Bound-out children must be guarded from neglect and cruelty by those responsible for binding out.

ALA.   Home of child preferred; if no parents, then to (a); may be apprenticed; foster home must adopt child: *1915*, no. 506.

ARK.   To reform schools or to suitable homes by county court: *1907*, no. 237.
                 Males 17, females 18, (a) (c) (d) (f) *1911*.

ARIZ.   At discretion of court: *1905*, ch. 16.

CAL.   At discretion of court: *P. C.*, sec. 273d.
                 (g) *1905*, ch. 418.

COLO.   (a) *Mils Supp.*, secs. 422a-v.
                 Board of Control has full discretion in keeping dependent or neglected children in institution or returning to parents or guardian: *1913*, ch. 50.

CONN.   Between 4 and 18, (b) until transferred to private home or to orphan asylum: *G. S.*, secs. 2788-2795, 2805, and *1907*, ch. 108.
                 Dependent minors must not be kept in almshouses: *G. S.*, secs. 2792, 2793.

DEL.   Guardian, asylum or home: *R. C.,* vol. 16, ch. 150, sec. 4; see also vol. 18, ch. 229, sec. 2.

(g) Child-placing agencies may remove child; refusal to deliver child after 3 days' notice a misdemeanor: *1919,* ch. 201, am. by *1921,* ch. 50.

D. C.   Probate Court may bind out: *Code of 1905,* sec. 411.

FLA.   May be bound out by county judge: *R. S.,* secs. 2639, 2640. Under 17, (a) (b) (c) (d) (e) (f) *R. S.,* sec. 3158, am. by *1911.*

GA.   To charitable society, institution or guardian: *Code,* secs. 2501-2505.

Between 4 and 14, to undenominational home: *1904,* p. 93; see also *Code,* vol. ii, p. 209, sec. 5.

IDAHO   Private society may receive neglected minor under 18: *1909;* see also *1919,* ch. 161.

ILL.

IND.   Under 15, to guardian or institution: *Burns,* sec. 2628.

IOWA   Bound out as apprentice to proper person: *Code,* secs. 3246-3248.

(g) *Code,* secs. 3255, 3256.

KANS.

KY.   Under 16 at discretion of court; (d) *Stat.,* sec. 3253.

(e) (g) By county boards of children's guardians (also "vicious and incorrigible"): *Stat.,* secs. 3274-3280, 5193.

LA.   At discretion of court: *R. S.,* p. 1055.

ME.   (a) (c) Of same religious faith: *1915,* ch. 320.

Parents have right of appeal in cases of dependent children to institutions: *1909.*

No child under 16 to almshouse: *1915,* ch. 320.

MD.   (a) Or other institution; (c); Court may remove: *1914,* ch. 171.

(f) Under 18: *1908,* ch. 626.

Child under 6 months may not be separated from mother and put into institution without court order or consent of physician or of Bd. of St. Aid & Char.: *1916,* ch. 210.

MASS.   Truant officers and officers of poor must make diligent search for such and make temporary provision: *1904,* ch. 356.

(c) Not to be kept in almshouse in any but exceptional cases: *R. L.* ch. 81, secs. 5-7, 28, am. by *1913,* ch. 117.

(g) And proper physical care: *R. L.* ch. 155, sec. 10. am. by *1909.*

MICH. (a) Under 16, or with guardian or indentured with family:
C. L., secs. 5563-5567; see also *1903*, no. 143, am. by *1907*,
no. 301, and *1913*, nos. 263, 300.

(g) May be returned to mother or sent to state institution
if ill-treated: *C. L.*, secs. 5568-5570.

Under no condition to be kept in almshouse: *C. L.*, sec.
5556.

MINN. (a) Under 17; temporary, then placed in homes: *R. L.*, sec.
1941, 1947, am. by *1909*.

(c) Of same religious faith: *1909*.

(e) Under 12, or adoption or otherwise with powers of legal
guardian; religious education not to be dictated; family
must be of same faith; agency may visit and investigate
child, and demand return: *1913*, ch. 314, am. by *1915*,
ch. 61.

MISS. See *1916*, ch. 111.

MO. (a) (c) *1913*, p. 131.

(a) Dep. and def. children: *1911*.

Bur. of Children created in St. Bd. of Char. & Cor. to
supervise treatment of dep. and neg. children; between 2
and 18, not to be in almshouse except temporarily with
parent: *1913*, p. 131.

MONT. (e) *1911*.

NEB. (a) Under 16, (e) *1909*.

Placing out work done under license by St. Bd. of C. & C.,
which keeps full record and inspects: *1903*, ch. 197.

NEV. (a) *1913*, ch. 243.

(g) By county commissioners: *C. L.*, sec. 628.

N. H. Under 17, (c) (d) (e) (f) *1907*, ch. 125, secs. 13, 14.

To St. Bd. of Char., or approved home-finding agency:
1917, ch. 74.

N. J. St. Bd. of Ch. Guar. places children in homes: *1899*, ch.
165, am. by *1902*, ch. 160.

To guardian or children's society: *1906*, ch. 84.

May not be committed to charitable institution under control of religious denomination: *1917*, ch. 226.

(e) State Home for Girls may parole and place in private
home any girl of school age; home pays board and may
send capable girls to higher institution of vocational
and educational training: *1917*, ch. 46.

N. M. "Indigent and orphan" to authorized charitable institutions; religious proselyting guarded against: *1915*, ch. 36.

N. Y.   Under 16, court may commit to any proper institution:
               P. C., sec. 291. Not to be sent to almshouse as pauper, nor
               committed to such or to jail: *C. & G.*, p. 607, sec. 2; p. 2712,
               sec. 56.

N. C.   Unlawful to separate a child under 6 mo. from mother
               to place in institution without consent of county health
               officer and clerk of court: *1917*, ch. 59.

N. D.   May be continued at home under probation or (a) (c)
               (d) (f) *1913*, ch. 68.

OHIO   (b) (c) Under 18: *1913*, pp. 889-893.
               "Bureau of Juvenile Research" to determine disposition
               of children: *1913*, p. 175.

OKLA.   (c) Boys under 15, girls under 16: *G. S.*, secs. 687-689.

ORE.   (g) *B. & C.*, sec. 5300.

PA.

R. I.   (e) (f) *1897*, ch. 475, sec. 3.

S. C.

S. D.   Under 18, (a) (b) (c) (d) Parents may be required to
               contribute; religious preferences taken into account: *1915*,
               ch. 119.

TENN.

TEX.   (c) (f) Under 16: *1907*, ch. 65.

UTAH   (c) Girls under 16, boys under 14: *C. L.*, sec. 720x29.
               (g) *C. L.*, sec. 77.

VT.   Under 16, (a) (c) (d) (e) *1915*, no. 92; *1919*, ch. 91.
               Town Overseer of Poor may not place for more than 20
               days in institution not approved by St. Bd. of Char.; does
               not apply to orphanage or home for dep. children: *1921*, no.
               220.

VIR.   Dep., del., or neg. children under 18 to St. Bd. of Char.
               or chartered children's agency; under 12 (d) (e) (f): *1914*,
               ch. 350.

WASH.

W. VA.   (a) (c) (d) (e) (f) *1915*, ch. 78.

WIS.   Under 16, (a) (b) (c) or on probation: *1913*, ch. 481.

WYO.   Under 16, to child-caring home, or (e) of same religious
               faith: *1915*, ch. 99.
               Cruelly treated children may be committed to guardian
               or to asylum, or, if possible and wise, may be returned to
               parents: *R. S.*, secs. 2296, 2297.

XI

REGULATION OF INSTITUTIONS CARING FOR CHILDREN

(a) Such must be licensed or approved by the requisite state authority.

Where the life or health of child is permitted to be endangered:

(b) The children may be removed from the custody of such by proper authority.

(c) Such authority may dispose of the children.

(d) Any improperly conducted institution or home may be closed as a public nuisance.

ALA.   (a) By the Child Welfare Department: *1919*, no. 457.
ARK.
ARIZ.
CAL.   (a) St. Bd. of Char. supervises: *1911*.
COLO.   (b) (c) (d) *Mills. Supp.*, sec. 412b.
CONN.   (a) Infant boarding houses by Conn. Hum. Soc., selectmen,
            and st. bds. concerned: *G. S.*, ch. 152; *1903*, ch. 22.
DEL.   (b) Bd. of Char. may remove, (c) *1921*, ch. 50.
D. C.
FLA.
GA.
IDAHO
ILL.
IND.   (a) *Burns*, sec. 1639. Infant boarding houses: *1909*, ch. 154.
            Bd. of St. Char. may appoint agents to supervise children
            in homes and institutions and provide temporary detention
            homes: *1913*, ch. 263.
IOWA
KANS.
KY.
LA.
ME.   (a) (b) *1915*, ch. 320. Everyone receiving two or more
            children comes under act: *1917*, ch. 149.
MD.
MASS.   (a) *R. L.*, ch. 83, secs. 1-19.
            (b) By agent of St. Bd. of Char.: *R. L.*, ch. 83, secs. 26-28.

MICH.	(a) *1919*, no. 136.
MINN.	Persons permitted to receive, secure homes for, or otherwise care for children must keep full record: *1919*, ch. 51.
MISS.	
MO.	
MONT.	
NEB.	(a) Maternity homes and infant boarding houses: *1911*. Placing-out societies: *1913*.
NEV.	
N. H.	(a) Infant boarding houses: *1911*.
N. J.	(a) *1915*, ch. 210.
N. M.	
N. Y.	(a) S. P. C. C. empowered to inspect: *P. C.*, sec. 288.
N. C.	
N. D.	
OHIO	
OKLA.	
ORE.	
PA.	(a) Infant boarding houses: *1911*.
R. I.	(b) (c) Infant boarding houses: *1897*, ch. 464.
S. C.	
S. D.	
TENN.	
TEX.	(b) Corporal punishment in state school only as last resort; must be no bodily injury: *1913*, ch. 6, sec. 15.
UTAH	
VT.	(a) All houses or institutions must keep a record open to inspection by authorities: *1912*, no. 132.
VIR.	
WASH.	
W. VA.	(a) Subject to inspection by St. Bd. of Ch. Guar.: *1921*, ch. 134.
WIS.	(a) Open to inspection: *1914*, ch. 350.
	(d) Officers shall be punished: *S. & B.*, sec. 4389.
WYO.	(a) Must receive annual certificates and make reports to St. Bd. of Char.: *1915*, ch. 99.
	(b) (c) *R. S.*, sec. 2300.
	(d) *1915*, ch. 99.

XII

S. P. C. C.s and Humane Societies

(a) May be appointed guardian of cruelly treated or neglected minor by court.

(b) May receive custody of same on application to court.

(c) Agent may not arrest without warrant.

(d) Fines for cases prosecuted go to society.

ALA.	Boards of county com. may enforce laws to prevent cruelty to children; they shall be vested with powers of deputy sheriffs: *1911*.
ARK.	(a) Under 14, (c) *1909*.
ARIZ.	
CAL.	(d) Such corporations operate under same arrangements as do S. P. C. A.s (*vide supra*, p. 259) : *P. C.*, sec. 273d. Police commissioner can grant agents police powers in cities of 1st Class: *1909*.
COLO.	(a) Under 14, Col. St. Bur. of C. & A. Prot.; (b) But may not be required so to act: *Mills Supp.*, sec. 412b; for powers of Bur. *vide supra*, p. 259.
CONN.	Conn. Hum. Soc. deals with both children and animals; *vide supra*, p. 259.
DEL.	(d) *R. C.*, vol. 16, ch. 477, sec. 2. St. subsidizes Del. S. P. C. C.: *R. C.*, vol. 18, ch. 229, sec. 6.
D. C.	
FLA.	(c) Peace off. may arrest minor under 16 without warrant: S. P. C. C. agents have powers of peace off.: *R. S.*, sec. 3158.
GA.	
IDAHO	(a) *1919*, ch. 161.
ILL.	(d) *S. & C.*, pp. 1413, 1414.
IND.	(a) Under 15, (b) Officers have police powers: *Burns*, secs. 2629, 2632. (c) Cities of 1st Class shall appoint 3 members of police force hum. off.: *1909*. (d) Apportioned among hum. soc. of county according to membership: *1913*, ch. 103.
IOWA	(a) Powers may be revoked if trust is abused; under supervision of St. Bd. of Control: *Code*, ch. 8, title 16, am. by *1902*, ch. 133.

KANS.   On application of S. P. C. C., court may appoint agent for protection of children; public officials must aid soc. in enforcing laws: *G. S.*, secs. 4436-4439.

KY.   (a) (d) Officers of S. P. C. C. have police powers: *Stat.*, secs. 3257, 3258.

LA.   (a) (d) *1908*, no. 83.
    La. S. P. C. C. may prosecute parents; officers may serve as peace off. in cities: *R. L.*, p. 1055.

ME.   (a) (c) Agents may serve in counties to which appointed by Gov. and council: *1905*, ch. 123, am. by *1915*, ch. 320.

MD.   See *1904*, ch. 77, am by *1906*, ch. 78.

MASS.   (a) Under 14: *R. L.*, ch. 83, secs. 29-35.
    (c) Agents may be appointed by Gov. for 3 yr. term: 1903, ch. 333.

MICH.   (a) *1909*.
    Agents may have police powers; in incorporated cities, they must be authorized by police officials: *C. L.*, sec. 8418; see also secs. 8419-8425.

MINN.   Minn. S. P. C. constituted a St. Bd. of C. & A. Prot.: *1905*, ch. 274.

MISS.

MO.   (a) Neg. and del. children under 16, (b) (c) (d) Officer of hum. soc. may act as probation officer: *1907*, p. 217.

MONT.   Mont. Bur. of C. & A. Prot.: *1903*, ch. 115.
    May appoint 6 deputies; monthly reports of persons prosecuted: *1911*.

NEB.   (a) Temporarily: *C. S.*, secs. 1747-1749.

NEV.

N. H.   (a) (b) (c) *P. L.*, ch. 178, secs. 15, 16, 17.

N. J.   May be incorporated to prevent cruelty, establish schools, erect and maintain asylums, receive custody of children, enforce laws, etc.: *G. S.*, pp. 1720-1722, secs. 42-49.
    (a) (b) (d) *G. S.*, pp. 1718-1720, secs. 33-40.

N. M.

N. Y.   Officers are peace officers: *P. C.*, sec. 688. May appear in court without belonging to bar: *1910*.
    (d) *P. C.*, sec. 293.
    Bd. of Co. Sup. may appropriate money for S. P. C. C.: *1911*.

N. C

N. D

OHIO (a) *R. S.*, secs. 3725-1, 2.
      (b) Must supervise where placed: *1913*, p. 876.

OKLA.

ORE. (a) Under 14: *B. & C.*, secs. 3605-3609.

PA. (a) (b) Officers have powers of peace off.; cities of 1st and 2nd class may aid by appropriations: *1879*, Act of June 11; *1887*, Act of May 25.
      Subject to state inspection: *1903*, Act of March 5.

R. I. (a) Under 16, " shall "; society may then deliver child under court order: *G. L.*, ch. 115, sec. 8.
      (d) *1897*, ch. 475, sec. 4.
      State may appropriate: *G. L.*, ch. 115, sec. 8. No recognizance for costs: *1910*.

S. C.

S. D.

TENN.

TEX.

UTAH All children's associations subject to county inspection and supervision: *C. L.*, sec. 720x36.

VT.

VIR. (a) Dep., neg. or del. children under 14; may control during minority, or place in homes, or apprentice, or send to ref. inst.: *Code*, secs. 3795a, cls. 4, 5, 6; sec. 3795b.
      Off. have powers of peace off.: *1908*, ch. 348.

WASH.

W. VA. (a) Under 16, (b) Children remain in custody until placed in inst. or private home: *Code*, secs. 489, 493; see also secs. 2619-2630, and *1907*, ch. 40.

WIS. County or city may appropriate not exceeding $1200 for work of S. P. C. C.: *1909*.
      Wis St. Hum. Off.: *1919*, ch. 359.

WYO. (a) Under 14: *R. S.*, sec. 2301.
      (d) Wyoming Hum. Soc.: *R. S.*, sec. 2294.
      Wyo. St. Bd. of C. & A. Prot.

XIII

CHILDREN'S CODE COMMISSIONS

(a) Children's Code Commission appointed by governor.

(b) Children's Code Commission provided for by legislative act.

ALA.
ARK.
ARIZ.
CAL.
COLO.
CONN. (b) " Child Welfare Commission ", *1919*, ch. 285, sec. 1, 2.
DEL.   (a) *1918*.
       (b) " Reconstruction Commission of the State of Del"
       1919, ch. 66.
D. C. Committee of five appointed by Att. Gen.: *1915*.
       " Children's Code Commission " appointed by Commis-
       sioners of D. C.: *1920*.
FLA.   (b) " Children's Code Commission ": *1923*, no. 155, ch. 9273.
GA.   (b) " Georgia Children's Code Commission ", *1922*, no. 300,
       p. 71.
IDAHO
ILL.
IND.   (b) " Commission on Child Welfare and Social Insurance ",
       1919, ch. 197, p. 771.
IOWA
KANS. (a) " Children's Code Committee ": *1918, 1920*.
KY.   (b) " Children's Code Commission ": *1920*, ch. 193, p. 725.
       " Kentucky Child Welfare Commission ": *1922*, ch. 107.
LA.
ME.
MD.   (a) " Children's Code Commission ": *1922*.
MASS.
MICH. (b) " Child Welfare Commission ": *1917*, no. 293.
MINN. (a) " Child Welfare Commission ": *1916*.
       (b) Joint Senate and House Committee: *1917*, p. 874.
MISS.
MO.   (a) " Children's Code Commission ": *1915; 1917; 1919*.
MONT. (a) " Committee to Standardize Children's Laws ": *1917*.
NEB.   (b) " Children's Code Commission ": *1919*, ch. 178.
NEV.   (b) " Children's Commission ": *1913*, ch. 72.
N. H.
N. J.
N. M.

N. Y.   (b) " State Commission to Examine Laws Relating to Child Welfare ": *1920*, ch. 669.

N. C.

N. D.   (b) " Children's Code Commission ": *1921*, ch. 29.

OHIO   (b) " Commission to Codify and Revise the Laws of Ohio Relative to Children ": *1911*, p. 123.
             Laws suggested by Commission passed en bloc: *1913*, pp. 864-914.

OKLA.   (b) " Children's Code Commission ": *1919*, ch. 58.

ORE.   (a) " Child Welfare Commission ": *1913*; *1915*.
             (b) Committee: *1917*, Sen. Res. no. 21, p. 941. " Oregon Child Welfare Revision Commission ": *1919*, ch. 299.

PA.   (b) " Commission to Suggest Revisions and Amendments to the Statutes Which Relate to Children ": *1923*, no. 411.

R. I.

S. C.   (a) " Child Welfare Commission ": *1919*.

S. D.   (b) " State Child Welfare Commission " with powers broadly interpreted so as to include suggestion for legislative revision: *Rev. Code (1919)* sec. 2., ch. 134.

TENN.   (a) " Child Welfare Commission ": *1920*.

TEX.   (a) " Texas Child Welfare Commission ": *1919*.

VT.   (b) " State Welfare Commission ": *1921*, ch. 56, secs. 1-6.

VIR.   (a) " Children's Code Commission of Virginia ": *1921*.

WASH.

W. VA.   (b) " State Child Welfare Commission ": *1921*, ch. 135.

WIS.   (a) " Child Welfare Commission ": *1918*.

WYO.

APPENDIX III

Recommendations of the special committee on Animal Transportation of the American Humane Association, reported at the Forty-First Annual Convention in 1917:

First—The revocation of the amendment of June 29, 1906, to the 28-hour law whch extended the time of confinement in the cars to 36 hours on the request of the owner or person in custody of the shipment. If this was done it would require all live-stock shipments to be unloaded for food, rest and water every 28 hours. The Department of Agriculture should be given power to issue and enforce rules and regulations consistent with and to insure the effective enforcement of the act.

This would restore the law to where it stood for 33 years prior to 1906. Shippers, stockmen and commission men admit that 28 hours is long enough. So do the government officials and many railroad men. Experience has shown that exactly the same conditions occur as to reaching the destination within the 36-hour limit, and similar circumstances would be met with were the legal time extended to 50 hours.

Second—A minimum speed limit should be fixed for the running time of cars between the hour of loading and the hour of unloading. Live stock should have the right of way over the dead freight and empty cars. With a minimum running time fixed at 16 miles per hour, and it is conceded that such speed is reasonably within the capacity of the railroad to maintain, a distance of nearly 450 miles could be covered in 28 hours, while at the rate of 10 miles per hour only 360 can be traversed in the 36 hours which the present law permits.

Third—The Department of Agriculture should be given the power to inspect the waybills and to examine any and all accounts, records and memoranda kept by the carriers relating to the transportation of cattle in interstate commerce. It has been shown through prosecutions made by the government that waybills are frequently falsified so that from one to 12 hours are gained by the railroad in the time allowed for shipment. Such a bill was before the last Congress and deserves the support of humane societies to secure its enactment at the next session of Congress.

Fourth—Poultry transportation should be under the control of the Department of Agriculture. The law should prescribe in general terms the conditions under which poultry can be transported, and should give to the department the authority to issue and enforce rules and regulations consistent with the act, enabling them to exercise a close supervision and intelligent direction over the humane treatment of the fowls.

Fifth—A law should be had prohibiting the transportation of immature calves.

APPENDIX IV

ILLINOIS HUMANE EDUCATION LAW OF JUNE 14, 1909

SECTION 1. BE IT ENACTED BY THE PEOPLE OF THE STATE OF ILLINOIS REPRESENTED IN THE GENERAL ASSEMBLY: That it shall be the duty of every teacher of a public school in this State to teach to the pupils thereof, honesty, kindness, justice and moral courage for the purpose of lessening crime and raising the standard of good citizenship.

SEC. 2. In every public school within the State not less than one-half hour of each week during the whole of each term of school shall be devoted to teaching the pupils thereof kindness and justice to and humane treatment and protection of birds and animals, and the important part they fulfill in the economy of nature. It shall be optional with each teacher whether it shall be a consecutive half hour or a few minutes daily, or whether such teaching shall be through humane reading, daily incidents, stories, personal example or in connection with nature study.

SEC. 3. No experimenting upon any living creature for the purpose of demonstrating in any study shall be made in any public school of this State. No animal provided by, nor killed in the presence of any pupil of a public school, shall be used for dissection in such school, and in no case shall dogs or cats be killed for such purpose. Dissection of dead animals, or any parts thereof shall be confined to the class room and shall not be practiced in the presence of any pupil not engaged in the study to be illustrated thereby.

SEC. 4. The Superintendent of Public Instruction of this State and the committee in charge of preparing the program for each annual meeting of the Illinois State Teachers' Association shall include therein moral and humane education.

The superintendent of schools of each county and of each city shall include once each year moral and humane education in the program of the teachers' institute, which is held under his or her supervision.

SEC. 5. The principal or teacher of each public school shall state briefly in each of his or her monthly reports whether the provisions of this Act have been complied with in the school under his or her control. No teacher who knowingly violates any provision of sections 1, 2, or 3 of this Act shall be entitled to receive more than 95 per cent of public school moneys that would otherwise be due for services for the month in which such provisions shall be violated. This Act shall apply to common schools only and shall not be construed as requiring religious or sectarian teaching.

Approved June 14, 1909.

APPENDIX V

Organization of Wisconsin humane work (from the 1920 *Biennial Report* of the Wisconsin Department of Humane work).

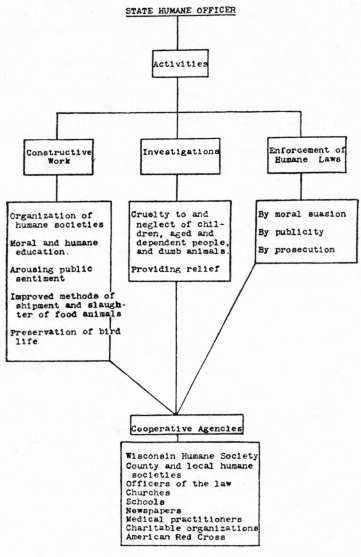

STATE HUMANE OFFICER

Activities

| Constructive Work | Investigations | Enforcement of Humane Laws |

Organization of humane societies

Moral and humane education.

Arousing public sentiment

Improved methods of shipment and slaughter of food animals

Preservation of bird life

Cruelty to and neglect of children, aged and dependent people, and dumb animals.

Providing relief

By moral suasion

By publicity

By prosecution

Cooperative Agencies

Wisconsin Humane Society
County and local humane societies
Officers of the law
Churches
Schools
Newspapers
Medical practitioners
Charitable organizations
American Red Cross

306

BIBLIOGRAPHY

GENERAL AND SECONDARY

Breckinridge, Sophonisba and Helen R. Jeter, *A Summary of Juvenile Court Legislation in the United States* (Washington, 1920).
Bulletin of Social Legislation, nos. 2, 3, 4.
Eliot, Thomas Dawes, *The Juvenile Court and the Community* (New York, 1914).
Hart, Hastings H., *Preventive Treatment of Neglected Children* (New York, 1910).
Hubbard, F. Morse, *Prevention of Cruelty to Animals in New York State* (New York, 1915).
——,*Prevention of Cruelty to Animals in the State of Illinois, Colorado and California* (New York, 1916).
Illegitimacy as a Child Welfare Problem (Washington, 1920), published by the U. S. Dept. of Labor, Children's Bureau.
Jeter, Helen R., *The Chicago Juvenile Court* (Washington, 1922).
Leffingwell, Albert, *An Ethical Problem* (2nd edition, New York, 1916).
Legislation for the Protection of Animals and Children (New York, 1914).
Lundberg, Emma O., *County Organization for Child Care and Protection* (Washington, 1922).
——, *State Commissions for the Study and Revision of Child Welfare Laws* (Washington, 1924).
Mangold, George B., *Problems of Child Welfare* (New York, 1914).
McCrea, Roswell C., *The Humane Movement* (New York, 1910).
Milne, Nora, *Child Welfare Work from a Social Point of View* (London, 1920).
Richardson, Charles S., *The Dependent, Delinquent and Defective Children of Delaware* (New York, 1918).
Ritchie, David G., *Natural Rights* (London, 1895).
Rowley, Francis P., *The Humane Idea* (Boston, 1912).
Rural Child Welfare (New York, 1922) published by the National Child Labor Committee.
Salt, Henry S., *Animals' Rights Considered in Relation to Social Progress* (2nd edition, London, 1915).
Slingerland, William Henry, *Child Welfare Work in Louisville* (Louisville, 1919).
——, *Child Welfare Work in Pennsylvania* (New York, 1915).

Standards of Child Welfare (Washington, 1919), published by the U. S. Dept. of Labor, Children's Bureau.

United States Department of Labor, Children's Bureau, Publications nos. 60, 66, 70, 104, 107, 116.

NEWSPAPERS AND PERIODICALS

Alabama Childhood, vol. i, no. 4.

Annals of the American Academy of Political and Social Science, November 1921, January 1923.

Charleston American, April 8, 1923.

Christian Science Monitor, February 17, 1918.

Community Chest Crier (Cincinnati), April 2, 1923.

Federal Republican (Baltimore), December 30, 1816.

Hospital Social Service, vol. vii.

Humane Monthly. vol. i.

Humane Record, vol. ii, no. 4.

Journal of the American Medical Association, vol. li.

Medical Record, January 31, 1880; March 31, 1880.

Mercy and Truth, vol. i, no. 14.

Minutes of the General Assembly of the Presbyterian Church of the U. S. A. for 1920, 1922 and 1923.

National Humane Review, vols. i-xi.

New York Evening Post, September 4, 1874.

New York Herald, July 8, 1909; February 6, 1914.

New York Times, May 21, 1912.

New York Tribune, December 18, 1881.

Proceedings of the National Conference of Charities and Corrections, vols. xl, xli.

Quarterly Record of the State Board of Charities, vol. i.

REPORTS OF ORGANIZATIONS, PAMPHLETS AND MISCELLANEOUS

American Humane Association, 34th to 46th Annual Reports.

American Humane Education Society, Annual Reports from 1910 to 1922.

American Society for the Prevention of Cruelty to Animals, 35th to 57th Annual Reports.

Animal Rescue League of Boston, 11th to 23rd Annual Reports.

Animal Rescue League of New Bedford, Annual Report for 1921.

Anti-Cruelty Society (Chicago), 11th to 23rd Annual Reports.

Auxiliary to the Pennsylvania Society for the Prevention of Cruelty to Animals, Annual Reports from 1917 to 1921.

California Society for the Prevention of Cruelty to Children, Annual Report for 1917.

Carstens, Carl C., "Development of Social Work for Child Protection," in *Annals of the American Academy of Political and Social Science,* November, 1921.

Chatanooga Humane Education Society, Annual Report for 1921.

Codman, J. S., *Human Vivisection and the American Medical Association* (Boston, 1923) a pamphlet.

Connecticut Humane Society, 30th to 42nd Annual Reports.

Defense of Medical Research pamphlets.

Dewey, John, *Ethics of Animal Experimentation* (1909) a pamphlet.

First Public Declaration of the Open Door in Laboratories for Animal Experimentation (1922) a pamphlet published by the Blue Cross Society of Springfield, Massachusetts.

Hearings on S. 758, 62nd Congress, 1st Sess.

Humane Society of Kansas City, Annual Report for 1919.

Humane Society of New York, 6th to 18th Annual Reports.

Humane Society of Rochester, Annual Reports from 1910 to 1922.

Juvenile Protective Association of Chicago, 21st Annual Report (1923).

Lehigh Humane Society, 15th Annual Report.

Los Angeles Society for the Prevention of Cruelty to Animals, 33rd to 45th Annual Reports.

Louisiana Society for the Prevention of Cruelty to Animals, 23rd to 35th Annual Reports.

Mansfield (Ohio) Humane Society, 1921 Booklet.

Massachusetts Society for the Prevention of Cruelty to Animals, Annual Reports from 1910 to 1922.

Massachusetts Society for the Prevention of Cruelty to Children, 30th to 42nd Annual Reports.

Medical Opinions Against Vivisection, pamphlet issued by the New York Anti-Vivisection Society.

New England Anti-Vivisection Society, Annual Report for 1919-1920.

New York Society for the Prevention of Cruelty to Children, Annual Reports from 1910 to 1922.

New York Women's League for Animals, 1st to 12th Annual Reports.

Ohio Humane Society, Annual Reports from 1910 to 1922.

Outline of Work (1923), pamphlet published by the American Humane Association.

Pennsylvania Society for the Prevention of Cruelty to Children, 34th to 46th Annual Reports.

Rhode Island Humane Education Society, 6th to 18th Annual Reports.

Rowley, Francis H., *Slaughter-House Reform in the United States and the Opposing Forces* (Boston, 1921) a pamphlet.

Social Service Bureau of Houston, Texas, Report for 1921.

Slingerland, William Henry, " Child Welfare Work in Colorado," in *University of Colorado Bulletin,* vol. xx, no. 10.

To the Fathers and Mothers of Colorado (Denver, 1915), a pamphlet issued by the Colorado State Bureau of Child and Animal Protection.

United States Department of Agriculture, Bureau of Animal Industry, *Order No. 264,* 1919.

Washington Humane Education and Anti-Vivisection Society, 1st Annual Report (1922).

Western Pennsylvania Humane Society, 36th to 48th Annual Reports.

What Vivisection Inevitably Leads To, pamphlet issued by the Vivisection Investigation League of New York.

Why It was founded (Boston, 1923), pamphlet issued by the Society of Friends of Medical Progress.

Wilson, Dalett H., *Statement on Behalf of Mr. August Heckscher* (New York, 1923).

Wisconsin Department of Humane Work, Report for 1920.

Wyoming Commissioner of Child and Animal Protection, Biennial Report for 1922.

Wyoming Humane Society and State Board of Child and Animal Protection, Biennial Reports for 1914, 1916, 1918.

Wyoming State Board of Child and Animal Protection, Biennial Reports for 1910 and 1912.

The session laws for all the states, and many other pamphlets and reports of societies not noted in the text.

INDEX

The more important passages are indicated by heavy type

Traps, setting of, 102, 250, 251, 253
Trapshooting at live birds, legislation against, 247-254
Twenty-Eight Hour Law, 109

U. S. Department of Agriculture, Department of Animal Industry, 111
United States Department of Labor, Childrens Bureau, 197-198
Utah, humane and anti-cruelty legislation in, 100, 101, 212, 217, 219, 232-301 *passim*

Vaccination and anti-vivisection, 144-145
Vehicle equipment of anti-cruelty societies, 31
Vermont, humane and anti-cruelty legislation in, 100, 101, 102, 212, 219, 232-301 *passim*
Virginia, humane and anti-cruelty legislation in, 100, 101, 212, 216, 218, 219, 232-301 *passim*
Vivisection, 141-161; legislation against, 254-256
Vivisection Investigation League, 154, 156
Vivisection Reform Society, 146

War. See World War
Washington, humane and anti-cruelty legislation in, 100, 101, 102, 136, 137, 212, 216, 217, 219, 232-301 *passim*
Washington Anti-Vivisection Society, 148
Washington Humane Education and Anti-Vivisection Society, 159
Washington Humane Society, 97
Watering stations for animals, 18, 31, 32, 33, 34, 37, 39, 40, 70, 71, 252
Watering troughs in cattle cars, 112
Western Pennsylvania Humane Society, 27, 89
West Virginia, humane and anti-cruelty activities in, 76, 81-82

West Virginia, humane and anti-cruelty legislation in, 100, 101, 212, 219, 232-301 *passim*
West Virginia Humane Society, 81-82, 224
West Virginia State Board of Children's Guardians, 224-225
White House Child Welfare Conference, 197
Wisconsin, Humane and anti-cruelty activities in, 45, 76, 82-83
Wisconsin, humane and anti-cruelty legislation in, 100, 101, 102, 211, 212, 217, 219, 232-301 *passim*
Wisconsin State Humane Officer, 82-83, 224, 306
Women's Auxiliary of the American S. P. C. A., 69, 126
Women's Auxiliary of the Massachusetts S. P. C. A., 37, 39
Women's Auxiliary to the Pennsylvania S. P. C. A., 39, 71-72, 74
Women's Club of North Carolina, 42
Work-horse parades, 39, 64, 69, 71, 72-74
World War, 17, 23, 31, 52, 54-63, 70. 158-159, 182
Wright, John D., 111
Wyoming, humane and anti-cruelty activities in, 48, 76, 80-81
Wyoming, humane and anti-cruelty legislation in, 100, 101, 136, 137, 212, 219, 232-301 *passim*
Wyoming Commissioner of Child and Animal Protection, 81, 224
Wyoming Humane Society, 80, 83
Wyoming Humane Society and State Board of Child and Animal Protection, 48, 80-81, 119, 120

Young Defenders' leagues, 69, 126
Youngstown Humane Society, 192